Mothers and Sons, Fathers and Daughters

Michael Psellos in Translation

Miniature portrait of Michael Psellos and his pupil Michael Doukas, Ms Pantokrator
234, fol. 254 (12th century). © Holy Monastery of Pantokrator, Mount Athos.
Used with permission.

Mothers and Sons, Fathers and Daughters

The Byzantine Family of Michael Psellos

edited and translated by

ANTHONY KALDELLIS

with contributions by David Jenkins and Stratis Papaioannou

University of Notre Dame Press

Notre Dame, Indiana

University of Notre Dame Press
Copyright © 2006 by University of Notre Dame
Notre Dame, Indiana 46556
www.undpress.nd.edu
All Rights Reserved

Published in the United States of America

Reprinted in 2014

Library of Congress Cataloging-in-Publication Data

Psellus, Michael.
    [Selections. English. 2006]
    Mothers and sons, fathers and daughters : the Byzantine family
of Michael Psellos / edited and translated by Anthony Kaldellis ;
with contributions by David Jenkins and Stratis Papaioannou.
        p.   cm. — (Michael Psellos in translation)
    Includes bibliographical references and index.
    ISBN-13: 978-0-268-03315-6 (pbk. : alk. paper)
    ISBN-10: 0-268-03315-3 (pbk. : alk. paper)
    ISBN-13: 978-0-268-02415-4 (hardback)
    1. Psellus, Michael—Family.   2. Psellus family.   I. Kaldellis, Anthony.
II. Jenkins, David (David Todd)   III. Papaioannou, Stratis.   IV. Title.
V. Title: Byzantine family of Michael Psellos.
    PA5355.Z5P74   2006
    189—dc22

                                                2006024194

I dedicate this book to
my father, mother, sister, and brother-in-law.

Contents

Preface and Acknowledgments

In addition to being actively engaged in the political intrigues of the Byzantine court of his time, the eleventh-century philosopher Michael Psellos (born Konstantinos) produced a vast corpus of writings that cover almost every field of knowledge and genre. Among modern readers, however, he is usually known solely from his masterly memoirs of the emperors of his time, known as the *Chronographia*. If this most fascinating of courtiers and thinkers is to be studied as broadly as he deserves—and not merely by professional Byzantine philologists who happen to specialize in his works!—it is necessary for more of his writings to be made accessible to a wider readership. The idea of a translation of works selected by genre, theme, or historical importance was accordingly proposed at the First Bi-Annual Workshop in Byzantine Intellectual History organized at the University of Notre Dame, 6–7 February 2004, by David Jenkins and Charles Barber on the topic of "The Play of Literature and Ideas in the Writings of Michael Psellos." The idea was received enthusiastically and the present book is the first offspring of what it is hoped will become a long-term and more broadly collaborative venture.

This volume presents in translation all the texts that Psellos wrote concerning his family. All together they present us with the most complete picture we have of any non-imperial Byzantine family, tracking its fortunes over the course of a century. This book, then, is one of the first and most comprehensive on the topic of the Byzantine family. Each text is annotated and prefaced by a special introduction, while the volume as a whole is introduced by an essay on Psellos' life, the history of his family, and the lives of women and children in eleventh-century Constantinople. Subsequent volumes in what we may loosely (and hopefully) call this "series" will focus on Psellos' career as a teacher in

Constantinople, on his writings on science and the occult, on literary criticism and aesthetics, and on friendship. No specific estimates can be offered yet regarding their completion, as much will depend on the schedules and initiative of the individual editors and translators. Obviously, these volumes will be finished sooner if additional qualified translators step forward and volunteer their services.

The author of this volume would like to thank David Jenkins (Byzantine Studies Librarian at the University of Notre Dame) and Stratis Papaioannou (Dumbarton Oaks Associate Professor of Byzantine Studies at Brown University) for contributing one chapter each, including both introductions and translations; David Jenkins and Charles Barber for flawlessly organizing and graciously hosting the workshop that was the forum for its inception; and all who took time from busy schedules to check the accuracy of the translations: Stephanos Efthymiadis, Stratis Papaioannou, and Jeffrey Walker read the encomium; Panagiotis Agapitos the funeral oration; and Antony Littlewood Psellos' address to his grandson. Alice-Mary Talbot in particular read the entire manuscript for the Press and made many suggestions for improvement. All saved me from errors and awkward expressions, especially Dr. Talbot, and none is responsible for the remaining imperfections. If translation is a thankless task, correcting another's translation is a courtesy beyond the call of duty. My sincerest gratitude goes to all.

A Note on the Spelling of Names: Greek and Byzantine names are here for the most part transliterated directly, without Latinization or Anglicization. In an age when scholars are trying to overcome or resist the ideological legacy of colonialism and cultural imperialism, when even newspapers are making an effort to spell correctly the names of the most "exotic" languages, Byzantium is one of the last remaining cultures whose names are routinely "translated" into their modern equivalents. No reader should have any difficulty in knowing who is meant.

General Introduction

The study of Byzantine women has been seriously underway for the past twenty-five years or so, yet it suffers from a debilitating lack of evidence. The vast majority of studies focus on empresses and saints (or at any rate nuns) for the simple reason that they are the only women we know much about. Alternately, they scrutinize the provisions of the various legal codes, though admitting the limitations of this kind of evidence, which is normative, often highly ideological rather than descriptive, and sometimes very much out of date. One is reminded of the man searching for his keys at night under a lamppost not because he dropped them right there but because that was the only place where he could see to look. Empresses and saints, however, were statistically insignificant and their lives were characteristically and even purposefully different from that of the majority of the population. "We admire rare things more than common ones," Psellos wrote in a playful treatise.[1] That majority, however, which consisted of agricultural families and the poor, will probably forever remain beyond our reach, with the exceptions, perhaps, of Egypt in late antiquity and of Makedonia in the Palaiologan period. Evidence about them in other times and places may be laboriously gleaned from archaeology or by searching through hundreds of texts for scattered references, but this will probably never yield a systematic picture because of its wide geographical and chronological distribution.

It is here that Psellos comes to our rescue, by casting some light outside the relatively narrow circle of hagiography and court history. Though there has been no systematic treatment of his life and his importance as a source for

---

1. Psellos, *Encomium for the louse* 15 (*Or. Min.* 28).

Byzantine history and culture, Psellos' name nonetheless appears in discussions of almost every aspect of Byzantine civilization. In particular, he often takes center stage in discussions of the family, although, because these discussions are almost always focused on the court or the upper levels of the aristocracy, he does so through his historical work, the *Chronographia,* and the letters and orations that he wrote to and for members of the court and aristocracy. Our focus here will be different. In a number of writings Psellos discussed many of the women in his own life, including his mother, his prematurely deceased first daughter, and his second (adopted) daughter (though, oddly, never his own wife). Taken together, as they are for the first time in this volume, these texts present, through a variety of literary perspectives, the history over the course of a century of a Byzantine family belonging to what we may call the upper middle class of Constantinople. These were not members of the imperial family or great lords who commanded armies and provinces; rather, we are dealing with the class of court functionaries, high officials in the civil bureaucracy, and intellectuals. They were relatively wealthy (they employed servants and owned slaves) and cultivated an ideal of bourgeois respectability. The evidence that Psellos offers is crucially important because it enables us to understand the norms taken for granted by almost all writers during the apogee of Byzantine power, the standard, in other words, against which they measured the aberrant eccentricities of empresses and saints. The women and children we encounter in these texts led, by the standards of their own class, relatively unexceptional lives.

Certainly, it is ironic that we should find an exposition of this norm in Psellos, who otherwise conformed to few of the norms of his society. And yet it is only here that we may obtain a sustained look at the life of an average Byzantine family of this most important class, a topic that has received little to no attention in scholarship. Psellos' evidence, coming as it does from the mid-eleventh century, is important as a corrective in another way as well. Too often historians assume that the paranoid and highly restrictive views about women expressed by the rather bitter Kekaumenos, a writer of advice-maxims of the exact same period, are indicative of Byzantine views in general. Like the works of Psellos presented here, Kekaumenos' treatise remains untranslated into the major languages of modern research; nevertheless, his simple Greek and aphoristic style have ensured that he is quoted often by way of illustration of prevailing social *mores,* especially in discussions of women and the family. Psellos, as will be seen, not only had a very different attitude toward women, his account of the circumstances of their lives is very different in tenor.

The order in which the present texts have been placed reflects the chronology of their subjects rather that their dates of composition; the same is true of the letters that have been included here, though they are gathered together in one chapter toward the end of the volume. Thus we move from Psellos' mother and childhood to the premature death of his daughter Styliane, the engagement of his second (adopted) daughter, and the birth of his grandson. Each of these texts, which vary greatly in size, purpose, and genre, is prefaced by a separate introduction. The introduction to the collection as a whole provides an overview of the background information that will be required by readers who are not specialists on Psellos. The topics covered here are (i) the life of Psellos; (ii) the history of his family from his grandparents to his grandchildren, so covering five generations; and (iii) a composite picture of the lives of women and children in eleventh-century Constantinople, with which topic all the following texts are concerned in one way or another. It is from these works that we obtain a more detailed and comprehensive picture of their lives than from virtually any other Byzantine source.

A Brief Biography of Michael Psellos

No biography of Michael Psellos exists in any language, though at least one has been formally announced and brief surveys of his life preface studies of specific aspects of his career and writings. None of these, however, is in English.[2] It was therefore decided to begin this volume with a brief biography, which will provide the necessary context against which to discuss his family life.

Konstantinos Psellos—the baptismal name of the later monk Michael—was born in 1018, so during the reign of Basileios II and the apogee of Byzantine power, to a "middle-class" family in Constantinople. Early on his mother Theodote perceived that he was a prodigy and encouraged his studies, possibly at the local monastery of *ta Narsou,* with which Psellos maintained a lifelong connection. He later boasted that school lessons were child's play for him and that by the age of ten he could recite and expound the entire *Iliad.*[3] He was also

---

2. For the state of the field, see Kaldellis (2006). The following survey of Psellos' life was originally written for my study on *Hellenism in Byzantium* (in preparation).

3. Psellos, *Encomium for his Mother* 5b, 6b–c. In the *Chronographia* 4.4 he implies that he started to study Homer when he was sixteen, but this is unlikely. For *ta Narsou,* see Hondridou (2002) 159–160, citing previous scholarship.

a purely urban creature, sixteen years old before he even set eyes on the fields outside the walls (probably only in Constantinople could this happen in all of Christendom). By that age he had begun to study rhetoric and joined the staff of a provincial judge, but this internship was cut short by the death of his beloved sister.[4] Psellos' instructors in rhetoric were Ioannes Mauropous, who was famous as a teacher but would not make his mark as a writer until after Psellos' rise at the court, and Niketas, who would later serve under Psellos in the reformed educational system.[5] As far as philosophy was concerned, Psellos claimed to have studied it largely on his own: whereas he was "a perfect philosopher," his friends were only "lovers of philosophy."[6]

After serving in a judicial capacity in Mesopotamia and Asia Minor,[7] around 1040 Psellos appears as a secretary at the court of Michael IV. Though only twenty, he already displayed a knack for making friends in high places, including Alousianos, son of the last Bulgarian tsar (Ivan Vladislav), who joined Deljan's revolt against the empire, deposed its leader, and betrayed it to Michael IV in exchange for titles; and the captain of the guard sent against Michael V in the popular riot of 1042, an event of which Psellos later wrote a dramatic firsthand account.[8] His standing at the court rose sharply under Konstantinos IX Monomachos (1042–1055), a charming if rather frivolous patron of the arts and of education whose wanton expenditures and neglect of the army would soon prove disastrous for the empire. Psellos became one of his intimate advisors and personal secretaries, a position earned largely by "the grace of my language. . . . For I am told that my speech is beautiful, even when making routine statements." He also acted as the emperor's spokesman, writing eloquent speeches in his praise and in support of his policies (regardless of whether he agreed with them personally).[9] He had by then been befriended by Konstantinos Leichoudes,

---

4. Psellos, *Encomium for his Mother* 15a.

5. For Psellos and Mauropous, see Karpozelos (1982) 26–28; Ljubarskij (2004) 70–83; for Niketas, Psellos, *Funeral Oration for Niketas* 3–6.

6. Psellos, *Chronographia* 6.192.

7. Psellos, *Letter S* 180; *Letters KD* 65 and 136. Weiss (1973) 22–23 suggested on the basis of the last two letters that Psellos served as *krites* (provincial judge) of the themes (provinces) of Boukellarioi and Armeniakon at the age of twenty (Ljubarskij [2004] 45–46 has Thrakesion and Boukellarion); but see Cheynet (1999) 233–234.

8. Psellos, *Chronographia* 4.47, 5.39. Fine (1983) 206 suspects that Alousianos was a Byzantine agent from the beginning, an early lesson in intrigue for Psellos, if so.

9. Psellos, *Chronographia* 6.14, 6.44–45, 7A.7. For Psellos' misgivings and his use of rhetoric at the court, see Kaldellis (1999a) c. 19–21. The orations are *Or. Pan.* 1–10.

Monomachos' "prime minister" and later a patriarch (1059–1063), whom Psellos admired for his urbane, philosophical, and flexible statesmanship. He had also facilitated the introduction to the court of his teacher Mauropous and his friend Ioannes Xiphilinos, another future patriarch (1064–1075), alongside whom he continued to teach privately. When a dispute broke out in 1047 among their students, the emperor intervened and granted official recognition to both schools. Psellos assumed the lofty title of Consul of Philosophers and seems to have exercised some supervision over higher education in the capital, though the institutional aspects of his position are unclear. Xiphilinos was made *nomophylax* (guardian of the laws) in charge of the new law school, whose foundation was chartered in a novel probably authored by Mauropous. Discussing these new foundations thirty years later, the historian Michael Attaleiates claims that Psellos "surpassed all of our contemporaries in knowledge." The late 1040s witnessed the reign of the philosophers at Monomachos' court.[10]

In those years Psellos laid the foundations of his philosophical revolution. He delivered hundreds of lectures on philosophical, theological, scientific, and exegetical topics, taking charge of the education of many who would go on to serve in the administration and the Church. He boasted of the diverse origin of the students who attended his classes: "I have made Celts and Arabs yield to me and on account of my fame they come here . . . While the Nile irrigates the land of the Egyptians, my speech irrigates their souls. If you ask a Persian or an Ethiopian they will say that they have known me and admired me and sought me out."[11] Psellos projected an ideal of vast polymathy subordinated to the queen of sciences, philosophy, and often barely discriminated between pagan and Christian wisdom. He also began to wield influence at the court, contracting an advantageous marriage and amassing patrons, clients, titles, a fine town house, and enemies against whom he wrote defensive tracts. Yet for unknown reasons he was forced to resign from the powerful and prestigious position of *protasêkrêtis* (head of the college of imperial secretaries) and settle for the title of *vestarchês*. The regime of the philosophers began to

10. For Psellos on Leichoudes, see Criscuolo (1981) 20–22; (1982a) 138–139, 160–162; (1982b) 207–214; and (1983) 15–16, 60–72; Ljubarskij (2004) 92–95. Various opinions have been expressed regarding the foundation of the schools: see Wolska-Connus (1976); Lemerle (1977); Agapitos (1998); and Hondridou (2002) 155–253. See also Michael Attaleiates, *History* 21. For Psellos and Xiphilinos, Ljubarskij (2004) 83–92.

11. Psellos, *Letter to Michael Keroularios* 3c. For the truth behind this boast, see Wilson (1983) 164–165; Volk (1990) 15–20. For Psellos' teaching position, see Kaldellis (2005).

unravel around 1050, under pressure by forces that we cannot identify: Leichoudes was dismissed; Mauropous was sent off against his will to serve as bishop of Euchaïta on the Black Sea coast; Xiphilinos became a monk on Mt. Olympos in Bithynia; Psellos clung to the court, but came under increasing fire and suspicion for his beliefs. In late 1054 he was tonsured and took the name Michael, while Monomachos' death in early 1055 only raised further suspicions: had Psellos predicted his death through astrology?[12]

Psellos detested both the false premises and hypocritical practice of Christian asceticism and so it is no surprise that his brief stay on Mt. Olympos (1055–1056) was not happy. He had previously composed a witty parody of the liturgy exposing one of the holy mountain's heavy drinkers. While there he composed a philosophical funeral oration for his monastery's recently deceased founder and a eulogy of the mountain itself, praising its natural beauties and defensively noting in the first few lines that the many stars of its night sky were only lifeless bodies! Unlike Xiphilinos, Psellos was not sincere in his new vocation and quickly returned to the capital when the empress Theodora (1055–1056) allowed it. For years afterwards he exchanged acerbic letters and poems with some of the monks on Olympos. "Father Zeus," wrote a wit among the latter, "you could not endure Olympos even briefly, your goddesses weren't there with you," to which Psellos responded with a torrent of abuse.[13] Yet his friendship with Xiphilinos seems also to have been damaged.

Psellos' return led to years of intrigue for him. Mistrusted at the court of Theodora, which was dominated by his enemies, he was appointed by Michael VI the Old (1056–1057) to head an embassy to the rebel Isaakios Komnenos. After two trips to Nikomedeia, Psellos finally negotiated an agreement, but meanwhile a faction in the capital, including the ambitious patriarch Michael Keroularios, deposed the weak emperor. After this was announced, Psel-

---

12. House: Psellos, *Chronographia* 7A.7; clients: Ljubarskij (2004) 49–51; defensive tracts: *Or. Min.* 6–10 (the chronology of these works is not secure); Mauropous: Karpozelos (1982) 33–40. For a cryptic account of his departure from the court, see *Chronographia* 6.191–200 (and see the introduction to the *Encomium for his Mother,* below); astrology: 6A.10–12.

13. For Olympos, see Psellos, *Funeral Oration for Ioannes Xiphilinos* (*Hist. Byz. et alia,* pp. 440–446); cf. Gautier (1974) 15–21. Parody: Psellos, *Poem* 22. See also his *Funeral Oration for Nikolaos, Abbot of the Monastery of the Beautiful Source on Olympos,* and *Regarding Olympos* (*Or. Min.* 36), on which see, in general, Weiss (1977) 283–291. For the bitter exchanges, see *Poem* 21 and *Letters S* 35, 166–167, 185, with de Vries-van der Velden (1996a) 119.

los spent the night in terror at the rebel camp, but the next day Isaakios made him one of his advisors and appointed him a President of the Senate before they entered the city together in triumph. Some, of course, suspected that Psellos had simply betrayed Michael VI and joined forces with Isaakios.[14]

The first Komnenos to rule Byzantium tried desperately to restore the army and finances. What endeared him to Psellos was his confiscation of monastic wealth and, above all, his deposition in 1058 of Keroularios, an arrogant, contentious, and bigoted prelate—in fact a failed claimant to the throne in 1040— who had wrecked the empire's relations with the West in 1054, and who was now encroaching on imperial authority. Keroularios was likely among those who had undermined Monomachos' cabinet of intellectuals in the early 1050s and had humiliated Psellos by forcing him to produce a public confession of faith.[15] Philosophy now went on the offensive. In a heavily sarcastic letter Psellos cast Keroularios as the embodiment of "angelic" obscurantism, inflexibility, and boorishness that he associated with Christian asceticism. Isaakios appointed Psellos to direct the prosecution of the recalcitrant patriarch, who, however, died before the trial could begin. Psellos greeted this piece of news as an *evangelia* and went on to write a long prosecution anyway (probably to cancel the odium of having to write a panegyrical epitaph for Keroularios, whose memory was popular in the capital and therefore a matter of concern and appeasement for the emperor). Keroularios was replaced by Leichoudes, Psellos' old friend and ally.[16]

In 1059 Isaakios fell ill and abdicated under mysterious circumstances. As his personal physician, Psellos encouraged this decision against the wishes of the emperor's wife and went so far as to personally invest his successor,

14. Psellos, *Chronographia* 7.15–42; Ioannes Skylitzes, *Historical Synopsis: Michael VI* 11 (Thurn 497). See Kaldellis (1999a) 150–154, 167–168, for Psellos' long and self-serving account of the embassy.

15. Monastic wealth: Psellos, *Chronographia* 7.59–60; cf. Michael Attaleiates, *History* 61–62. For Keroularios in general, see Tinnefeld (1989); for his limitations, Kolbaba (2000) 33, 36, 94, 134; for his imperial pretensions, Dagron (2003) 235–247. Confession: Psellos, *Theol. II* 35, with Garzya (1967); Hondridou (2002) 238–239; cf. Psellos, *Encomium for the Blessed Patriarch Michael Keroularios* (*Hist. Byz. et alia* p. 355), for a possible allusion to this examination. For the relations between the two men, see, in general, Ljubarskij (2004) 125–140.

16. Psellos, *Letter to Michael Keroularios* passim. *Evangelia* and Leichoudes: *Chronographia* 7.65–66, with Kaldellis (1999a) 174–175. Cf. the extravagant *Accusation of the Archpriest before the Synod* (*OFA* 1) with the vapid *Encomium for the Blessed Patriarch Michael Keroularios* (*Hist. Byz. et alia* pp. 303–387).

Konstantinos X Doukas (1059–1067), even before Isaakios had made up his mind. Psellos then wrote the proclamation of the new emperor's accession to be distributed to the provinces. Psellos was a close friend of the Doukai, especially the emperor's brother, the Kaisar Ioannes.[17] The good-natured, deeply pious, but unwarlike new emperor did little to halt the empire's rapid decline as the Seljuks raided Asia Minor and sacked major cities. Psellos, now in his forties, spent the 1060s as an honored member of the imperial family, wielding considerable influence behind the throne. He was appointed to tutor Doukas' son and heir, Michael, for whom he composed a number of didactic and relatively superficial works on legal, historical, and scientific topics, sometimes rededicating to him works originally presented to Konstantinos IX. We can safely detect his hand at work in the choice of Xiphilinos to replace Leichoudes as patriarch in 1064. In the early years of the reign he also completed the first edition of his *Chronographia,* covering the emperors from Basileios II to Isaakios. Beyond its ambitious philosophical message, this text employs masterly and virtually unprecedented literary techniques verging on the postmodern to demythologize the imperial position and expose the all-too-human qualities of God's anointed. This by itself implies a political theory, as Psellos did not believe that "ideal" emperors were possible—all were both good and bad—but there is also a more subversive theme running through the work: the empire must be governed by soldiers, not civilians, and its resources should be used to support the army, not the civilian administration, the Church, or the monasteries.[18]

Konstantinos' death in 1067 precipitated a crisis in the Doukas regime. His widow, Eudokia Makrembolitissa, a niece of Keroularios and opponent of Ioannes Doukas and Psellos, broke her oath to her husband, marrying and elevating to the throne the handsome general and former plotter Romanos Diogenes (1068–1071). Romanos tried to restore the military situation by conducting long and determined albeit poorly planned and indecisive campaigns against the Seljuks. Ioannes Doukas was forced to the sidelines and Psellos

17. For Psellos' medical knowledge and practice, see Volk (1990). Isaakios' wife, Aikaterine, was the sister of Psellos' friend Alousianos. Proclamation: *Or. Min.* 5. For Ioannes Doukas, see D.I. Polemis (1968) 34–41; Ljubarskij (2004) 111–119.

18. The literary qualities of the *Chronographia* are slowly gaining attention: see Macrides (1996) 211–217; Ljubarskij et al. (1998) 13–15; and the unsystematic but often insightful "Afterthoughts" of Karalis' translation, v. 2, 469–503. Mixture of qualities: 6.25–28. Political theory: Kaldellis (1999a) c. 5–6, 9, 24.

himself was distrusted, despite the fact that he continued, as always, to praise the emperor in public orations and to draft his pronouncements. Romanos even compelled him to accompany his second expedition to Syria in 1069, joining Michael Attaleiates in the emperor's council of advisors. Psellos disagreed utterly with Romanos' strategy and tactics and proffered his own, based on his superior understanding of the "science" of war.[19] But it was intrigue that restored the Doukai and sealed the fate of Byzantine Asia Minor. Many suspected that Ioannes' son Andronikos betrayed Romanos at the battle of Manzikert in 1071 (though there were additional reasons for the defeat). Psellos and Ioannes promptly deposed Eudokia, elevated her son Michael VII Doukas (1071–1078) to the throne, and declared Romanos an outlaw, refusing to recognize his surprisingly favorable agreement with Alp Arslan. A civil war conducted by the Doukai resulted in the surrender, tonsure, and brutal—in fact, fatal— blinding of Romanos. In the brief supplement to the *Chronographia* that he wrote in 1075, whose purpose was to expose the frivolity of his patrons the Doukai through sarcastic praise, Psellos boasted of the power that he personally wielded at the court in those critical days.[20] A moving letter of consolation to the blinded Romanos—that referred to God as the "Sleepless Eye that watches over all," encouraged him to find his "inner sight," and that was written soon after a bombastic congratulatory letter to his conqueror Andronikos— cannot divert our attention from the damage done to the empire by the Psellos-Doukas regime, nor does Psellos' devastating sarcasm regarding his patrons mitigate his role in those events.[21]

Michael VII was an utterly incompetent and corrupt ruler. Attaleiates said that he was fit only to be a bishop! Psellos continued to write various treatises for his education and edification and to draft his diplomatic correspondence, but little seems to have been done to halt the decline of imperial authority.

---

19. Psellos, *Chronographia* 7B.12–16. Panegyrics for Romanos: *Or. Pan.* 18–21. For philosophers as armchair generals, see *When he resigned from the rank of* protasêkrêtis 33 ff. (*Or. Min.* 8); see also his *On Military Formation* (*De oper. daem.* pp. 120–124). For an anguished letter that Psellos wrote during the campaign of 1069, see Snipes (1981). De Vries-van der Velden (1997) has a different view of the relationship between Psellos and Romanos; the matter certainly requires further study: see Ljubarskij (2004) 55–56.

20. Psellos, *Chronographia* 7B.27–30. For Andronikos and Mantzikert, see D. I. Polemis (1968) 55–59.

21. Psellos, *Letters S* 82 and 145 respectively. Cf. Skylitzes Continuatus (Tsolakes 152), based in part on Psellos' own admissions.

Certainly, we do not know what kind of influence Psellos had at this time as the court politics of the period remain very little understood, yet contemporaries did complain that the emperor was spending all his time "on the vain and useless study of letters, trying constantly to compose iambic and anapestic verses . . . deceived in this by the Consul of the Philosophers."[22] To this ignoble end had Psellos, charmed by the mystique of the palace, led a career that had promised so much for philosophical renewal under Monomachos, ultimately betraying his own astute analysis of the empire's practical needs. Moreover, the consul's days were numbered. The emperor's favor was usurped by a crafty and hugely corrupt eunuch named Nikephoros, who led the empire to the nadir of its fortunes. The position of Consul of the Philosophers was eventually given to Psellos' student Ioannes Italos. Psellos himself is not heard from again after 1075–1076, when he left off writing his sarcastic account of the Doukas regime, delivered a funeral oration for Xiphilinos, and welcomed back to the capital his old teacher Mauropous.[23] By his own arrangement, he was buried at a famous monastery of the Theotokos, the *Zôodochos Pêgê* situated just outside the walls of the city.[24]

The Family History of Michael Psellos

We know very little about Psellos' grandparents and have only hints about ancestors prior to them. Our information comes from the *Encomium* for Psellos' mother. His maternal grandparents were native Constantinopolitans who came into life and died at roughly the same time (2b), though Theodote, their first child (2c), died after her father but before her mother (24d). The dates of these deaths cannot, however, be established precisely (see the introduction to

22. Michael Attaleiates, *History* 303. Complaints: Skylitzes Continuatus (Tsolakis 171). Cf. Psellos, *Chronographia* 7C.4 for Michael's intellectual interests, including iambic verses. For Psellos' writings associated with Michael VII, see D. I. Polemis (1968) 44–45.

23. Italos: Anna Komnene, *Alexiad* 5.8.5. The latest discussion of Psellos' death places it in ca. 1078: Karpozelos (2003), examining previous proposals (but see the next section below). Mauropous' return: Karpozelos (1982) 46. For the last section of the *Chronographia,* see the notes of the Karalis tr., as well as Criscuolo (1982b) 201–206. Various pieces of evidence have been put forward to show that Psellos lived past 1080, e.g., by Ljubarskij (2004) 58–63, but all are dubious and none may be accepted at this time.

24. Psellos, *Letters KD* 177, 228; for the monastery, see Janin (1969) 223–228.

the *Encomium,* below). This side of the family, Psellos broadly hints, was not so-cially distinguished (2a). Theodote had at least two brothers, given that Psellos refers at one point to the youngest of them (5d).

Psellos' father, on the other hand, came from a more distinguished family, which included both consuls and *patrikioi* among its ancestors (4b)—or so his son boasted. In this connection, we should note that a younger contemporary, the historian Michael Attaleiates, refers to the death in 1078 of "the monk and *hypertimos* Michael, who had been in charge of political affairs." He goes on to characterize him as an "unpleasant" man whose family originated in Nikome-deia (296–297). Some historians—including the latest discussion—have taken this as a reference to Michael Psellos.[25] But the identification is doubtful. First, Attaleiates refers to this man elsewhere as Michael of Nikomedeia (181), though no source refers to Psellos in this way. Second, Attaleiates does refer to Psellos elsewhere in his *History,* in connection with his assumption of the post of Presi-dent (i.e., Consul) of the Philosophers. Without naming him, which itself ad-ditionally militates against the identification, he says that he "surpassed all of our contemporaries in knowledge" and claims that he was a good teacher (21). This does not accord with the negative portrayal of Michael of Nikomedeia later in the work. In fact, Attaleiates may have studied under Psellos during the reign of Monomachos.[26] Third, in his voluminous and autobiographical cor-pus, Psellos never refers to a family link with Nikomedeia, not even in the trea-tise that he wrote regarding a puzzling natural phenomenon that occurred in that city which he claims to have witnessed personally.[27] In short, it may be a sheer coincidence that the monk Michael of Nikomedeia was politically active and held the title of *hypertimos* (which was not uncommon).

Allusions in the *Encomium* indicate that Psellos' parents were affluent (4b, 11d), though we know nothing of the source of their wealth. It was probably not agricultural, for Psellos claims that he was sixteen before he even set eyes on the fields outside the city (15a).

Theodote's first child was a daughter. If we assume that the latter was some five years older than Psellos (cf. 13b–c), we may place her birth in ca. 1013. Psellos claims that his mother was only "a few years older" than this sister and

---

25. Esp. Karpozelos (2003) 673–675, citing prior discussions of the question and rightly disposing of other arguments regarding Psellos' death; *contra:* Ljubarskij (2004) 61.

26. Krallis (2006) chs. 3–4.

27. Psellos, *On the echo-chamber in Nikomedeia* (*Phil. Min. I* 31).

that it was difficult to tell them apart (13b)—a universal compliment, it seems—
so we may place Theodote's own birth in ca. 998. Her husband seems likewise
to have been a teenager when they married (4a), though we do not know for
how many years, if any, they remained childless together. Her second child was
also a daughter (4d), but given that nothing more is said of her we may assume
that she died in infancy. Psellos was the third child and the first son, though it
is not clear whether there were any more after him. He does not mention any
in the *Encomium*, but his own death is the subject of a brief letter of consolation addressed by his student Theophylaktos Hephaistos, later archbishop of
Bulgaria, to "the brother of Psellos." Theophylaktos' modern editor maintained
that this is a mistake, as Psellos does not mention brothers in the *Encomium*.
But the contents of the letter, especially its many uses of *adelphos*, indicate that
a literal relationship is meant (see below, p. 176) and, besides, we should not
rely too much on the silences of the *Encomium*.[28] In *Letter S* 17, Psellos mentions how he took care of his parents in old age, loved his brothers, and treated
his friends fittingly (see below, p. 169). The term "brother" in Byzantium, as in
many other societies, was often used in a non-literal sense—this very letter
in fact is addressed to a "brother" who is clearly only a friend—but here these
"brothers" are clearly differentiated from friends and come between them and
Psellos' natural parents, so it is possible that natural brothers are meant. Can
this refer only to a sole sister who had died decades ago? It is not impossible, as
Psellos is speaking in very general terms, but it does seem unlikely.

Psellos' sister was married (13a) and delivered a baby (14d) shortly before
dying in Psellos' sixteenth year (15a), so in 1034. We do not know her name or
that of her husband or anything about the fate of Psellos' nephew. Psellos' father died "soon" after the death of his daughter (18b), his mother long afterwards (22d), but it is impossible to fix these dates with any greater precision
(see the introduction to the *Encomium*, below).

It is odd that the woman in Psellos' life we know the least about is his wife.[29]
She is mentioned (though not by name) in the *Funeral Oration* that Psellos
composed for their daughter Styliane, who died around the age of nine (68).
What we have for the most part are generic references to her moral qualities,
but one passage stands out: Psellos claims that Styliane was descended from em-

28. Theophylaktos Hephaistos, *Letter* 132 (Gautier 588–589, with reservations expressed at 23 n. 4, 113–116, 588 n. 1). For the letter, see Mullett (1997) 143.

29. De Vries-van der Velden (1996b) 244–245 has argued that she is the subject of
Letter KD 34. The case, though quite plausible, is not conclusive.

perors on her mother's side, specifically from "the fathers of emperors" (63), i.e., presumably from the father of an imperial bride. Various suggestions about his identity have been made, including that of Stylianos Zaoutzes, one of the fathers-in-law of Leon VI (886–912), who gave his name to Styliane.[30] At the end of the text, Psellos notes that he and his wife had long been without children (87), and twice suggests that Styliane was their only child (80, 81), but he also hints that she had siblings (86). It is, however, difficult to be certain about the latter passage given the rhetorical nature of the praise that it contains (and we will see below that shortly after Styliane's death Psellos had no other children left to him). His wife was certainly alive when Styliane died, as numerous references in the oration attest.[31]

It is difficult to assign dates to Psellos' marriage and the life of Styliane. It is likely that the girl's death occurred before Psellos left the court of Monomachos in late 1054 to become a monk, because his account of her sickness suggests a normal household life and conjugal relationship. In a letter written probably soon after his tonsure, and possibly on Mt. Olympos in Bithynia, Psellos wrote that new monks do miss their wives and native lands.[32] As we saw, he himself would later be compared to Zeus and ridiculed by a fellow monk for being unable to endure Olympos without his "goddesses." Though Psellos did take up politics after his return from Bithynia, it is unlikely that he took up residence with his wife. Still, in a letter from the 1060s to his friend Konstantinos, nephew of the former patriarch Keroularios, he sends the greetings of his "women," children, free dependents, and slaves, including his oven-man and baker. It is unclear who these "women and children" are.[33] Another letter to Konstantinos, in which Psellos contrasts his friend's household to his own lack of conjugal company, dates to an even later period. This is shown both by what we know of the career of Konstantinos, whose elevation to the post of *epi tôn kriseôn* (a

30. Leroy-Molinghen and Karlin-Hayter (1968). Sathas (1874) xxxvii n. 5 suggested the family of Argyros on the ground that Psellos refers to one of its members as an *anêpsios* ("nephew"). But he uses this term as well for Konstantinos, the nephew of the patriarch Keroularios: Volk (1990) 20–21 n. 69, e.g., Psellos, *Letter KD* 31 and 214 (Kurtz and Drexl 46 and 254). *Anêpsios* is a term that he seems to have used for the sons of his dear friends: de Vries-van der Velden (1996a) 112.

31. Number of children: Sideras (1994) 119–120 n. 86; Leroy-Molinghen (1969a) 155 n. 2; Psellos' wife: ibid. 156 n. 1.

32. Psellos, *Letter S* 54 (Sathas 285).

33. Psellos, *Letter KD* 31 (Kurtz and Drexl 49, lines 19–23); for Psellos and Konstantinos, see Ljubarskij (2004) 102–111.

judicial office) occurred after 1074, and by Psellos' reference to his dear ones, some of whom were dead—was Styliane on his mind twenty-five years later?—while others—his wife?—were lost to him. This letter, in any case, cannot be used to question the historicity of his marriage and, by extension, the authenticity of the *Funeral Oration*.[34] After all, in the *Encomium* Psellos admits that he has not conformed to his mother's exaltation of virginity (8b), which may refer only to marriage.

Moreover, Psellos' (feigned) concern in the *Encomium* to avoid praising his mother's physical beauty on the ground that such non-spiritual topics must be avoided now that he has become a monk (see the introduction to that text, below), has no counterpart in the *Funeral Oration,* which, in sharp contrast to the *Encomium,* gives no rhetorical sign that Psellos has formally renounced worldly life. This allows us to conclude that the *Oration* was written prior to 1054. Subtracting nine years and, say, five years of childless marriage, we arrive at 1041 as the latest date for Psellos' marriage. He would then have been about twenty-two, so an even earlier date may be postulated given the early date of marriage among the Byzantines (e.g., Psellos' father was probably in his mid-teens when he married Theodote). By 1040 Psellos had already secured a post as secretary at the court of Michael IV, a secure enough position from which to plan a marriage and obtain a good match (to say nothing of the possibly independent financial standing of his parents). This means that the death of Styliane may have occurred as early as 1050.

The third text translated in the present collection is a *hypomnêma,* a court memorandum regarding the dissolution of the engagement of Psellos' adopted daughter to a certain Elpidios Kenchres, the son of the high official Ioannes Kenchres. This is perhaps not the only text in which we hear of this daughter, who unfortunately also remains anonymous, as the three texts that relate to Psellos' newborn grandson probably refer to her as well (see below). The details regarding her engagement, its dissolution, and her fiancé, may be found in the *hypomnêma* and the introduction below.[35] What interest us here are chiefly questions of chronology and family history. The memorandum, then,

34. Psellos, *Letter KD* 214 (Kurtz and Drexl 255, line 22 ff.), *pace* Vergari (1988) 155–156; cf. eadem (1985). For the letter's context, see de Vries-van der Velden (1996a) 145–146 n. 79, though the date she offers (1078) is open to debate; for the career of Konstantinos, see Oikonomidès (1963) 119–120; Gautier (1970) 212–216; and Snipes (1981) 102–103. At *Fun. Or.* 85 Psellos promises that his grief for Styliane will have no end in time.

35. For adoption in Byzantium, see Macrides (1990), for this case 116; Kiousopoulou (1990) 158–162; for engagements, ibid. 31–36; Papadatos (1984), 231–233 for this case.

specifies that Psellos had no other children when he made the adoption (144), late in the reign of Monomachos. Pained by the death of Styliane before the age of marriage, a fact plaintively noted in the very title of her *Funeral Oration,* Psellos moved quickly to arrange the engagement of his new daughter, as he notes, "when she was still a child and not yet old enough to marry." Her fiancé was exactly twice her age (144). From the fact that Psellos used his influence to obtain titles and posts for him, we may postulate their ages at about nine and eighteen. In other words, after the death of Styliane, Psellos immediately adopted a daughter of exactly the same age and rushed to arrange for her marriage, a sequence of events that affords curious insights into his state of mind. The memorandum, interestingly, makes no mention of his wife, from whom he would have been separated when he was tonsured. There is no reason to believe that she had died in the meantime.

The betrothal was finally dissolved in court in August of 1056, following the intervention of the empress Theodora. Psellos' adopted daughter would then have been about thirteen. It would seem that Psellos did subsequently manage to find her a more acceptable husband than Elpidios Kenchres, as she produced a son whose birth Psellos announced in *Letter S* 72 to the Kaisar Ioannes Doukas (see p. 172) and whose infancy he described in the charming address *To his grandson* and then again later in *Letter S* 157 to his friend Konstantinos (these are translated below, pp. 162 and 173). We know of no other child by Psellos to whom this grandson can be assigned; such a child would have to have been born between the adoption of Psellos' second daughter in the early 1050s and 1054, which seems unlikely and is in any case unattested. A recent study has argued that Psellos' son-in-law was Basileios Maleses, a close friend and colleague of the historian Michael Attaleiates who made his career in the 1060s as a provincial judge, benefiting from Psellos' patronage at the court of Konstantinos X Doukas. Though Maleses was away for most of that decade at his posts in Anatolia and the Peloponnese, he may have fathered children in the mid to late 1060s.[36] In his *Letter S* 157 to Konstantinos from the mid-1070s, Psellos alludes to the children (plural) of the *vestarchês,* probably a reference to the grandchildren fathered by his son-in-law. This use of the plural may be only a rhetorical trope, but Psellos refers to his great concern for the "children of the *vestarchês*" in *Letter KD* 268 as well (for the circumstances, see p. 160).

36. The argument was made by de Vries-van der Velden (1996a), esp. 142 n. 74 for the date (see also pp. 157–160, below, for a discussion).

In *Letter S* 146, probably from the 1060s, Psellos informs his son-in-law that the *magistrissa*—the wife of a *magistros*[37]—was both physically sick and worried about the slanders being spread about her husband. The casual manner in which Psellos here discusses his close relationship to another man's wife indicates that she was almost certainly his own daughter. There is no reference to children in this letter, though there is no reason why there should be. The history of the relationship of the two men is a matter of ongoing speculation and need not detain us here (see below, p. 159). What matters for our purposes is that from Psellos' loving address *To his grandson, who was still an infant,* we may infer that the child was born into a fairly prosperous household, with a nursery, servants, a doting grandfather, and, through Psellos, a connection to the court, most probably that of Konstantinos X Doukas and Eudokia Makrembolitissa; the latter in fact sponsored the child's baptism.

If Maleses really was Psellos' son-in-law, Maleses' son would have been involved in Maleses' own disgrace by the emperor Michael VII in 1074 and the gradual destruction of the faction of Psellos and the Kaisar Ioannes Doukas. Attaleiates specifically states that Maleses was deprived of his property and children, probably for being captured by and then seeming to join the renegade mercenary Roussel de Bailleul (see below, p. 159). We have no way of knowing exactly how harmful and how permanent this turn of events was for Psellos and his grandchildren. By 1093–1094, his grandson had fallen on hard times or was seeking advancement by evoking pity (a common enough solicitation). A letter of the aforementioned Theophylaktos Hephaistos, archbishop of Bulgaria, pleads with the official Gregorios Kamateros to find a job for the son of the daughter of the great Psellos, to whom Theophylaktos felt that he owed a debt.[38] This, then, is the last reference in the record to the family of Michael Psellos, whose fortunes we have traced for exactly a century. There is unfortunately no way to know whether the teacher and philosopher Michael Psellos, active in Constantinople in the mid-twelfth century, was descended from his illustrious namesake. He is mentioned fondly in a letter of Ioannes Apokaukos, bishop of Naupaktos in the early thirteenth century.[39]

---

37. See Margarou (2000) 72–74 for this and other attestations.

38. Theophylaktos Hephaistos, *Letter* 27 (Gautier 218–221; for Gregorios and the letter, see 73–75, but Gautier wrongly assumes that Psellos' grandson was born of the union between his adopted daughter and Elpidios Kenchris). For the letter, see Leroy-Molinghen (1969b) 295–296; and Mullett (1997) 136, 138.

39. See Lambropoulos (1988) 41–42 n. 15 for sources and discussion.

Daughters and Wives in Eleventh-Century Constantinople

The aim of this section is not to draw together sources that relate to women and children in Byzantium in general, but to offer a composite picture of their lives in eleventh-century Constantinople based on the texts translated in this volume. This exercise is justified by the fact that these texts deal with the same family and social class and come from the same author. We therefore avoid the danger of blurring the differences among periods, regions, and levels of society. Moreover, the majority of evidence that we have for the lives of women in Byzantium relates either to saints or to empresses. We are here offered the unique opportunity to study in detail the life and history of a family of the upper middle class in the capital in a time of peace and relative prosperity (the closest parallel to this multi-generational family portrait is probably the *Life of St. Philaretos* written by the saint's grandson Niketas, though this text reflects a very different setting and period and is informed by a different set of concerns). Besides, there already exist many general surveys of women in Byzantium and interested readers may consult those.[40]

In the case of Psellos' family, we are probably dealing at all times with an extended household, including, as he notes at the end of a letter to his friend Konstantinos, women, children, free dependents, and slaves, including skilled workers and craftsmen such as oven-makers and bakers and, probably, their families

---

40. For a compound picture of the life of a Byzantine woman, albeit indiscriminate in its use of evidence and drawing heavily on the Church Fathers, see Koukoules (1948–1955) vol. 2.2, 163–218. For prolegomena to the study of Byzantine women, focusing on social and economic questions, see Herrin (1983); for a brief and entertaining survey of women in late antiquity, Clark (1993); for the middle and late periods, see the lucid summaries of Laiou (1981) and Talbot (1997); for the eleventh and twelfth centuries, Garland (1988) and Nardi (2002) (though both rely on uncritical reporting of the sources; the latter offers mostly typologies); for an attempt on the basis of monastic *typika* to discover how Byzantine women of the middle and late period thought of themselves, Laiou (1985); for women in Epeiros in the early thirteenth century, see Kiousopoulou (1990) 115–130, based on legal sources. Connor (2004) covers the entire period, alternating between brief syntheses and biographical portraits (mostly of the usual empresses, nuns, and saints). Though well-written, the book is probably intended for a general audience and approaches its subjects piously, even whitewashing some of them. For the catalogue of an exhibition devoted to Byzantine women, with visual imagery and discussions of many aspects of their lives, see Kalavrezou (2003). Bibliography on more specific issues will be cited at the relevant points of the discussion below.

as well (*Letter KD* 31). Psellos' own class, then, were people who could not easily live without servants. His mother still had an attendant waiting on her even after she had entered a convent (though she had not yet taken the habit: *Enc.* 22a–b).[41] It was a sign of humility and charity on her part that she made clothes for her servants with her own hands (4b). The extended household (*oikos*), then, could comprise upwards of twenty people and perhaps many more. Unfortunately, we know little about its physical setting, as we know little in general about Byzantine housing.[42] In the *Chronographia,* Psellos notes that his advancement at the court under Monomachos brought with it a fine town house (7A.7), more likely a compound housing a small community of men, women, and children whose fortunes depended largely on Psellos' ability to gain and keep the emperor's favor.

The communal environment of the household marked virtually every aspect of life. Psellos' sister gave birth while surrounded by a team of midwives who "assisted in the delivery, tended to her needs, and comforted her, by stimulating and relaxing the labor pains." Presumably men were excluded, as were other pregnant or young married women (14d).[43] The *omphalotomos* presumably specialized in cutting the umbilical cord, and fathers either rushed in to embrace their newborn child immediately, covered in blood as it would have been, or waited for it to be washed and swaddled first (*Letter S* 157, which concerns the birth of a son to Psellos' friend Konstantinos[44]). Labor was very dangerous for the mother. It is not clear whether Psellos' sister died as a result of such complications, but at the very moment that his adopted daughter was giving birth some forty years later, Psellos was writing a letter on truffles to the Kaisar Ioannes Doukas, in which he pauses to remark fearfully that "my baby daughter is pouring her life out" (*Letter KD* 233). When he was told that it was not going well, he says he nearly died; he began to pace outside her room,

41. For this practice in late antiquity, see Clark (1993) 103; in the middle and late periods, Laiou (1981) 242.

42. For the Byzantine *oikos,* see Magdalino (1984); Patlagean (1987) 567–579; Neville (2004) 66–77; for Byzantine houses, Koukoules (1948–1955) vol. 4, 249–317; Oikonomides (1990); Sigalos (2004); Dark (2005); for female domesticity in late antiquity, Clark (1993) 94 ff.; in the middle period, Kazhdan (1998); A. Walker (2003).

43. For midwives in the Roman empire, see French (1987); in late antiquity, Clark (1993) 67, 69–70; in the middle and late periods, Laiou (1981) 245 and n. 62; Margarou (2000) 235–236. For various sources describing birth, see Koukoules (1948–1955) v. 4, 21–29, who concludes that Psellos' sister may have given birth while standing up, supported on either side.

44. See de Vries-van der Velden (1996a) 141–142, esp. n. 74, who rightly corrects Leroy-Molinghen (1969b).

hanging on her cries. When the women about the new mother announced the birth, adding that the baby looked just like him—a lie, he knew, but a pleasant one—Psellos rushed in to hug and kiss his grandson (*Letter S* 72). Newborns were washed by the *balaneutria* with hot water and swaddled as the midwife (*maia*) sang a lullaby (*Letter S* 157).[45]

Male children were certainly preferred. Perhaps the entire household was required to pray that Theodote deliver a boy after giving birth to two girls, and many would have joined in the hymns of thanks when she did (*Enc.* 4d). Regarding the birth of a son to his friend Konstantinos, Psellos claims that he himself, at any rate, was indifferent to the gender of infants—"male or female: what's the difference?"—but nevertheless admitted that he was more pleased that it was male and congratulated his friend accordingly (*Letter S* 157). To be sure, Psellos really liked babies and wrote about making baby-faces at them, calling this his feminine side.[46]

These babies enjoyed specialized care. They were breast-fed by wet nurses (*têtthê, thêlazousa*), swaddled and bathed in tubs regularly, and, at least in the case of Psellos' grandson, doted upon by adoring grandfathers who burst into the women's chambers in order to kiss and play with them (*Letter S* 157; *To his grandson,* passim). In his *Funeral Oration for Styliane,* Psellos mentions as being present at her death "friends, relatives, male and female slaves, free dependents, nurses and wet nurses, who . . . had swaddled her and breast-fed her and nourished her and raised her to this age, everything short of actually giving birth to her" (79–80). It is unclear how much contact such children actually had with their parents. Psellos' daughter appears in the work that he addressed to her son only to dress the baby in fancy clothes (*To his grandson* 154); everything else seems to have been taken care of by others, except, of course, the audience with the empress. It seems, however, that it was considered a good sign if a baby did not accept a wet nurse, only its mother's teat (*Enc.* 5a). These texts afford us rare and precious glimpses into the Byzantine nursery.[47]

---

45. For additional sources on the treatment of newborns and mothers, see Koukoules (1948–1955) v. 4, 29–35. For these female professions, see Margarou (2000) 214–215, 235–236.

46. Cf. Papaioannou (2000).

47. Leroy-Molinghen (1969b) 297–299. For breast-feeding in Byzantium, see Beaucamp (1982); for Byzantine childhood in general, Koukoules (1948–1955) vol. 1.1, 138–160, followed by a long section on children's games; Antoniadis-Bibicou (1973); and Moffatt (1986); Kiousopoulou (1990) 131–139 for thirteenth-century Epeiros. For perceptions of childhood in late antiquity, see Kalogeras (2001), citing previous studies (though relying exclusively on religious texts); for childhood in the Latin West in late antiquity, Nathan (2000) ch. 6.

Girls were educated chiefly in piety and in the practical skills and authority of household management. As mentioned above, we are not dealing here with the atomized, suburban, nuclear household of the 1950s that did so much to spark the feminist movement in the U.S. The *oikos* had the size of a small village and being confined to it hardly amounted to boredom and isolation. When Psellos says that as she grew up his daughter Styliane talked with her wet nurses, spent time with children her own age, and played with the servant-women (63–64), he need not imply that she ever stepped foot outside the *oikos*. Practical skills learned by girls, often from their own mothers, included working the loom, embroidery, and weaving fine textiles with silk threads (*Fun. Or.* 66; *Enc.* 3b).[48] From one of Psellos' brief works we learn of a festival named Agathê that was celebrated every year in Constantinople on the day after the commemoration of the city's foundation and that involved song and dance. The participants were chiefly women who seem to have been professional weavers. It is unclear whether private women such as his own mother could participate or whether it was reserved for members of a guild, as has been proposed (see below, p. 179 for a translation and discussion). From a very early age, girls were also habituated to the practices of the Orthodox Church, attending service regularly, learning the Psalms, and joining in the chanting of hymns (*Enc.* 3c; *Fun. Or.* 67, 74–76), none of which required literacy. As mothers, they would later teach their children stories from Bible, as Theodote did to Psellos; she also forbade his nurse from telling him fables about Greek monsters (*Enc.* 8a). In general, religious inculcation seems to have been more thorough and systematic with girls than with boys. These two aspects of girls' education, which Psellos philosophically viewed as the active and the contemplative parts of their lives respectively (*Enc.* 4a), came together in the practice of charity. Theodote wove beautiful garments that she gave to servants and the poor (*Enc.* 4b, 12a–b) and attended to the needs of monks and nuns (11c–d, 12c). Styliane did the same even before the age of eight (*Fun. Or.* 75).

Opinions differed regarding the degree of affection that should be shown to children. Theodote apparently believed that too much was not good, and hugged and kissed Psellos only when she thought he was asleep (*Enc.* 8b; cf. 13c). It is hard to believe that Psellos himself maintained such a stance toward

---

48. For these female occupations, see Laiou (1981) 243–254; Nardi (2002) 43–45; Heinz (2003) 140–141; for the upbringing of girls in this period, see Garland (1988) 368–370.

his daughters, given his behavior toward his grandson later (*To his grandson,* passim; *Letter S* 157). And it does in fact seem that he and his wife were very affectionate toward Styliane (*Fun. Or.* 75). It should be noted that one aspect of family life in the middle Byzantine period, the castration of boys, is never mentioned in connection with any member of Psellos' family.[49]

There was also in general no consensus about the literary education of girls. Theodote, for instance, was not allowed to learn how to read on the explicit grounds that she was woman; nevertheless, she secretly found someone to teach her the letters and then made her own way from there (*Enc.* 3b). Her parents' attitude would be shared by Alexios I Komnenos and Eirene Doukaina toward their daughter Anna, while Theodote's initiative in learning how to read finds a much earlier parallel in Theoktiste, the mother of Theodoros Stoudites, who taught herself to read at night so as not to upset her husband or allow education to interfere with her household duties.[50] Later Theodote became very active in Psellos' education, testing him after school, listening to him recite his lessons, and staying up with him at night as he studied (10a–b). Most importantly, it was she who finally persuaded the family to allow Psellos to continue his studies and make a career of them (5b–6d). It seems that, like many other mothers in Byzantium (and modern Greece), she pushed him to acquire an education by which he could then secure a well-paying job in the state bureaucracy (cf. *Chronographia* 1.29). More generally one can say that the personal influence of mothers was greater upon their children than that of their fathers, though this is difficult to quantify and access. Still, one does gain the impression that many sons in Byzantium worshipped their mothers more than they idolized their fathers, which testifies to the strength of these women's personalities and, often,

49. For this practice, see Ringrose (2003) 61 ff. and passim.

50. Georgios Tornikes, *Funeral Oration for Anna Komnene* (Darrouzès 245). For the same attitude, see Jeffreys (1984) 205 for the monk Iakobos; for a general survey, see Reinsch (2000), here 87. In the *Preface* to her *Diataxis* 16 (Kurtz 99), Anna says that her parents did not prohibit her from learning, but her testimony on family issues is not necessarily preferable to that of Tornikes (or any other source, for that matter) and is, moreover, suspiciously defensive in this case. For the authorship of this text, see Buckler (1929) 9–10. Theoktiste: Theodoros Stoudites, *Funeral Oration for his Mother* 3 (= *Or.* 13 in *PG* 99, col. 885b). For education of women in late antiquity, see Clark (1993) 135–138; in the middle and late periods, Laiou (1981) 253–257; Nardi (2002) 46–55 (mostly reporting what the texts say); for Psellos on his mother's education, with an eye on patristic models, see Vergari (1987b) 217–221.

their dominant position in the household.[51] This impression of matriarchy is certainly the one that we gain from the *Encomium.*

Psellos' own attitude toward female education was the opposite of that of his maternal grandparents. When he states that men are stronger or superior to women what he almost always has in mind are their bodies (e.g., *Enc.* 7b, 13b). As a Platonist philosopher, he was entirely convinced that women are in no way inferior to men as moral agents and rational beings.[52] He affirms this strongly toward the end of the *Encomium*: "if the two genders differ in the tenor of their bodies, nevertheless they possess reason equally and indistinguishably" (25b). This notion, which seems to have been gaining ground in the middle and late Byzantine periods,[53] may explain Psellos' generally favorable portrayal of the sole reign of the empress Theodora (1055–1056) in the *Chronographia* and, more relevant to our theme, the provisions that he made for the education of Styliane. By her sixth year she could read and began her study of the Psalms; we hear of teachers and female classmates over whom she excelled (*Fun. Or.* 65–66). These teachers were no doubt privately hired and the reference to classmates implies that at least some other parents in the city took a similar approach to the education of their daughters as did the Consul of the Philosophers.[54]

In general, the education of girls had two goals that were usually, though not always, in agreement. The first was to produce women who could effectively run the household of their husbands by acquiring and allocating resources so as to increase the prosperity of the *oikos* (*Enc.* 4a). In *Letter KD* 70,

51. In general, Byzantines wrote about their mothers, not their fathers. In addition to Psellos, see Theodoros Stoudites, *Funeral Oration for his Mother,* and Christophoros Mytilenaios, *Poems* 57–60 (Kurtz 33–36). See also the relationships of the emperors Alexios I Komnenos and Ioannes VI Kantakouzenos to their mothers. Augustine was no Byzantine, but conformed to this pattern. For this phenomenon in general, see Kazhdan (1998) 11–12. For maternal education, see Patlagean (1987) 605 (and 597–598 on choosing a career for a son) and Herrin (1999), who add material from hagiography but oddly omit Psellos' mother.

52. I intend to discuss this aspect of the philosophical tradition in late antiquity and Byzantium in a separate work focusing on Plato's *Republic.*

53. Laiou (1981) 258–259.

54. For a comprehensive survey of education in eleventh-century Constantinople, citing previous studies, see Hondridou (2002) 151–253. For the schooling of children, see, in general, Koukoules (1948–1955) vol. 1.1, 35–105, and, for the middle period, Kalogeras (2000).

probably addressed to his son-in-law Maleses stationed in Greece, Psellos refers to his daughter as the "mistress (*despotis*) of your *oikos*" and indicates that she was making independent decisions about her husband's finances.[55] This kind of administration was no mean feat and was probably only a few steps away from governing the empire itself, as the empire discovered when Alexios I turned it over to his mother Anna Dalassene.[56] Second, children were expected to become virtuous, something that to most parents today is merely an abstraction. Girls in particular had to learn piety, charity, humility, and moderation, to say nothing of celibacy before marriage. Psellos presents this moral dimension of education in Platonic language, but was probably only expressing what his contemporaries understood in equivalent Christian terms when raising their daughters. A reputation for virtue was required to secure a favorable match.[57] It also enabled girls to become efficient household managers and honorable wives. However, the pursuit of virtue could take on a life of its own and undermine the social ambitions of this bourgeois class. From St. Thekla onward, girls could refuse to marry out of devotion to ascetic ideals (or exploit them to evade undesirable unions), which inevitably led to conflict with their parents. This is a common theme in the hagiography of female saints.[58] Though Psellos was embellishing his mother's biography to enhance her reputation for piety (see p. 34), he mentions precisely such a conflict between Theodote and her father regarding marriage: in the end, she submitted piously (3d). Styliane died before she ever faced this choice, but Psellos, as her father, was very eager for her to marry and even made her *Funeral Oration* into something of a tragic advertisement for the perfect bride (74–77).

At an early age daughters went from being girls to being wives and mothers. For Psellos, nine was apparently not the age of childhood but the age that came immediately before that of marriage. Girls were married away as early as

55. For the context, see de Vries-van der Velden (1996a) 123. For the practical responsibilities of such wives, see Xenophon, *Oikonomikos*; Apuleius, *Apology* 87; Christophoros Mytilenaios, *Poem* 57 (Kurtz 33–34).

56. Anna Komnene, *Alexiad* 3.6–8; see Hill (1996) and Malamut (1999); in general, Laiou (1981) 242–243.

57. Cf. Ioannes Chrysostomos, *Encomium for Maximos and regarding the kinds of women that one ought to marry* (in *PG* 51 cols. 225–242). For a typology of feminine virtues in the eleventh and twelfth centuries, see Nardi (2002) c. 5.

58. Clark (1993) 131, citing previous discussions; Talbot (1990); Connor (2004) 10–11, 15–17, 170–171, 194.

the age of twelve, and sometimes even earlier,[59] and soon began having children of their own. There is every indication that this is what Psellos' mother and older sister did. He himself betrothed his second (adopted) daughter to Elpidios Kenchres when she was perhaps nine and he eighteen (see p. 140). The choice of groom was made very carefully. The daughters of well-to-do families, especially if they had ties to the court, were highly prized, particularly if they were known or believed to be beautiful (personal attraction certainly played a role in these decisions, at least for the grooms). Psellos managed to secure a range of highly lucrative and prestigious titles and positions for Elpidios before the contract was broken. A number of suitors applied and competed for the hand of Theodote (*Enc.* 3d); their wealth, connections, and morals were scrutinized, probably in that order. Psellos likewise expected many to sue for the hand of Styliane and mentions the services of professional matchmakers (*Fun. Or.* 76: *nymphagôgoi*), though he had no intention of using them. Engagement involved a detailed contract that specified the dowry to be provided by the father of the bride and the penalties to be paid by either party in the event of termination. The legal memorandum (*hypomnêma*) translated in this volume that documents the dissolution of the agreement between Psellos and the Kenchres family constitutes unique evidence regarding the legal aspects of such transactions in the period before 1204.[60]

We have already touched upon many aspects of married life for the women of eleventh-century Constantinople. How restricted were their lives? In general, the more respectable they were the less they were to be seen outside or by other men. Such, at any rate, was the ideal. In the eleventh century the *gynaikônitis,* the women's quarters, is still attested but it was either going out of fashion or had already become a rhetorical commonplace with little relation to the

---

59. Patlagean (1973) 90–93; Kiousopoulou (1990) 28–30. So too in late antiquity: Clark (1993) 13–14, 80.

60. For betrothal in late antiquity, when the rules were established that were still valid in the eleventh century, see Clark (1993) 14; for the middle and late periods, Patlagean (1973) 87–88; Kiousopoulou (1990) 31–36; Talbot (1997) 121–122; for a comprehensive legal discussion of *mnêsteia,* Papadatos (1984), esp. 231–233 for this case; for *nymphagôgoi,* Koukoules (1948–1955) vol. 4, 78–80. Various aspects of marriage in the middle period are treated by Patlagean (1987) 592–609 and Laiou (1992), esp. legal (c. 1) and the relations between spouses (c. 3), but the focus is almost always on the aristocracy and the imperial family. For the impact of Christianity on Roman marriage in late antiquity, see Nathan (2000), though the emphasis is on law and the West.

lives of actual women. There is evidence that women enjoyed considerable freedom of movement, which perhaps shocked only the most prudish. By no means were Byzantine women confined to the household.[61] Modesty certainly required that a proper daughter or matron not be seen much, but it really could not be avoided. For instance, Psellos notes that a few did catch glimpses of his mother before her marriage and word of her beauty spread (*Enc.* 3c–d). At the funeral of her daughter, she was "possessed by madness and then for the first time displayed her beauty in public, indifferent to the gaze of men" (15d), which probably means that she allowed the scarf to fall from her head and reveal her hair. This behavior at funerals was specifically condemned by Ioannes Chrysostomos and frowned upon by other Fathers of the Church, as Psellos certainly knew.[62] Furthermore, his sister, despite being married, managed to befriend and convert a prostitute from the neighborhood (14a), which would have required some degree of freedom of movement. Such conversion entailed the rejection of cosmetics and jewelry, which had long been associated in literature with actresses and prostitutes, and the wearing of a veil (14b; cf. 7b and *Fun. Or.* 76). Psellos claims that the latter "covered her entire face" and other sources indicate as much (though often in highly unusual contexts),[63] but no representation of this has come down to us and there was probably a range of options. There is abundant evidence that Byzantine women dyed their hair or wore it down or in elaborate coiffures, all obviously meant to be seen.[64] A veil was usually a scarf that framed the face, as we observe in so many images of female saints, but penitence may have called for extreme measures (the prostitute in the story eventually took up her old ways). It seems that with female dress we are dealing not with a strictly monitored and enforced system

61. Psellos (*Chronographia* 5.26) and Michael Attaleiates (*History* 88) discuss dramatic events such as revolutions and earthquakes that brought women out into the streets who had never been seen before (the latter passage, we should note, is modelled, as in other respects, on Agathias, *Histories* 5.3.7); gradual obsolescence of the *gykaikônitis*: Laiou (1981) 249, 252–253; no real evidence for it to begin with: Kazhdan (1998) 2–10; for relative freedom of movement, see A. Walker (2003). A century later, Anna Komnene boasted that she had not been brought up in the women's quarters: *Alexiad* 14.7.4.

62. Spyridakis (1950) 121–122; Koukoules (1948–1955) v. 4, 163; Emmanuel (1995) 776. Many additional texts may be cited, e.g., Gregorios of Nyssa, *Life of Makrina* 10, 26–27.

63. Garland (1988) 371–372 and n. 37; Kazhdan (1998) 15. For veils and cosmetics in late antiquity, see Clark (1993) 108–109; for dress and jewelry in the middle and late periods, Talbot (1997) 127; Nardi (2002) 35–41.

64. Koukoules (1948–1955) vol. 4, 361–394; Emmanuel (1995).

but with a range of options plotted on a complex grid denoting social class, personal piety, circumstance (e.g., at a funeral), and profession. Girls, women, and wives had many choices (and were judged accordingly and variously by the men).

Marital relationships were of course hardly equal. Theodote fully accepted the "divine decree" that women should be their husbands' helpmates (9a) and regarded herself as inferior to him (9d). Some modern readers have concluded on the basis of a passage toward the end of the *Encomium* (25b) that Theodote held revolutionary views regarding gender equality,[65] which they link to the undeniable impression that we gain from the text that she was the dominant force in the family. However, the views are probably Psellos' own: the point of the passage is that Theodote's life and virtue proved to be valid in practice. It should also be noted that Psellos praises her for looking after her *own* elderly parents (8c–d), not those of her husband, as would have been expected of a married woman in antiquity.[66] Divorce her husband deemed tantamount to apostasy, even if only to enter the monastic life (11b). We have little evidence from the eleventh century for this practice. Legal sources of the early thirteenth century suggest that ordinary men and women were aware of their legal rights in this respect and initiated divorce proceedings under a variety of terms and pretexts, and obtained just and sympathetic verdicts from at least two bishops whose dossiers have been preserved.[67] When Theodote finally made up her mind, she made arrangements that her husband take precedence in this respect too (16d). In Byzantium, it was not uncommon for married women to join convents (as did Theodote) or for couples to do this jointly when their children matured or died prematurely. Many entered monasteries in order to grow old and die in a community that would care for them in both body and soul (*gêrokômia* and prayer were thereby combined), though some lived there without actually taking the tonsure (as did Theodote for years before her death).[68] No doubt the monks and nuns looked after some such people out of compassion and charity, but in many cases, as in this one, the resident

---

65. E.g., Garland (1988) 377 ("the unprecedented view of Theodote herself"); Angold (1995) 437 ("some of her opinions were extremely radical").

66. For Theodote, see Nardi (2002) 118–121; for married women and their fathers, Connor (2004) 16; for marital relations in thirteenth-century Epeiros, Kiousopoulou (1990) 107–114.

67. Kiousopoulou (1990) 60–73.

68. Talbot (1984) 275–278, (1990), and (1997) 138; Connor (2004) 171, and esp. 270.

"novice" brought property to the community and his or her own servants (22a–b; for skepticism regarding Psellos' account of his parents' conversion, see the introduction to the *Encomium* below.)[69]

In times of relative peace and stability, women who never left the capital died usually of disease or old age. Psellos' family never experienced wars or murders or feuds and was probably typical in this respect (history tends to record dramatic and aberrant cases). Still, death could come at any age. Theodote's second baby daughter disappears in Psellos' account immediately after birth (4d); Styliane died of disease, perhaps of smallpox, at around the age of nine (Psellos, a physician in his own right, gives a detailed and lengthy account of her illness and last days: *Fun. Or.* 77–79); Psellos' elder sister died soon after giving birth, probably in her late teens; and Theodote seems to have destroyed her health and killed herself through excessive asceticism (though this may be an exaggeration by Psellos).

The moment of death was marked by an outpouring of lamentation on the part of everyone present.[70] The body was washed, dressed for burial (*Fun. Or.* 80), and then placed on a bier (*skimpodion*) and carried to the cemetery where it was buried under a slab after those present had partaken of communion (82). The funerals of such respectable matrons were elaborate and drew crowds and onlookers even from the third floor of buildings along the processional route (*Enc.* 16c, 24c–d). There was more lamentation at the grave site on the day of burial as well as on the days of commemoration prescribed in Orthodox tradition (Psellos happened to return to the city when his parents were lamenting the death of his sister on the seventh day: *Enc.* 15c). Yet there was no rest for the virtuous: the deceased often appeared in dreamvisions to assure those still living of their blessed state in the afterworld and promise to intercede on their behalf (*Fun. Or.* 86–87; *Enc.* 15d, 19b, 20a–d, 24b, 26b–27a; see the introduction to the *Encomium* below, p. 45); sometimes visions were granted to them soon before they died (*Fun. Or.* 82–85) or to

69. For such practices in late antiquity, see Clark (1993) 103; in the middle and late periods, Laiou (1981) 242; Connor (2004) 172.

70. See here *Fun. Or.* 79–82; *Enc.* 15d (sister), 19b-d (father), 24b (mother). For the ritual lament, see Alexiou (1974) and Derderian (2001); for rituals of death in the middle period, Spyridakis (1950); Koukoules (1948–1955) vol. 4, 148–227; J. Kyriakakis (1974); Abrahamse (1984); and Barbounis (1994) 75–81; for images and conceptions of death, Agapitos (2001). A detailed description, parallel to those in Psellos, can be found in Gregorios of Nyssa, *Life of Makrina* 28–34.

others who would then relay the dire, albeit in a different sense hopeful, message to them (*Enc.* 22d).

To conclude, it is from this handful of writings by a Byzantine intellectual that we may reconstruct the most comprehensive picture of the life of daughters and wives in average middle- to upper-class Byzantine households of the capital. It is our hope that the present translations will allow these fascinating texts to escape the obscurity to which they have been condemned by a learned language.

Encomium for his mother

Introduction

Psellos' *Encomium for his Mother* is one of his longest, most rhetorically complex, and personally revealing narrative works after the *Chronographia*. No less than the latter work, it is also highly idiosyncratic (in ways that we will discuss below) and was studied and admired by later generations of Byzantine writers. "The most wise Psellos" is cited as a model in a treatise on composition attributed to Gregorios Pardos, bishop of Corinth in the early twelfth century and author of various technical philological treatises (including one on the dialects of ancient Greek). Pardos ranked the *Encomium* among the four best orations ever written (along with works by Demosthenes, Aristeides, and Gregorios of Nazianzos).[1] Anna Komnene, in her well-known digression on Ioannes Italos, compared him unfavorably to his teacher Psellos, who had "attained the peak of all knowledge" and "become famous for his wisdom," though this achievement, she notes, was in part due to his mother's prayers to the icon of the Theotokos on his behalf.[2] This is certainly one way of reading the *Encomium,* one that Psellos seems to have encouraged; below we will consider some others.

---

1. Gregorios Pardos, *[On Composition]* 31–33, 36, 38 (Donnet 320–322; see 110–111 for this work in general). For a sympathetic attempt to explain Pardos' choice, see J. Walker (2004).
2. Anna Komnene, *Alexiad* 5.8.3 (Reinsch and Kambylis 162); at 5.8.5 Anna misdates Psellos' tonsure to the reign of Michael VII (probably assuming that he fell out of favor only once).

Content.   The work is at once an encomium and a funeral oration for Psellos' mother Theodote (who is named only once, at 22d). Theodote is one of
very few Byzantine women we know something about who was neither an empress nor a saint (though, as we will see, Psellos tried to depict her as a saint).
Roughly, the *Encomium* focuses first on her domestic and then on her ascetic life, at all times linking her to Psellos' own educational and spiritual development. But unlike other works of this genre, this oration has a wider cast of
characters, including Psellos' unnamed father and sister, who, like Theodote,
are praised in similar terms and given extended and dramatic death scenes
followed by Psellos' own laments (cast as his reaction to the events at the
time). The work is therefore unique in that it constitutes a laudatory "family
portrait" as well as a kind of literary mausoleum. Nevertheless, everything—
except Psellos' extended list of his own intellectual interests at the end of the
work (27–30)—is arranged around the family life, conversion, and death of
Theodote.

   The *Encomium* is not an "autobiography," as its last editor enticingly albeit
inaccurately entitled it. It does, to be sure, contain many autobiographical
elements, but this is only to be expected given Psellos' relation to its subject
and the reasons and circumstances that impelled him to write it in the first
place. For instance, it affords us precious glimpses into private domestic life in
Constantinople as well as a firsthand account of childhood education; these,
however, are precisely what modern psychology valorizes and encourages us
to regard as more deeply confessional than, say, a political *res gesta.* However,
no ancient or Byzantine author would have accepted this set of priorities
(with the possible exception of Augustine).[3] The *Encomium* tells us little or
nothing about Psellos' career at the court, his friends, or his enemies. This may
be due in part to the possibility that the events recounted in the oration do
not extend past Psellos' teenage years. For these other aspects of his life, which
at the time that he wrote the *Encomium* he would surely have considered more
important, we must turn to his other works, each of which presents us with a
different "Psellos." There may come a time when we are in a position to synthe-
size them into a more or less coherent portrait; for now, however, we still are
a long way from understanding each individually.

---

   3. For autobiography in Byzantium, see, in general, Angold (1998) and Hinterberger (1999) esp. 41–43 for the *Encomium*; also idem (2000) 141 for the difference between autobiographical texts and an autobiographical mode.

The following outline of the contents of the *Encomium* has astutely been divided into thematic sections by its editor, Criscuolo.

1:	exordium
2a–3c:	Theodote's parents, birth, physical and spiritual virtues
3d–4d:	her marriage to Psellos' father and their children
5–6:	Psellos' childhood and education
7–8:	Theodote's virtues and spiritual qualities
9:	her husband's qualities
10:	her encouragement of Psellos' studies
11–12:	her asceticism and charity
13–14:	Psellos' sister, her conversion of a prostitute, and her pregnancy
15:	his lament for his sister's death
16a–c:	his sister's death described in retrospect
16d–17d:	Theodote's conversion and pious longings
18:	Psellos' father as a monk
19:	his father's death and Psellos' lament
20:	Psellos' vision of his saved father
21–22:	Theodote's asceticism
23:	her formal consecration into the religious life, and her death
24:	Psellos' lament for his mother's death
25:	Theodote as saint and martyr
26:	Psellos' different conception of philosophy
27–30:	his philosophical and scholarly interests
31:	his plea to be released from the court

Date, Occasion, and Purpose.   Psellos wrote the *Encomium* at the very end of the reign of Konstantinos IX Monomachos (1042–January 1055), probably in late 1054, immediately after he had accepted monastic tonsure in an effort to escape from the crumbling regime of the ailing and weak emperor. The year 1054 had been an eventful one for Psellos in any case (he was thirty-six years old at the time). The circle of "intellectuals" that had enjoyed the emperor's favor from the mid-1040s—including Psellos' friend Konstantinos Leichoudes, his teacher Ioannes Mauropous, and his colleague Ioannes Xiphilinos—had, for reasons that remain unclear, gradually lost its influence: one by one they were either dismissed from the court or retired "voluntarily." The emperor's position had moreover been shaken by the rise of the ambitious patriarch Michael Keroularios and the events of the so-called Schism of 1054. Also, in the last years of Mono-machos' reign Psellos' faith was publicly questioned. The emperor demanded a signed confession to silence the critics, who may have included the patriarch himself. Psellos had in any case always been defensive about his philosophical pursuits and had probably always been perceived as flirting with paganism, Neoplatonism, theurgy, and astrology.[4]

In the chapters of the *Chronographia* devoted to the final months of the reign of Monomachos, written in the early 1060s, Psellos attributes his deci-sion to become a monk to the instability of the emperor's character (6.191–203). He, Xiphilinos, and one other man who cannot be safely identified, made a pact to retreat from the court in this manner. Xiphilinos was the first to go through with it. Thereupon, Psellos very conveniently became sick and used the possibility of his imminent death as a pretext to follow the same course. The emperor, he claims, at first tried to dissuade him with promises and threats but finally acceded when the deed was done. To be sure, in one passage (6.199), Psellos notes that he had wanted to embrace the monastic life since his child-hood, but this we may take to be nothing more than a passing nod to the lies he must have told at the time to make his decision more credible. There was little in monastic life that would have appealed to Psellos: soon after Mono-machos' death he fled from Bithynia and returned to the capital, where he again took up court intrigue, philosophy, and teaching.[5] But at the time, and for a while thereafter, he had to keep up appearances. These are reflected, for instance, in the *hypomnêma* concerning the dissolution of the engagement of his daugh-ter to Elpidios, where sickness is cited as the sole reason for his tonsure (see below, p. 151).

The *Encomium,* which is in all likelihood the first text we have from Psellos' hand after his tonsure (excepting perhaps certain letters), was written be-tween his "recovery" and his departure from the capital. Yet he makes no men-tion here of his sickness and presents his decision to become a monk as the natural outcome of his mother's lifelong saintly influence. In the final para-graph, he indirectly begs the emperor, who apparently wanted to retain him at the court despite his tonsure, to cease disputing with his monastic superiors

---

4. For the regime of the intellectuals, see Lemerle (1977). See Hondridou (2002) on the reign of Monomachos in general (Hondridou speculates that the intellectuals were linked to Zoe and lost power after her death in ca. 1050). Accusation against Psellos: Garzya (1967); the text is now *Theol. II* 35.

5. For Psellos' view of contemporary monasticism, see Kaldellis (1999a) ch. 10 and passim.

and allow him to depart (31a).[6] It is here that we gain a glimpse of the immediate intended audience of the work. Psellos has throughout maintained the
appearance (or the fiction) that the *Encomium* is a funeral oration being addressed to relatives and others who wish to know about the saintly qualities
of his mother (e.g., 1c–d, 7c, 17b). Only at the end do we realize that it is a political document that has as much if not more to do with Psellos' career than
with his family. Theodote's refusal to moderate her asceticism or change her
way of life in response to the threats and blandishments of her spiritual father
seems to highlight and justify Psellos' refusal to do the same in response to the
emperor's threats and blandishments (22a). There is, moreover, a passage (29a)
in which Psellos aims the defense of his intellectual pursuits at those who would
question them, invoking his saintly mother in defense of his philosophical
motivation. We are dealing, then, with a text written at a time of personal crisis that reflects a specific image that Psellos was keen to propagate in order to
respond to the circumstances of the moment, an image that he later discarded
when it was no longer convenient. We should therefore approach this oration
with considerable caution and even skepticism (as, indeed, we should every
text written by Psellos).

It has escaped the attention of most scholars that the *Encomium* effectively
canonizes Psellos' mother. At her funeral, Psellos has her spiritual father pro-
nounce her both a saint and a martyr (24b), a judgment that Psellos immediately goes on to defend in his own voice (25c: she was martyred in her fatal
struggle with the tyranny of matter).[7] This family hagiography would later be
complemented with a more playful autohagiography: after his brief withdrawal
from political life, Psellos wrote a new version of the *Life of St Auxentios,* in
which he reworked crucial details of the saint's life to match those of his own![8]
But the intent of the *Encomium,* at any rate, is serious. By focusing throughout

6. In my view, the passage does not suggest that he is asking the emperor to intercede on his behalf with his monastic superiors: J. Walker (2004) 64–65. Arguments against
the proposed date of 1054 rest on the assumption that Psellos wrote the *Encomium* at
Olympos; it seems, rather, that he is here pleading with the emperor to allow him to depart for Olympos by *ceasing* to exert pressure on his monastic superiors. Besides, no alternative date better fits the tenor and hints of the oration. Psellos' alleged "incarceration" in
the monastery of *ta Narsou* during the years 1059–1064, taken seriously by Walker, is
based on a single letter misunderstood by Joannou (1951) 287.

7. Cf. Hinterberger (1999) 92.

8. Kazhdan (1983); see also Hinterberger (1999) 233–234, and 230–238 for autohagiography in general; idem (2000) 147 for the *Life.*

on his own close relationship to his mother, he effectively appropriates her sanctity for himself and wraps himself in her piety. This is perhaps why he refers to her by name only once, and that only tangentially in a vision seen by a third party (22d), ensuring that she would be remembered less as Theodote than as "Psellos' mother," a term used throughout and most emphatically in the first words of the oration. In this way, Psellos hoped to counter the suspicions that were certainly being raised at the court regarding the sincerity of his conversion. This oration would silence those doubts, while a proclamation of filial piety on his part would dampen the accusations of cynicism and heterodoxy. In fact, with the *Encomium* Psellos hoped to kill two birds with one stone. In addition to its exaltation of ascetic ideals, the oration constantly traces the origins of Psellos' own intellectual pursuits to the initiative and piety of his mother (5b ff., esp. 6a, 10a–d, 24b). As we will see below, Psellos makes it clear that his own brand of philosophy was not the same as that of his mother, but her sanctity is meant to protect his eccentric and broad interests. That is why the *Encomium* ends with the long and defensive list of his own studies (27–30), which follows his accounts of her death and posthumous appearance to Psellos in a dream.

In short, the emphasis in the *Encomium* on asceticism and the justification of Psellos' own philosophical studies closely tallies with the pressures to which he was subject in 1054. This suggests that political worries were more important than filial piety in prompting its composition. Let us note that a similar argument has already been made regarding one of the orations that Psellos used a model, Gregorios of Nazianzos' *Funeral Oration for his Brother Kaisarios.* Gregorios goes out of his way to present his rather unsaintly brother as a saint in order to strengthen his hand in dealing with officials who were investigating some irregularities in Kaisarios' will and estate.[9]

There are additional reasons why skepticism is in order, beyond even the fact that Psellos does not ascribe any miracles to his saintly mother. First, the ideals to which Theodote devoted the later and saintly portion of her life were precisely those that Psellos himself opposed in a variety of works not subject to severe political and ecclesiastical pressure. Second, it seems that Theodote had died some time before 1054, making her *Encomium* a belated and therefore somewhat opportunistic work. To be sure, Psellos gives no indication of the date of her death, only that it happened some time after the death of his sister in 1034

---

9. McGuckin (2001) 33. For Psellos' models, see below.

(22d). But this omission probably means that it was not recent. Accordingly, the grief expressed in the work is set entirely in the past, at the time of her death, and not in the rhetorical present. We should also note that Theodote's own mother, Psellos' grandmother, was still alive at the time of Theodote's death (24d) but not when the *Encomium* was composed (2a–b). This establishes only a relative temporal framework, but militates against a recent bereavement.[10]

Third, the narrative of Theodote's monastic career is unconvincing. Psellos would have us believe that she had ascetic aspirations as a child (3c), resisted the idea of marriage initially (3d), and began to contemplate retiring from the world even before the death of her daughter in 1034 (11b), though she did not want to separate from her husband. It was the death of her eldest child that strengthened her resolve (16b–d) and enabled her to persuade her husband to do likewise. But now the logic breaks down. Theodote made sure that her husband was tonsured first (16d) and, curiously, though he died soon thereafter (18b), she herself was not properly consecrated until long afterwards (21a, 22d), in fact immediately before her own death. At that point she was almost too weak to go through with the ceremony; more to the point, she *knew* then that she was dying (23a). One can be skeptical of this narrative. Why did she wait so long for something she had allegedly desired since childhood? It is more likely that she and her husband, like so many other Byzantines of perfectly ordinary faith, took monastic vows only when they perceived that their end was near (and her husband had grave doubts about this decision even at the very end: 18b, 19b). Monasteries for such affluent families served as homes for the retirement and care of the elderly and infirm. But Psellos, for purposes of his own, has worked his family up into an assembly of saints, transforming, in accordance with the rules of rhetoric, minor virtues into a full-fledged encomium.[11]

In doing so, moreover, he has adapted traditional hagiographic motifs. The hagiography of female saints in Byzantium followed a curious trajectory.[12] Beginning with the martyrs of the persecutions, it moved on to women who broke with their families and social expectations in order to suppress their femininity through extreme asceticism or by dressing as men and joining monastic communities. But the years after ca. 800 witnessed the rise of the pious housewife, who had monastic aspirations but largely conformed to social

10. So too J. Walker (2004) 65.
11. Cf. *Chronographia* 6.161 and Kaldellis (1999a) 136.
12. See Patlagean (1976).

conventions regarding marriage and childbearing. In the *Encomium*, we witness the reversal of this process: Theodote begins as a pious housewife but gradually gives rein to her ascetic impulses and ends up denying her femininity by an excess of renunciation. In terms of the saints of Lesbos, Thomaïs has turned into Theoktiste. Finally, at her death she is proclaimed a martyr to the flesh. To the learned Byzantine reader, the *Encomium,* even beyond its rhetorical strengths, is a masterpiece of typological allusion.

Literary models and Psellos' originality.   It is clear upon a first glance that the *Encomium* combines aspects of various genres, especially panegyric, e.g., in the title, in the disclaimer of the orator's ability (1c), and in the mention of Theodote's ancestors (2a); *epitaphios* (this requires no illustration); hagiography, e.g., in the description of her asceticism and funeral; consolation, especially in the visions that attest to the salvation of his loved ones; and lament (*monodia*), especially in the three major laments that Psellos attributes to himself upon the deaths of his sister (15d), father (19b–d), and mother (24b) (another can be found toward the end of the *Funeral Oration for Styliane*: 79–82).[13] The standard rhetorical models for non-imperial subjects were the funeral orations by Gregorios of Nazianzos for his father Gregorios, brother Kaisarios, and sister Gorgonia (which also refer to his mother Nonna often along the way), and for Basileios of Kaisareia (*Or.* 7, 8, 18, 43). Psellos used these directly, to judge from the frequency of his borrowings from them throughout the *Encomium.*[14] As with most of the literary works he used there, these allusions will not be marked in the translation, for that would clutter the text and make it difficult to read (though it should be borne in mind that the effect of multiple allusions cluttering the text would surely not have been lost on the very educated Byzantine reader, probably the only kind who could read a text as difficult as the *Encomium* in any case). Those who are interested in the specific passages in question should consult the apparatus of Criscuolo's edition, where they are conveniently listed.

Other models included Gregorios of Nyssa's *Life* of his sister Makrina and, a much later text, Theodoros Stoudites' funeral oration for his mother Theoktiste (*Or.* 13, in *PG* 99, cols. 883–901). But generic analysis, for all that it is both easy and popular, reveals little about authorial intentions and strategies. It is

13. For questions of genre in response to death, see Agapitos (2003).
14. For this question, see Criscuolo 29–44; for a few case studies, see Vergari (1987b).

more illuminating to ask why Psellos imitated the Fathers and, more importantly, to what degree. Between them, as we saw, the two Kappadokians offered a complete portfolio for the praise of deceased relatives as model Christians. These works, for instance the oration for Kaisarios, were themselves self-serving and not always truthful. Just as does Psellos' *Encomium,* they too reflect the political pressures of their immediate circumstances. On the whole, they represent the effort of prominent churchmen to sanctify deceased members of their own families in order to thereby augment the status of the living ones.[15] Many Byzantine saints were in fact promoted or even created by the efforts of their relatives and it seems that this too was Psellos' intention in the *Encomium,* though he did not pursue it beyond his immediate advantage in 1054. But his reliance on Gregorios of Nazianzos was not merely rhetorical or the product of historical coincidence: his need in 1054 to associate himself with a saintly mother was perhaps equaled by his need to associate himself with the chief Theologian of the Orthodox tradition, the model Christian orator who combined perfect doctrine with Hellenic *paideia.*

Psellos' complex relationship to Gregorios has not yet received systematic attention. I plan to argue elsewhere that the common view that Psellos followed the Theologian in most important aspects of his thought in addition to esteeming him highly as a stylist is exaggerated and probably wrong. Granted, Psellos did esteem Gregorios' style and learned from him how to deploy Hellenic *paideia* in addressing Christian audiences. But his frequent invocation of Gregorios as an authority was, I believe, cynical: Psellos' ethics and metaphysics were in most respects consciously opposed to those of the Church Father.[16] We can therefore allay the suspicion that in the *Encomium,* for instance, Psellos is only an unoriginal and even slavish imitator based on the face that he follows Gregorios in praising his relatives as exemplary and ascetic Christians by deploying a heavily philosophical vocabulary. There are crucial differences, however, which in my opinion constitute deliberate corrections to the models that Psellos and the rest of the Byzantine world were compelled and inclined to follow. These corrections, in turn, reinforced his revolutionary program to revive ancient philosophy.

---

15. For the world, writings, and families of the Kappadokian Fathers, see McGuckin (2001); Van Dam (2002), (2003a), and (2003b).

16. I argue this in a study of *Hellenism in Byzantium* (in preparation). The chapter on Psellos is complete.

For instance, Psellos is the first writer in the Byzantine tradition (in fact the only one known to me) who praises Christian asceticism in the strongest terms while at the same time constantly distancing himself from it and admitting his failure to attain its perfection (of course, in other works he more or less openly rejected it as a human ideal).[17] The praise can be attributed to his circumstances and the political goals of the work whereas the distancing is part of Psellos' campaign to revive non-ascetic varieties of philosophy. This theme recurs throughout the work, gradually acquiring a force beyond the customary protestations of humble inadequacy. At 8a he admits that he has not lived up to his mother's expectations and has not lived in accordance with her instructions. Thereupon he admits that he has not embraced virginity or purity (8b; of course, neither did his mother, but this is a separate problem, as we have seen). Again, "I have entirely fallen short of the example set by her and failed to live up to it" (9c). At 23d he again admits that he has not attained monastic perfection (though we must remember that he would then have been a monk for only a matter of weeks or even days). At 20d he laments that "God wanted all the most beautiful things for me, but I have always acted against His views." He therefore personally accepts the blame for his own fall from grace. As we saw, this can be viewed as a traditional acknowledgment of sinfulness and display of humility. But it is too closely linked to Psellos' conscious election of a different "philosophy" and, in addition, the sincerity of his lament is questionable. At 11c he describes what he self-consciously labels as his mother's "philosophy" in a way that makes it perfectly clear that it is not the same as his own. At the end of the oration, he confesses that he cannot emulate his mother (23b) and explicitly states that "I do not entirely philosophize according to that philosophy which is so dear to you, and I do not know what fate took hold of me from the very beginning and fixated me onto the study of books, from which I cannot break away" (27a).

In short, even in a quasi-hagiographic work in which he was compelled to pay tribute to the ascetic ideals of the Orthodox tradition, Psellos contrived to maintain a distance between them and his own brand of bookish philosophy. Ironically, then, his dishonesty was not total and I believe this was deliberate. Consider, for example, the self-conscious emphasis in the *Encomium* on the physical beauty of the members of his family (not excluding himself). Such descriptions are altogether missing from the orations of Gregorios, in full ac-

17. See Kaldellis (1999a) c. 23; cf. Vergari (1987b) 219.

cordance with their radically spiritual orientation. By contrast, Psellos gushes over his mother's physical beauty and uses both metaphors and colorful language in order to describe it. What is more important, he knows and acknowledges repeatedly at the beginning of the oration that as a "philosopher," i.e., a monk (at this stage of the work's argument), he must not now pay attention to such matters (2c–d), but he does so anyway, at great length and repeatedly (3a, c–d; see 4c for his sister as an infant; 9b for his father; 13a–b for his sister and himself). He does not hesitate to intrude this theme even into his funeral laments. Above the grave of his sister he saw fit to wonder about "the beauty of your body, has nature received, guarded and preserved it, or has the earth entirely destroyed it, extinguishing the blaze in your eyes, removing the bloom of your lips . . . ? Or is your beauty still intact, preserved in the grave as in a treasure-box?" (15d) The funeral oration that he wrote for his own daughter Styliane likewise includes an *ekphrasis* of her physical features and beauty to complement her spiritual and intellectual qualities (see below, pp. 123 ff.), an extended passage that does not lack an undercurrent of sensuality.[18] The initial disclaimers in the *Encomium* therefore, only serve to draw attention to the extensive attention that he devotes to this theme thereafter, forcing us to consider the extent of his commitment to these "philosophical" principles. This was Psellos' method of introducing the body back into Orthodox discourse, a goal that was one component of his broader project of philosophical and ethical reform (see below for the union of body and soul). In short, he advocates a radical Christian position but in reality practices a mediation between it and what his contemporaries would have viewed as an all too Hellenic devotion to the body. But Psellos had the last word here: Komnenian and later literature was again seduced by the charms of the body and restored to beauty its standing as a virtue. This process has unfortunately not yet been studied.[19]

Philosophical aims and rhetorical style.   In part because of our empiricist belief in the independence of content and form, we do not ordinarily think of these two categories as related, far less as fundamentally interdependent, but many

18. Ljubarskij (2004) 341–342.

19. Nardi (2002) 31 ff., 183–184 misses the revolutionary nature of Psellos' insistence on physical beauty and treats it as a staple of the Byzantine mentality. The only parallel I have found is in Gregorios of Nyssa, *Life of Makrina* 2, 4–5 (brief mentions of the beauty of his mother and sister). For Psellos' descriptions of physical appearance, see Ljubarskij (2004) ch. 7.

ancient thinkers did so, and close connections can be established between them in the *Encomium*. The *way* in which Psellos chose to write in this work subtly reflected some of the aspects of his underlying philosophical agenda.

First, the vocabulary used in the *Encomium* and many of the expressions are lifted from a wide variety of classical texts, including Plato and Homer, tragedy and comedy, the Church Fathers (especially Gregorios of Nazianzos' funeral orations), Neoplatonic philosophers and, most inappropriately at times, the ancient romance novels and erotic poetry. In this respect the text is a showcase of classical learning. As noted above, few of the sources of these allusions and quotations are listed in the footnotes of the present translation. Interested readers should consult the apparatus in Criscuolo's edition. But a word of caution is in order. Many, perhaps the majority, of parallel texts cited by Criscuolo contain only vaguely similar texts or stock phrases that many Byzantine authors would have known independently of their provenance.[20] However, some of these allusions are significant, such as, for instance, those to the works of Gregorios of Nazianzos, which establish a (rather ambiguous) relationship between Psellos and the Theologian. Moreover, the language of the *Encomium* is heavily philosophical and abstract, lapsing at times into direct discussions of technical questions of an ethical or metaphysical nature. At 7a Psellos states that the account of his mother's life will have a philosophical slant and, accordingly, a great deal of the text concerns the relationship between body and soul and the elevation of the soul (see, e.g., 11a). One might almost say that this oration is a philosophical treatise in the form of a funeral oration. I propose that what we have here is an example of Psellos' intention to infuse rhetoric with the sublimity of philosophy and promote philosophy through the power of rhetoric. His intention to mediate between these two disciplines, which had traditionally been considered distinct, is announced, among other places, in the *Chronographia* (6.41). It is elaborated in the closing sections of the reign of Konstantinos IX Monomachos (6.197), in other words in those sections that cover the exact period in which Psellos wrote the *Encomium*.[21]

What is especially noteworthy in this regard is Psellos' reliance on terms and notions from non-Christian Neoplatonic thinkers. His presentation of his

20. See Kaldellis (2006).

21. For the theory itself, Kaldellis (1999a) c. 19, 22. Cf. Psellos' synthesis of poetry, rhetoric, and philosophy in *Chronographia* 5.24, on which see ibid. ch. 14 and Dyck (1993).

mother's Christian beliefs and ascetic practices is often couched in the philosophical language of Plotinos and others, and at one point he directly compares her to Plotinos himself (see especially 17b, 18a). In other words, just as the
Encomium attempts to mediate between philosophy and rhetoric, so too it attempts to mediate between Christianity and (pagan) Neoplatonism, which,
we know, Psellos was eager to rehabilitate among contemporary Byzantines.
That is why he makes Neoplatonism complicit in the very articulation of the
most Christian beliefs and practices of his mother, formulating the latter in
such an abstract manner that the differences between Christian and Hellenic
thought essentially vanish into insignificance.[22]

   The rhetorical style of the *Encomium* is moreover extremely complex and
often obscure, and philosophy is only one source of this. There are few sentences in which the meaning is stated directly and without elaborate artifice.
For the most part, the reader must struggle to grasp or to guess the concrete
import that lies behind the twists and turns of the syntax. This is very difficult
rhetorical Greek. The purpose of this must have been, at least in part, to dazzle
the reader with the breadth of Psellos' philological expertise, the awesome
subtlety of the arrangement and expression, and the profundity of the philosophical exposition. The oration would have impressed and perhaps even intimidated contemporary readers. As we saw, it was soon accepted as a canonical
model on a par with works by Demosthenes and Gregorios. The present translation aims to capture the terseness and convoluted periods of the original,
which, whether we like it or not, constitute its literary distinction. For this reason, Latin and pompous terms have been preferred over English and common
ones. Some phrases inevitably remain obscure and my renditions will no doubt
be contested. I suspect that it will take time for the profession to digest this
work, to establish the meaning of all its passages and ferret out its nuances, assuming that these were ever meant to be pinned down in the first place.[23] Hopefully, the present translation will provide the launching point for this long-
delayed enterprise.

   There is an additional feature of Psellos' style in the *Encomium* that seems to
reflect and reinforce his philosophical project. One of the devices that Psellos

---

   22. A more detailed study of this project will appear in my study on *Hellenism in Byzantium* (in preparation).
   23. See the remarks of J. Walker (2004) 58 on the deliberate polyvalence of such literature.

relies on frequently is apparent inversion and contrast, in which the original formulation is seemingly subverted and yet in reality extended in the reformulation, sometimes through a reinterpretation of the key terms.[24] There are, to be sure, many simple contrasts in the text, clauses introduced by a "but" or an "and yet." Often, however, these are additive rather than negational: "it was *not only* the case that *x*, but it was also the case that *y*." The terms of the initial contrast are thereby subtly resynthesized. On other occasions, denial is followed by reinterpretation through a "transposition," i.e., a new and superior understanding of the original terms that is not, however, completely unrelated to their common sense. At 2a, for example, Psellos applies this to the "prominence" of Theodote's parents and refers to Aristotle's theory on words (cf. likewise 5b on the transposition of "playfulness" and "study" in Psellos' youth). The world of the *Encomium* is one of apparent antithesis always leading to synthesis. In the first paragraph, for instance, Psellos disjoins the subjective motive for writing the oration (natural affection) and the objective one (tribute to a life of virtue), only to reunite them "by assigning what is fitting to each in the course of a single exposition," thereby "making them more beautiful through one another" and "entwining them together" (cf. likewise 6a on whether the subject of the work is Theodote or Psellos himself and 10c on Psellos' twofold debt to her). At 14c Psellos comments that "here [the death of his sister] my narrative becomes at once most sweet and highly painful, but my speech will arbitrate between the two." This "arbitration" closely parallels the "entwining" of affection and virtue in 1a: the narrative will be painful because of Psellos' love for his sister and sweet largely because of her virtue.

This device of unifying apparent opposites occurs even in passages that do not bear heavy philosophical weight. For example, mourners at Theodote's funeral were opposite in quality and origin but united in their grief and reverence (24c). But often these passages go right to the heart of Psellos' general attempt to mediate between "opposite" things (such as rhetoric and philosophy, Hellenic and Christian philosophy). Consider, for instance, Psellos' effort to rehabilitate the body in defiance of the philosophical and religious ortho-

---

24. See Hunger (1984) for antithesis, conceptual polarity, paradox, and comparison in Byzantine literature, but this is more a survey of examples by genre and rhetorical type than an analysis of the underlying mentality (as promised in the title). Maguire (1981) ch. 3 ("Antithesis") is more insightful in this regard, but limited to paradox and juxtaposition in theological contexts.

doxy that effectively viewed it as evil or at best as of no account in comparison with the soul. We saw how Psellos pointedly elaborates on the bodily beauty of his mother, father, and sister. In fact, he does much more here than merely correct an imbalance: he intertwines the two. "It was *not just* that her bodily beauty formed an image of the quality of her soul . . . but the soul itself made its own qualities shine forth in the body" (3a; cf. likewise 9b–c for Psellos' father and 13a for his sister). The relationship between the two was direct and real, not just symbolic. As a result (the passage in 3a continues),

> it was not possible for the many to discern whether the maturity of the body precedes the graces of the soul, or whether the latter dawn before the grace of the body, or whether both of them run together and are equal with respect to their speed and comparable with respect to their dignity, each reflecting off the other, with the one attracting to itself the gaze of all, the other astounding their intellects.

The final possibility, apparently endorsed by the attention that Psellos devotes to its implications and nuances, cuts against his earlier assertion that spiritual things are inherently more valuable than bodily ones and that, as a "philosopher," his proper business is to ignore the latter and devote all his attention to the former (see above, p. 38). Psellos is in fact attempting to "mediate" between the body and the soul (cf. below and 4a on the harmony of his parents: "it was as though two souls came together and recognized each other through the medium of the body").

The connection is deepened soon afterwards, in a passage that makes full use of the rhetorical techniques under discussion here.

> *It was not* her visible beauty that so entranced the many *as much as it was* the hidden and invisible one, I mean that of the soul, whence it happens that, even if the former is not present, the latter can by itself astonish those who hear of it or see it. I am distinguishing here between those who view from the outside and those who look into the soul. Yet since both aspects were present in her and both kinds of person existed around her, *both those who* embrace the phenomenon and those who espouse the nooumenon, *but also* the third and middle kind of person, who cling to and excel at both aspects, her father then for the first time suggested to her that she marry . . . . (3d)

We have every reason to think that Psellos himself belonged to this third and middle group of people.[25]

Such synthesis informs Psellos' characterization of his mother throughout. In addition to overcoming the polarity of body and soul (at least before her decision to embrace the monastic life), she united the active and the contemplative lives: in her case "there was no division between them as everything found expression in her at the same time" (4a). In general, "whoever managed to mix together the opposites in a more suitable way, I mean precision and simplicity, an appropriate degree of authority and a well-balanced mildness, a lofty sentiment and a restrained intelligence?" (7a) In particular, Theodote mixed the two different types of virtue that Psellos had identified among his contemporaries, the one gentle and the other bitter, the latter "hating evil more than it adapts to virtue. Her virtue was a mixture of both of these two types" (8c). She was both gentle and a stern teacher.

Yet, significantly, at the point in the narrative "when she entered the spiritual life," the language changes and becomes harsher; no longer interested in mediation, it imposes unilateral, one-sided judgments.

> She was no longer divided between body and spirit . . . her every desire, her every impulse inclined and directed her toward God . . . . Without hesitation she spurned the flesh, demolished its pretensions, and altogether deserted the body, . . . gathered her soul into itself and removed it from her senses, subjecting every desire to it, and enslaving everything irrational within her; . . . she lived by her mind alone and relied on it to effect her divine ascent. (17a)

As we have seen, this attitude cuts against Psellos' own "humanism," expressed both in the *Encomium* and in many other texts. The language in which he describes here the subjection of the body and its senses is likewise reminiscent of his bitterly ironic attacks against the otherworldly pretensions and inflexible "spiritual" stance of men such as his enemy, the patriarch Michael Keroularios. Psellos goes on to elaborate on Theodote's rejection of the body, which, in her view, dulled the soul's perception of God (17b–d). Unlike Psellos himself, who passionately lamented the death of his father, she managed to terminate the "contest of numerous oppositions that raged within her" and

25. Cf. Kaldellis (1999a) ch. 23.

impose a unilateral "philosophical" solution (19c). This denial and mortification of the body, Psellos more than hints, brought about her physical death (21b–c). Those who warned her to moderate her asceticism and practice virtue in a timely fashion, including her spiritual father, offered advice that sounds suspiciously similar to what the mature Psellos would have said (22a). But she continued to "cause her flesh to waste away though self-control and to neutralize her body" (25d). It is therefore something of a paradox that when Psellos summarizes her qualities after the account of her funeral, he reverts to the language of reconciliation and mediation among opposites. "Dissimilar things were established in her alongside each other and their opposition was reconciled for her alone, or else contrary things were seen in one and the same nature to have become conformable" (25a). He refers in particular to her mastery of nature and her reconciliation of feminine and masculine qualities.

> She advanced steadily in the contemplative life through the illumination given by contemplation ... wisely arbitrating between matter and immateriality and distributing whatever is suitable to each part or, rather, mixing immateriality into matter, rendering it more sublime and splendid through its participation in the higher element. (25d)

The *Encomium,* then, seems to vacillate between a philosophy that views body and soul as partners that reflect the same qualities and a different one that views the body as the natural enemy of the soul that must be subdued for immortality to be procured. Is this a product of the tension between what Psellos had to say in late 1054 and what he believed otherwise? In conclusion, it has recently been suggested that "the praise of Theodote's virtue works as a foil for tacit denunciation of the Christian asceticism that, in Psellos' view, destroyed her."[26]

Folk beliefs?   Unlike the vast majority of learned Byzantine writers, Psellos paid attention to popular beliefs, customs, and superstitions. What he wrote about them may not amount to much in length, but it is still more than we have from most writers of his caliber, excepting perhaps Eustathios of Thessalonike. So, for instance, we have two brief discussions of the creatures Baboutzikarios and Gillo; an account and philosophical interpretation of a women's festival

---

26. J. Walker (2004) 76, who makes (independently) a similar argument. This essay was brought to my attention after I had finished writing the present introduction.

in Constantinople; and some scattered notices in the *Chronographia* regarding popular songs and dances.[27]

Despite the *Encomium*'s high level of abstraction and the prevalence in it of philosophical terminology, it is nevertheless still possible to discern colorful and even concrete images of daily life in eleventh-century Constantinople. Given its subject matter, many relate to burial practices and to notions regarding the afterlife. For example, a crowd gathered at Theodote's funeral, trying to touch her body and grab shreds of her clothes (24c); her spiritual father pronounced her a martyr and saint before the crowd (24d); Theodote's decision to enter the monastic life after the death of her daughter was announced by cutting and suspending her own hair from the catafalque (16b–c); and the customary seventh-day commemoration sets the scene for Psellos' lament for his sister at her tomb (15c). That emotional outburst, which Psellos repeated later for his father and mother (19b, 24b), in fact belonged to a very popular genre, despite the classical garb with which it is invested here.[28] Both of his parents chose to end their days in monasteries and were tonsured shortly before their death. In a passage that is unfortunately obscure, Psellos suggests, regarding his grandparents, that the member of a couple who dies first may somehow "prepare" a position in the afterlife for the other (2b). In the lament for his sister, he expresses the pious hope that by being buried along with her he might be joined with her in their eventual resurrection (15d). In his three laments, he often begs his departed relative to watch over him or communicate with him, yet at times he is worried that the dead may have no recollection of their earthly lives (15d, 19b, 31a). His father subsequently appeared to him in a dream and revealed both his own fate as well as that which God had in store for Psellos himself (20b–d). In the lament for his mother, Psellos specifically requests that she appear to him in a dream and reveal her fate to him. He then relates a dream-vision in which she appeared to him and proclaimed that she had been watching over him ever since (26a–27a).[29]

27. Baboutzikarios and Gillo are *Phil. Min. II* 48 and 49 respectively; for Psellos' work *On the festival of St Agathe*, see pp. 179–186, below; and *Chronographia* 5.38. For Psellos and others' investigations into popular sayings and practices, see Megas (1953); Angold (1995) 457–464.

28. For the commemoration of the dead in Byzantium, see Spyridakis (1950) 166–171; Angold (1995) 453–457; for the ritual lament in general, see Alexiou (1974). For additional bibliography on death, see p. 27, above.

29. For the diversity of Byzantine notions regarding death in this period, see Angold (1995) 442–453.

The six dreams of the *Encomium* have already been studied,[30] though hardly conclusively. Likewise, there is still much room for the study of popular beliefs and practices in Byzantium, even in such classicizing authors as Psellos. What we need most urgently are analyses of their *literary* function rather than, say, of what they tell us about Byzantine mentalities and superstition.

Psellos' intellectual interests (sections 27–30).   The end of the *Encomium* deserves special attention and future study. It is nothing less than a comprehensive list of subjects that Psellos claimed to have studied up to 1054 and includes virtually every one known to antiquity and Byzantium. This was no idle rhetorical boast. We can document Psellos' interest in these subjects in the vast corpus of his works (in size between those of Plato and Aristotle, or about fifteen to twenty Teubner volumes), which truly does cover every field of knowledge. Elsewhere I have attempted to show that his references in the list to Christian topics, specifically the (allegorical) treatment of scriptural terms in 29b–d, seems to reflect the content of his lectures on patristic texts and passages of Scripture (the so-called *Theologica*), which must then, on the evidence of the *Encomium,* date prior to 1054 and may plausibly be ascribed to his teaching in the capital under Konstantinos IX.[31] It is likely that future studies will demonstrate that his references in the list to other topics, e.g., philosophical and scientific, correspond to other extant treatises and lectures.

The list at the end of the *Encomium* is clearly defensive. In 1054 Psellos was evidently under pressure to justify his eccentric, wide-ranging, and dubious pursuits, perhaps after having recently been accused of lapsing from the Christian faith (see above, p. 32). He is therefore careful to repudiate astrology, divination, Hellenic doctrines, and theurgy (28c–29a), while finding reasons to explain why he dabbled, or more than dabbled, in them in the first place. His interest in other, more innocuous, subjects he ascribes to the persistent questions of his students and of others (30a–d). Some years later, in the *Chronographia* (6A.11), he would obliquely deploy this line of defense for the more heretical fields as well. He also makes it seem throughout the *Encomium* that his love of learning was incited by his pious mother with divine approval, yet

---

30. Criscuolo 51–63, cites general bibliography on the topic and relevant ancient sources, but (again) does not elaborate on the literary function of the dreams in the *Encomium* itself; Vergari (1990) for 5c. For a recent groundbreaking attempt at a literary interpretation of the visions, see J. Walker (2004) 91–94.

31. Kaldellis (2005).

at the same time, as we saw (p. 38), he insists that his own bookish philosophy was different from the ascetic variety that she practiced (27a). As further proof of his piety, he offers within the list a long catalogue of Christian terms on which he expounded (29b–d). But his allegorical and Neoplatonic treatment of them hardly establishes the purity of his faith; quite the contrary, one suspects. When he wrote the *Chronographia,* he largely omitted Christian topics from the intellectual autobiography that he placed toward the middle of that work (6.42).[32]

The final pages of the *Encomium* constitute an extraordinary document by Byzantine standards. Yet they were not entirely without precedent. In his *Life of Nikephoros I,* Ignatios the Deacon (early ninth century) devoted many pages to the patriarch's studies, producing a list not unlike the one in the *Encomium* in breadth, detail, and content. As always in Byzantium, Ignatios is likewise defensive about his hero's involvement with Greek wisdom. But his list differs dramatically from that of Psellos, first in the omission of explicitly pagan subjects and second in that it leads into an exposition of Nikephoros' very Christian virtues: knowledge only enabled the patriarch to "devote himself to the much-honored practice of silently contemplating God and demonstrate a humility that raised him toward heaven."[33] This was a path which Psellos was both unable and unwilling to tread. Still, a historical comparison may be made between the two texts, as the generation of Nikephoros and Ignatios was the first after the so-called Byzantine Dark Ages (ca. 640–780) to acquire, value, and flaunt its classical learning. Psellos likewise (and famously) believed that he had single-handedly revived ancient philosophy after a period of darkness, ignorance, and neglect (in the *Chronographia* 6.37). He presented himself as a model philosopher of the future who had mastered a wide variety of disciplines.[34] In this sense, the end of the *Encomium* is both a defensive justification and a positive advertisement linked to his broader project of philosophical reform.

A major difference between Psellos and Nikephoros is of course that Psellos took it upon himself to advertise his learning in the first person, whereas Nikephoros, at least in this respect, did really practice the virtue of humility ascribed to him by Ignatios in the passage quoted above. There was no prece-

32. See Kaldellis (1999a) 130.
33. Ignatios the Deacon, *Life of Nikephoros I* (Fisher 52–56).
34. See, e.g., *On Incredible Reports* 100–106 (*Phil. Min. I* 32) as well as *Chronographia* 6.36–43.

dent in Byzantine literature for such a systematic exposition of one's own intellectual interests (and I suspect that the innovation could only have been made
by a professional teacher with philosophical ambitions). As with so many of
Psellos' literary innovations, it fell on fertile ground and found many imitators
(though not necessarily at firsthand). The scholars of the Komnenian empire
constantly flaunted their learning, emphasizing both its breadth and expertise.
In time, the figure of the public intellectual that was created in Psellos' after-
math seized upon the traditional hagiographic motif of the saint's learning—a
few paragraphs are devoted to that topic in the lives of learned saints—and,
in time, the genre (or subgenre) of the intellectual biography made its appearance. By the late thirteenth century, the acerbic Nikephoros Blemmydes (who
partially canonized himself) and the patriarch Gregorios of Cyprus were com-
posing their intellectual autobiographies.[35] The causes of this development,
however, are linked to the intellectual history of Byzantium in the centuries
after Psellos, which has yet to be written.

Editions, translations, and discussions.   For a list of manuscripts and all studies
referring to this text, see Moore (2005) 385–387. The *Encomium* was first published in its entirety by Sathas (1876) 3–61. The critical suggestions of Vergari
(1987a) were followed by an improved edition by U. Criscuolo, *Michele Psello:
Autobiografia, Encomio per la madre* (Naples: M. D'Auria Editore, 1989). However, I have been unable to find any reviews of this edition. It features a long introduction that focuses more on the various backgrounds, historical and literary, against which the oration should be understood than on interpreting it as
a work of literature. It also includes a good, if at times periphrastic, translation
(from which I have dissented on occasion), as well as an extensive and detailed
commentary on the origin and significance of almost all of the literary, philosophical, and religious terms employed by Psellos. This is a very useful guide to
the *Encomium*. The present translation is based on Criscuolo's edition.

---

35. For the intellectual biography of learned saints, see, e.g., Michael the Monk's *Life
of Theodoros Stoudites* (in *PG* 99 117b-124c). For its elaboration and development after
Psellos, see Nikolaos Mesarites (early thirteenth century), *Funeral Oration for his Brother
Ioannes* 8–19 (Heisenberg 22–33). For the late thirteenth century, see Nikephoros Blemmydes, *A Partial Account,* on which see Munitiz (1981); and the patriarch Gregorios of Cyprus,
Concerning His Own Life, on which see Hinterberger (2000) 141. Additional parallels may
be cited. The scholars of the Komnenian empire will be examined in my study on *Hellenism in Byzantium* (in preparation).

Apart from a few scattered notes, especially in broader works on other themes, e.g., Angold (1995) 436–437, and its inclusion in Sideras' standard catalogue of Byzantine funeral orations ([1994] 130–133), the *Encomium* has received virtually no attention from historians, in large part because it has not been translated into the major languages of modern research (Criscuolo's Italian translation is both recent and relatively inaccessible). Byzantinists are familiar with its contents only from the uncritical and romantic biography of Theodote in Diehl (1925), which, by contrast, has been translated into many languages. A subtle and sympathetic reading of the text by J. Walker (2004), which comes to many of the same conclusions, reached me after I had finished this introduction. Walker (2005) has made an able translation of his own with extensive philological commentary in the notes, whose readings differ in places from mine. Students of the text will benefit from a variety of interpretations.

Two numbering systems have been incorporated into the present translation: the bold numbers in brackets correspond to the page numbers of the Sathas edition, which is still the most widely used and, in any case, was universally cited by scholars before the appearance of Criscuolo's edition. The parallel division of the work into thirty-one sections, each of which is subdivided by letters into four paragraphs, follows the latter edition. I have, however, been informed that the forthcoming edition of the text in the Teubner series by P. Agapitos and I. Polemis will not retain this numbering system. The editors have announced that it will be numbered as *Or.* 18 in the corpus of Psellos' *Funeral Orations*: Agapitos and Polemis (2002) 152.

The Most Wise and Hypertimos Psellos, Encomium for his mother

[3] **1.** For my mother, this encomium. But this speech is no special favor, just because she brought me into this world, nor am I eager for praise;[1] rather I am both repaying the just debt to nature and rendering the appropriate tribute to virtue, not by separating the two,[2] but just as it in fact happened, by assigning what is fitting to each in the course of a single exposition. For if it is the case that even when they are separate they still draw out words of praise, the one through the necessity imposed by nature, the other through the dignity of character, how then is it not necessary, when they are entwined together and made more beautiful by one another, to grant them the praise of discourse in a superior form? For those who have earned the good through their own efforts and in great measure should be praised by skilled speakers in a more brilliant way, all the more so when the one who fashions the discourse is not drawing upon the experience of others but upon that which is intimate and familiar to him. And this is the happy position I find myself in now.

[4] **(b)** We must not be bold in praising people who are foreign and distant to the family when they provide brilliant opportunities for encomia yet overlook those who are most intimately related, and, on account of the suspicions of outsiders, deprive our relatives of the praise to which they have a rightful claim, so that in this way foreignness gets the better of intimacy and strangers gain the advantage over relatives. Given that it has been nobly agreed upon by all that we must requite the boon as much as possible for fathers and mothers

---

1. Namely by flaunting his gratitude toward his parents (a standard virtue).
2. Namely nature and virtue.

and all who are otherwise related to us, how are we to acquit ourselves of this charge, we who keep our compacts perhaps at other times, but fail at critical moments, and while they are living we furnish them with reasonable offerings, but when they are dead we neglect the demands of piety and deny them the speech that adorns them, which is the only thing left behind by those who have departed for the other life?

(c) This fear, moreover, should be feared[3] by those who have composed encomia of distant ancestors, whose virtues are perhaps unknown to the audience of the oration that only now and for the first time hears the eulogy, at once a historical narrative and an adornment. But herein I have been emboldened in devoting a discourse to my mother being among those who knew her, attributing to her those things for which there are many witnesses. At the same time I would also be doing an injustice to my mother by neglecting to perform this service, given that I learned my letters from her, as I will describe below, and by not repaying at least a small part of that debt. I, however, do not fear this fear, namely that someone may suspect that my encomium is for the most part false,[4] but rather that many may indict the insufficient power of my speech, as I rush to repay the innate debt that I owe to my mother and yet am shown to be inferior to my own desire, giving not what it is proper to give, but only as much I want or, rather, can.[5] And I would have shrunk from this enterprise, if this also did not give my mother the honor of greater virtue, namely that she would be shown to be superior to my own will and power.

(d) Since I have proven that this speech addressed to her [5] is most free of risk and highly proper in every respect, let the encomium begin. And you, mother, be gracious if I do not make my eulogy equal to the level of your virtue. For this is not the task that I have set out to perform; my purpose is rather to draw a shadow-outline of the image of your virtues for the benefit of those who are ignorant of them. Those who do know them will not pay much attention to the speech, but will give testimony to the truth.[6] To those

---

3. For this expression, common in Gregorios of Nazianzos, see Criscuolo 233 n. 31. The beginning of the *Encomium* echoes the beginning of Gregorios of Nazianzos' *Funeral Oration for his Sister Gorgonia* (*Or.* 8).

4. The dubious truth value of encomia was of particular interest to Psellos; see Kaldellis (1999a) ch. 19–22.

5. The contrast between the ability and the will to praise the honorand was a rhetorical *topos*.

6. Cf. John 18:37.

who come afterwards I explain this much in advance, namely that the speech will be measured not by your standards and your power to do good, but by the measure of my willingness to praise you.

2. Virtue came to my mother from her ancestors and her family, as an inheritance, so to speak, from the union of both her parents, just as two rivers flow together into a single ocean. That much do I grant to her with respect to the authors of her birth. Their concern was not to have prominent careers and conduct themselves in a brilliant way. Here I mean by prominence and brilliance those things which the many so designate, who form their opinions hastily and erroneously. Better people, however, are accustomed to 'transpose words'[7] to different meanings: prominence and brilliance do not merely tinge their external surface nor do these things barely touch upon them from the exterior, but, rather, the spring of brilliance actually gushes up from below and from inside themselves. For such people speeches of praise are not mere formalities, but rather they are adorned and made to shine by contrast to the others. Each of her parents had known only the other; through one another, as though they were most familiar examples, they regulated their lives toward the good, at the same time shaping and being shaped, being archetypes to one another and models for emulation. What is even more marvelous is that they receive what they give and straightway give what they receive.[8]

(b) Though limited to this glorious city, their fatherland, they were yet entirely limitless in the magnitude of their virtues. They were equally adjusted to the measure of each life, both of the present one that is dissolved and of the other one, which forms the image of a different life and which foreshadows to a great degree that limitless and boundless one.[9] In accordance with this, as it were, they had come forward into this life and came to light at around the same time. [6] It was also at about the same moment in time that they brought to an end that segment of eternity that had been allotted to them, one of them leaving in advance by just enough time to prepare for the other that higher life that was most fitting and to receive the other, as it were, with suitable preparation.

7. Cf. Aristotle, *Topics* 112a32, referring to the original meaning of a word.
8. For this expression, common in Gregorios of Nazianzos, see Criscuolo 235 n. 76.
9. It seems that we have three kinds of lives: the active life in the first part of the sentence and then the contemplative life, which is the image of a third life, the eternal afterlife.

(c) It is from ancestors of this kind and age that my mother sprang forth, being the first to release her mother from the pains of childbirth, the first also to obtain the paternal prayers, as was the custom. And if I were not a philosopher, a praiser and lover of the hidden beauty alone, not associating with the beauty that resides in symmetry and colors, I would repeat what they say, that at the very moment of her birth beauty spread to every part of her body. For the beauty that was in her soul was yet invisible, as age could not yet contain its power. Just as some flowers show the full temper of their beauty as soon as they spring forth from the earth and the first to appear is such that it can be seen already to be in full bloom, so too am I told that beauty was diffused all about my mother, in the symmetry of her limbs, in the blossoming of her hair, in the shining color of her skin, and I would say still more of what I have heard from her mother and father, who were startled with delight at the comeliness of their daughter.[10]

(d) But since my present condition shackles my tongue,[11] I think that I will leave aside this theme and turn to the subsequent portions of my speech. And if here too I seem to be somewhat out of line, may my speech be pardoned as it treats from this point onward, to whatever extent is possible, the most essential parts of my theme. If, however, I have attempted at the same time to narrate and to praise those things of which I do not have personal experience, there is no need to marvel. For I have heard the majority of them from the mouth of my mother herself while the rest, those which testify to her refinement and elegance, I have learned from family members.

3. They said that just as from a powerful lamp, or from a conspicuous and celestial firebrand, or from the rising of a pellucid star,[12] certain rays and beams flashed forth from her and announced her future virtue. And it was not just that her bodily beauty formed an image of the quality of her soul,[13] or that her spirited glance indicated [7] the maturity of her character, or that the whiteness of her color imprinted the purity of her disposition, or that the steadiness of her speech echoed the stability of her reasoning, but the soul itself made its own qualities shine forth in the body, though the latter was still incomplete, so

10. This is a typical instance of Psellos talking at length about things that he had told us he will not talk about.
11. I.e., his monastic vocation.
12. Or, "a pellucid star of the east."
13. Cf. Marinos, *Proklos, Or on Happiness* 3.

that it was not possible for the many to discern whether the maturity of the body precedes the graces of the soul, or whether the latter dawn before the grace of the body, or whether both of them run together and are equal with respect to their speed and comparable with respect to their dignity, each reflecting off the other, with the one attracting to itself the gaze of all, the other astounding their intellects.[14]

(b) Regarding the working of the loom and whatever the hands of women weave or whatever clever minds create, of which things even I myself often became a witness, not a single woman could have competed with her, not even the one who is attested by Solomon in these matters.[15] I would go so far as to say that those things which that wise man's account fashioned regarding the other woman are attested in my mother in double measure. But she paid less attention to these things lest she overlook greater matters.[16] The fact that she happened not to be a man by nature and that she was not allowed to study literature freely caused her anguish. Evading the attention of her mother whenever she could, she picked up the basic principles of letters from someone and soon began through her own efforts to join them together and to form syllables and sentences, without having any need for an instructor in the basics.

(c) She was consecrated to the holy temples but not by her mother, nor was she dedicated to them as though she were a lifeless votive object, but, rather, she went to them out of her own free choice, anticipating her mother's pledge and serving and worshipping God of her own accord. Henceforth she neglected her body, but the latter required no artifice, for it was like a rose in that it had no need for additional beauty. In fact, this neglect and lack of concern for her appearance were more of an artless complement and a kind of natural increase. Mist creeps up and obscures the sun and a cloud sweeps upward and blocks its rays, [8] whence at those times we do not know how the light-giver of heaven shines forth. But in her case there was nothing that could veil her beauty, not even that most attentive lack of attention to her bloom, because of which she was noticed everywhere just as is the light of the sun, so that nearly everyone was either held fast with amazement at the sight of her likeness or astonished to hear it described. To some indeed this seemed to be a piece of

---

14. For this passage, see the introduction above, p. 43.

15. Proverbs 31:10 ff. In all likelihood, Psellos is here following Gregorios of Nazianzos' *Funeral Oration for his Sister Gorgonia* 9 (*Or.* 8).

16. Or, "to the point that she even overlooked them most of the time."

really good fortune in another sense if they happened to catch a glimpse of her somewhere. I speak not only of the lovers of external beauty, but also of those who are philosophically conveyed from perceptible reality in this earth to that which is intelligible and invisible.

(**d**) But O for this digression in the speech, to which the necessity of continuity drew and diverted me. This very beauty, however much I have dishonored it with my speech, I still ascribe to my mother, bearing witness to it as the ultimate adornment, not from my own desire, but because from it proceeded her inclination to embrace life.[17] Her fame reached all and bound them to her, attracting one after the other; it held everyone with mouth agape or rather suspended with bewilderment, the majority through what they heard but some through what they saw. But why should I not also add that too, which, in fact, it is even my duty to say? It was not her visible beauty that so entranced the many as much as it was the hidden and invisible one, I mean that of the soul, whence it happens that, even if the former is not present, the latter can by itself astonish those who hear of it or see it. I am distinguishing here between those who view from the outside and those who look into the soul. Yet since both aspects were present in her and both kinds of person existed around her, both those who embrace the phenomenon and those who espouse the nooumenon, but also the third and middle kind of person, who cling to and excel at both aspects,[18] her father then for the first time suggested to her that she marry and he developed many arguments to that effect.[19] But she was not convinced and so he set aside the attempt to persuade her with words and inclined towards the use of force, even to the point of pretending to utter curses against her. But she forestalled the pretense by assent; indeed, she was innocent of dissimulation, as the narrative will later relate in detail.[20] [**9**] Now, as it happened, there were many who were running together in the race for her favor or rather who were running ahead of the others;[21] yet the winner had not the better fortune but rather the most virtue. I am speaking, of course, of

17. I.e., to create life and have children, the author among them.

18. Psellos here creates theoretical space for a mean position between absolute devotion to the body and absolute devotion to the soul.

19. In hagiography, parents often object to the young saint's desire to embrace asceticism, especially against the attempt by daughters to renounce marriage; see p. 35 above.

20. Cf. 8b, below. For this passage, see Vergari (1987b) 222.

21. For the expression, cf. John 20:3–4; for suitors enthralled by the girl's beauty, cf. Gregorios of Nyssa, *Life of Makrina* 2, 4–5.

my father, for whom this was a deficiency in his happiness, namely to remain deprived of such a woman, just as by gaining her he attained fulfillment.

4. At that time he was, as they say, 'with a newly grown beard'[22] and beautiful as a statue, although it was not only in this respect that he was similar to her, for the concurrence of their characters virtually eliminated any differences between them. It was as though two souls came together and recognized each other through the medium of the body.[23] In this way then, from being similar they came together into an equal concord. Each age is not suited to every circumstance, but immaturity is suited to playfulness, the prime of youth to the affairs of life, and maturity to higher pursuits; in turn, one is more advantageous for one kind of activity, another for another. Also, since lives are divided into action and reason,[24] one of them is eminently practical while another inclines toward the opposite direction. In the case of my mother, however, there was no division between these aspects as everything found expression in her at the same time and this was already the case even in the flower of her youth. She had both intelligence and wisdom, order in her thought and reason in her conduct, and she knew how to divide the two opposite principles and how not to divide them, how to hold to the one while seeming to hold to the other, so as never to be separated from God or from the meticulous care for her household.[25] She drew near to God or, rather, was always at His side, and, thinking that it was not necessary to be mindful of material things, she dealt with them in no other way than as a follower of God. So she both increased in age and also made her household increase in prosperity, making skillful use of whatever goods lay at her disposal as well as diligently acquiring those that did not.

(b) Now in the case of my father, whose family could trace its descent from consuls and *patrikioi,* matters were not arranged in so fitting a manner. If one were to place him and my mother on one side of the scales and the rest [10] of his family on the other, he would win by far thanks to the weight of my mother, but in other respects he would fall short of them. In fact, the woman praised by the wise man seems to me to have undertaken her actions in an altogether mean and shabby manner, just enough to work the 'spindle' and to 'make two

---

22. Homer, *Iliad* 24.348; *Odyssey* 10.279.
23. Psellos again involves the body in the moral and intellectual activities of the soul.
24. For the same distinction, see *Chronographia* 7.28.11–12.
25. The latter apparently qualifies as the "active" component of a woman's life.

cloaks for her husband,'[26] as though she did not want to do anything more or could not do other similar things. My mother, however, was more magnificent than that woman by far not only in turning the spindle but also in using any other instrument that pertains to the women's chambers. She did not 'make cloaks for her husband,' for his fortune in life was not that low, but rather wove them for herself, for her maidservants, for many relatives, and for the majority of others who were in misfortune. Most of these garments in addition happened to be extraordinarily beautiful.

(c) And then she gave birth to a child, a daughter unlike any other, if one excludes her mother, and what I say is no boast. For already at that time her beauty caused amazement to the majority, as the course of the speech will reveal more clearly. When, therefore, she became a mother and the first-fruits of her womb seemed fitting to the God who grants them, she concentrated upon herself to an even greater degree and directed more attention to how she conducted her life, not as the majority of women do who from that moment on abandon the strict life and live in indolence, for she reinforced her efforts rather than slackened them and strengthened both her nature[27] and her mind. And then Nature, as though being in love with herself and amazed that she could bring forth such beauty (I am referring, of course, to my mother), reasoned that it would not be possible to produce anything similar, except through this woman. Hence she modeled my sister on the image of my mother so that she might have, even if the prototype were lost, a faithful likeness. Thus Nature; God, however, arranged matters differently, as my speech will relate at the appropriate moment.

(d) Straightway there was a second birth, and once again the child was a girl.[28] This fact was not pleasing either to the parents or to the rest [11] of the family, for just as barren women long for a child of whatever gender, in this way did my mother all the more want her second to be a boy. But the throes of labor on both occasions were protracted[29] as though Nature herself were making preparations and needed a certain amount of time for the delivery. Since, however, it was necessary for God to listen and respond to her petitions, her womb was made to conceive and the time of birth drew near. The present

26. Proverbs 31:19, 31:22. The wise man is Solomon.

27. Presumably by "her nature" Psellos here means her body.

28. Nothing more is said about this other sister of Psellos nor of any children that may have been born after the author himself.

29. Cf. Kleophantos in Soranos, *Gynecology* 4.1.3.

author then burst out from nature, preceded by many prayers and hopes and while a great and divine paean was chanted on account of the childbirth, even though a labor such as this did not accord with the causes of birth.[30]

5. I will set my part in the story aside now and confine the speech to my mother. But should I narrate something about myself, let no one censure me, for it would not be an autobiography[31] but rather an explanation, to whatever degree is possible, of my mother's virtues. For I would be committing an injustice by depicting her as completely deprived of everything that she had hoped for and unsuccessful in her prayers.[32] But this will not be the case at all if what she had hoped for is shown to have had some measure of success and not to have been at variance with her desires.[33] Now whatever my relatives wished for me when I was born, for instance that I would never cry, not even in the most pressing demands of nature;[34] that I would never accept another woman's breast but only that of my mother; and that I would recognize her as my mother through intuition and not habit, as well as all the other things about which there is no need to say anything, these, then, I leave to the women's chambers.[35] On the other hand, whatever I happen to know for myself about both me and my mother from the time that I entered the age of understanding, this I will reveal more clearly, with no reservations and no fear for the tongues of slanderers.[36]

(b) My mother was led to accede to my literary studies both by the very loveliness inherent in cultivated discourse and the desire for its practical benefits, but even more so it was my own nature that strengthened her resolve in this matter since it was immediately admired for readiness of mind and, through practice, was fortified by aptitude for learning. Indeed, most of my relatives claim that even when I was a child [12] nothing was said to me in vain and that

30. This statement is obscure.

31. Psellos uses the term *periautologia* in the *Chronographia* (6.46.11) in connection with his autobiographical digressions; for this term, see Hinterberger (2000) 150–151.

32. I.e., Psellos has to mention his own birth, for it fulfilled his mother's hopes and prayers.

33. I.e., Psellos' own success and glory is a reflection of his mother's prayers and hopes and is therefore admissible material.

34. Psellos presents himself as weeping as a child later in this oration (8a), contradicting his family's wishes here.

35. Psellos nevertheless reveals quite a few of those things "about which there is no need to say anything."

36. In the course of his prestigious, controversial, and tumultuous career, Psellos had to defend himself frequently against *baskania* and *loidoria*: see *Or. Min.* 6–12; *Chronographia* 6.191, 6A.14, and probably also 6.74.

everything said to me became a true imprint on my soul.[37] Therefore, my mother, who was being led on to higher things, took me to a teacher in my fifth year and the lessons there were not only easy for me, they were even more pleasant than any other kind of childish game. In fact, I was distressed if he did not play with me for the entire day, given that for me study was play and play study, not in the sense that some things were games for me while others studies, but rather I was devoted to the latter on account of their pleasant quality and rejected the former because of their roughness. I say these things not in an effort to praise myself, but to indicate the source of my pursuit of literary studies.

(c) A short period of time flowed past and I had entered upon my eighth year. My nature now urged me onward to higher lessons. But to many in my family it seemed best not to send me off upon this sea or, rather, to surrender me to it, but instead to set me upon a different and easier course and, having seen me to its completion, to anchor me in a safe harbor.[38] I, however, was pained even to hear the suggestion that I might have to follow a different career than that of letters. My mother most readily inclined to my point of view, but for a while was undecided between my preference and the decisions and dispositions of the majority. And she made the decision, one might say if my mother had obtained a resurrection from one of the supreme beings and were present here at this speech.[39] For she would have interpreted for us the vision which she saw in a better way. There were actually two visions: I heard about the one from her, while the other I learned later by asking someone in whom she had confided. My mother used to tell me that once, when she was deeply immersed in sleep, she felt as though she were again in doubt about the proper course that I ought to pursue. After she had been repeatedly driven in confusion between the opposing considerations, a man of those who are assimilated to God,[40] who was familiar to her and made to look like the one with the golden tongue, I mean the Antiochene one of our faith,[41] said to her, "Waver no longer, O woman,

37. Note that in the previous paragraph Psellos claimed that he will not divulge any information provided by his relatives about his infancy and that he will rely solely on his personal recollections.

38. This image was one of Psellos' favorites; cf. *Chronographia* 6.34.1–3, 6.72.2–3; Littlewood (2006) on imagery in Psellos, including this one. This entire passage is also highly dependent on Lucian's autobiographical and yet ironic *The Dream*. See Misch (1962) 770; Vergari (1990).

39. This passage is problematic: see Vergari (1990) 317–318 n. 2.

40. I.e., a monk. For the expression, see Criscuolo 245 n. 310.

41. I.e., Ioannes Chrysostomos rather than Dion Chrysostomos.

in your thoughts, but [13] through one victorious decision choose to 'teach your son letters.'[42] I myself will follow him as his tutor (*paidagôgos*), and as his instructor (*didaskalos*) I will fill him with learning."

(d) I was told about that vision by my mother herself. The one which I am about to relate, however, was recounted to me by the younger of her brothers after she had passed away and he swore awesome oaths. He claimed that on one occasion his sister told him that when she was still divided in her deliberations about my future a dream of the following kind led her to make the final decision. It seemed to her that she had solemnly entered the shrine of the Apostles,[43] accompanied by some men whom she did not recognize. When she approached the sanctuary—her boldness stemmed from the presence of divinity, even in the shadows[44]—she thought that she saw a woman of those who are indistinct to the sight and who approached from within and ordered her to wait for her outside as she was leaving. That woman, then, when she reached the specified place, said nothing to my mother but turned to address those who stood on either side of her. "Fill," she said, "her son with the knowledge of literature. For you see how he embraces me!"[45] She also described the appearance of the men who stood on either side of her. Both of them, she said, were gray with age but one had a large and round head with thinning white hair, a nose that was not hooked and a beard that was not too long or thick, while the other had a smaller head and body, except that his beard was much longer than that of the other man.[46] These two visions gave my mother confidence in my future and she cast her vote in my favor, leading me to my initiation into higher culture.[47]

42. Cf. Deuteronomy 4:9.

43. This is almost certainly the church of the Holy Apostles in Constantinople, one of the city's most important churches, attributed (perhaps wrongly) to Constantine himself: see Janin (1969) 41–50.

44. I.e., in a dream. Women are forbidden from entering there. With a different punctuation, the phrase may be rendered, "she confidently believed that, even in the shadows, she was seeing a woman . . . ."

45. Or, "how she [i.e., Psellos' mother] embraces me." This could then be the Theotokos, but why is she not described? J. Walker (2004) 77–78 plausibly suggest that this is Lady Rhetoric or Lady Philosophy.

46. Probably saints Paul and Peter; cf. the descriptions by Elpios (or Oulpios) the Roman, *Ecclesiastical Antiquities: On the Physical Appearance of the Saints* (Chatzidakis 411–412; Winkelmann 119–121).

47. Psellos uses the same term (*proteleia*) to describe his initiation of Konstantinos IX Monomachos into the mysteries of philosophy: *Chronographia* 6.45.5–8; cf. Kaldellis (1999a) 132–133.

6. But I know not what has come over me. How should I continue this discourse? For I resolved to treat one theme but now the speech itself has carried me over to another, and, although I prefer not to mix any of my affairs with her virtues, nevertheless I cannot think of any other way for me to fulfill this encomium in her honor, or rather this truthful account of actual deeds, if not by intruding myself into it. How else could I demonstrate that she was the cause of my distinction in letters, if not by showing the origins [**14**] of my involvement with them? And if someone should prefer this, let the matter be distinguished in the following way between us: to her belongs the choice and decision to lead me to higher things, to me the fact that I did not ever resist her decisions. I appeal now to men who love scoffing and accusing, since the listener who is not hostile would not blame me at all for deriving advantages from my mother's virtue even if in accounts and stories about her.

(**b**) But the speech must again return to its proper theme and what follows must conform to the occasion. Or, rather, now that I have reached this point, let also those bear witness on my behalf who imparted the first lessons to me, on the speed with which I traversed them, on how I understood them better than most, and, lest I say anything more than is necessary, on the natural ease with which I learned, the tenacity of my memory, the eloquence of my recitations, on how over the course of a single revolution of the sun my orthography was perfected and I recited the entire *Iliad,* knowing not only the epic verses, but also the figure of speech, style, poetic diction, opportune metaphor, and harmony of composition.[48] And if you refrain from saying that I am addicted to dreams, I will briefly recount for you one of the visions I have had.

(**c**) I was not yet ten years old or, rather, I had just embarked upon that age, when a hunt swept me up at night and carried me into the open air. Whether I too was hunting I do not know, but it seemed to me that I had captured two birds of those that sing, of which the one seemed to be a parrot while the other was unquestionably a jay, and both pressed close in the folds of my garments. At this my soul relaxed and was gladdened, and I petted them often with my hands and smoothed their feathers. But the birds said, "Do not seek to tyrannize over us in so human a manner, nor seize us by force. Rule us as a master, as is right by law. Let us go and then converse with us logically and dialectically. If you persuade us, thenceforward you shall rule over us. Otherwise, grant us the free use of our wings."

---

48. For the study of Homer in Byzantium, see Browning (1975) esp. 16.

(**d**) It seemed to me that what they were saying was valid and so, using both hands, I held on tightly to the wings of each, and responded to them, I believe, with some philosophical arguments. [**15**] It was as though then, for the very first time, that the shadowy mists were lifted with which birth had clouded my soul.[49] The discussion was at first evenly balanced among us, as they too were developing arguments and syllogisms and replying to my counterpositions. But as the conversation stretched out into an extended debate and I was babbling on more than they were, they said, "Cease now, since even we acknowledge that you have defeated us." At that time I did not wholly understand the vision and so I thought that it was a product of the more irrational part of the soul. Later, however, after I had grasped musical theory and the more exact teachings, I assigned the dream-birds to the realm of rational discourse, given that they too babbled and used music and often spoke with a human voice.

7. But now that my speech has come to this point I will initiate the encomium for my mother. For I have not yet touched upon matters of which I have direct knowledge; instead, some of them I heard from the father, and some from the mother—I am referring to her parents—some from others who knew her well, and some I myself have recalled to mind and portrayed in this speech. That which I will relate henceforth, however, I have seen and heard and understood in a more philosophical way. I would even declare, to summarize everything into a single formulation, that there is not a single mortal woman who could compete with her, for I exclude those only who are reputed to be immortal. Who had a more ready mind than her or a more graceful character, and who a more steady ability to reason or a greater discerning sense in both speech and action? Who more than she managed to keep her tongue within bounds, in both speaking and being silent? What other woman was adorned with natural humility in quite the same way? Who ever managed to mix together the opposites in a more suitable way, I mean precision and simplicity, an appropriate degree of authority and a well-balanced mildness, a lofty sentiment and a restrained intelligence?

(**b**) O, her wise eye lowered towards the earth yet able to apprehend even the most distant things; O, hands which were soft by nature and age, but which became rough through the bending of the knee and bowing before God; [**16**] O, her every sense, exactly attuned to that which is dear to God, and her every

49. For the Neoplatonic background of this sentence, see Criscuolo 248 n. 380. For a reading of the vision as a whole, see J. Walker (2004) 91.

inclination, straining toward that end alone; O, the painted lines and eye-liners unknown to my mother alone;[50] O, the deceitful bloom and counterfeit white-ness, which paled in her presence and retreated from her; O, the added hair that adds nothing, but was incomparably inferior; O, the intelligence of her eyes and the gravity of her brows and the wisdom that resided in every one of her senses; O, for one who knew nothing feminine, except what was decreed by nature, but was in all other respects strong and manly in soul and even showed herself to be more resilient than the other portion of our species, pre-vailing over all men and women, over the latter by her incomparability, and over the former by her superiority!

(c) But how is one to describe the 'hidden life'[51] that you conducted in God's presence, the nocturnal vigils and early rising, the flight of your soul, the 'ec-stasy of mind,'[52] the illumination, the ascent? O, how could I neglect any of your qualities? I wanted strangers to know about them and I wanted them to want to praise them, so that this encomium in your honor does not come under suspicion. I should have added by "impartial judges" and by "arbitrators be-yond suspicion," lest anyone doubt my account. But now I am failing in two of the greatest respects and I am pressured from both sides. For I recounted your virtues in a restrained way and was silent about the majority and the best of them, and yet still my account of the least of them will be doubted, if not by those who knew you, then by the majority. Having fallen into the depths of your virtues, I do not know which of the oncoming waves to drive back first and which to admit in a smooth and even manner.

(d) But how am I to swim through this and resist the currents that assault me from both sides? Nor do I know to which one I should give precedence, since all have won the right to be first and have surrounded me all around: each attracts me and draws me towards itself. When I want to admire your moderation, I am attracted by the ascent of your soul toward higher things;[53] elevated to that point, I am then drawn down to the depths of your humility. From here, in turn, your gentleness transports me over to itself, [17] and, again, other virtues, one after another, lead me in different directions and convey me to new places. Therefore, it is quite impossible to praise adequately even a tiny

50. For the language of cosmetics used in this paragraph, see Philostratos, *Letter* 22.
51. Colossians 3:3.
52. Plotinos 5.3.7.14.
53. For the ascent of the soul in Neoplatonic thought, see Criscuolo 252 n. 444.

portion of your qualities, as I am pulled and transported in different directions, tracing the steps of this fruitless dance or, rather, of this endless journey. For the infinite extent of your virtues offers no prospect of a focus on the principal ones.

8. I fell far short of your expectations and so I will submit to chastisement, since my conduct has not been in accordance with your instructions. Right from the beginning, just as midwives do to the newly born infants, you trained my every sense and instilled in me every divine utterance without permitting the nurse to indulge me with fables. For I remember, bringing it up, as it were, from the depths, that even when I was crying and you wanted to put me to sleep, instead of the myths and the horrific Lamia[54] you would narrate at one time the story about Isaak, how he was led by his father to the sacrifice and how he obeyed him in all matters,[55] at another time about Jacob, who received the blessing of his father because he followed the instructions of his mother,[56] while on other occasions you would tell me about the more sacred things, I mean about 'the new Adam,'[57] your God and Master,[58] who also submitted to his parents in all ways.[59]

(b) I also remember what you used to say about virginity and all the pure advice you gave, even though my life has not conformed to it. Nor have I forgotten your talk of fire and light, the latter to illuminate the moderate, the former to burn the licentious. Nor will I overlook that deed which you desired to conceal from me, but which did not escape my notice. For my mother loved me—how shall one say it?—exceedingly and dearly, and often sought to cling to my neck and embrace me, but restrained her desire through the higher law and her better judgment, lest I grow overbold and become less obedient to her commands. As affection compelled her, however, on one occasion when I seemed to be asleep—my state had reached the closing of the eyelids—she, entirely unaware of my pretense, came near to me and ever so gently took me in her arms, [**18**] kissed my face many times, and then wept in floods, saying, "O my dear child, though I love you so, I cannot kiss you often." In this way

---

54. A monster of legend, used to frighten children. This passage contradicts the prediction by Psellos' family that he would not cry as a child (5a).

55. Cf. Genesis 22:1–19.

56. Cf. Genesis 27:1–40.

57. Gregorios of Nazianzos, *Or.* 30.1; cf. 1 Corinthians 15:45 and Lampe (1961) 28 (I).

58. Cf. John 20:28.

59. Cf. Luke 2:51.

she both restrained her affection and kept diligent watch over my upbringing. For such, in truth, was the character of her soul, but before I discuss this,
I should expound on this matter in a more general way.

(c) I do not regard all the souls that seek virtue as conforming to a single
pattern, but some are simple in their own way and full of grace and look upon
those who come near them with gentleness, while others are bitter and sullen and take offense at the greater part of human life, are rougher in character,
unapproachable to the majority, and become irritated and disgusted at anything whatsoever that does not conform to their will, for they hate evil more
than they turn it to virtue.[60] The virtue of my mother was a mixture of both
of these two types. For who had a more cheerful glance than hers, conversed
with more grace, or corrected error in a milder spirit? This part of virtue was
innate in her, while the other was gained by frequent practice, through intercourse with many people, but the dread that she inspired went no further
than the contraction of the brows. That which in others is added to the awk-
wardness and roughness of character, I mean being inaccessible or difficult to
approach, and which discourages some from drawing near, that was given to
her by the superiority of her own virtue. In short, it was not only the majority of people who feared her and held her in awe, but also her own parents,
and this even in the depths of their old age, as though they were paying their
respects to a superior nature which they revered and regarded as a living law.
They regarded her as a model of action and speech and silence, although they
fell far short of the archetype. And if she appeared suddenly before them when
they were disturbed, she would quiet the unrest in their souls; if they were
angry, she would dispel their anger; and if they were suffering or doing something else unpleasant, she would transform their disposition for the better.
But if they did something wrong and it escaped her notice, they took care lest
[**19**] she discover the event.

(d) I have not said these things to indicate that she boasted of being superior to her parents. For of all women, who attended and honored them more?
She supported them when they were old, comforted them with speech and
deed, sat beside them in their sickness, shared in their grief and suffering, and
kept a sleepless eye over them when they could not sleep. Not, indeed, that she
believed herself to be wiser than her parents, but they themselves honored her

60. The latter group exemplifies the inflexibility of virtue that Psellos attacked in the
person of Keroularios (see his *Letter to Keroularios*); cf. Kaldellis (1999a) ch. 23.

more than they did anyone else, even when she was acting in the way I have described, not because they could see what a high opinion she had of them but rather because they were astonished at the surpassing nature of her virtue. Her character was able to adapt to all people and to differentiate itself in such a way as to match the various dispositions of those who lived with and near her or who spoke with her, not by speaking sophistically to the many, but by determining what was suitable to each and acting accordingly, as circumstances required.[61]

9. To my father she was not only a helpmate and an aide, in accordance with divine decree, but also a prime agent and discoverer of the most noble things. His character also was such as none I have yet observed in others, indeed many knew the man and will testify on his behalf, should they choose to do so. He was at once simple and noble, having nothing feminine about him, tempered by an unaffected mildness, incapable of anger, reacting quietly to anything that might happen. I for one never saw him in an angry or disturbed mood, nor did he ever strike anyone with his hand or ever order others to do this. His soul was always graceful and his speech, though not ready for any occasion, he could imbue with pleasing charm whenever necessary. His conduct in life was highly industrious and his hand was not the instrument of a speedwriter, yet he was more winged than speech itself, not by using a foreign instrument but by relying on himself alone. He passed through life lightly, smoothly, and 'without stumbling, as noiselessly as flows a stream of oil.'[62]

(**b**) As for matters of the body, how am I to discuss them, how am I to make a digression in the speech, when to praise them is such an extremely difficult task? His stature resembled that of a large cypress tree, shooting up [**20**] to about the same height, and his limbs were suitably long and broad. His eyes beamed with brightness and, as someone else might put it, radiated lovely grace. The eyebrows which topped them were not haughty and conceited, but rather finely drawn and direct, indicating the decency of his character.[63] For truly he revealed the nature of his soul even to a passing glance.

(**c**) And, if one of those who can discern the nature of the soul by looking at the body had seen him, but before hearing him speak and even before gaining

---

61. An ideal of flexibility to which Psellos himself aspired. For sophistical imitation, see Eunapios, *Lives of the Philosophers and the Sophists* 16.1.9–12 (495–496), on Libanios.

62. Plato, *Theaitetos* 144b, a proverbial saying.

63. For elevated brows as a sign of pride, see *Chronographia* 1.35.

any experience of him in any other way, he would declare, concerning things that were for a time hidden, that my father showed forth in his life a spark of that ancient simplicity, so that if indeed some portion of this quality in some way characterizes me as well, it has been conveyed to me from him as though from a model. For I have entirely fallen short of the example set by my mother and failed to live up to it, since the way she lived was less suited to imitation than to amazed admiration. But as for my father, I fly alongside him as an eaglet or, rather, I follow him about like a shadow, or even less than that, since I do not orient myself or conform to his example in every way.

(d) Since my father was such a man, on account of the equability of his soul everyone felt confident in approaching and speaking to him and not a single person feared to do so. Only my mother, on account of the sublimity of her virtue, did not associate and converse with him on an equal level, but as though she were inferior to him. It was only in this respect that she maintained an incongruity between them and did not speak to him in a manner according to his nature, since she did not seek to conform to his character, but rather to the ancient commandment.[64]

10. But O, what can I say that will touch upon her virtues in even a superficial way? For I do not want my speech to fall far short of what she deserves and this I will attempt and strive for, or at least so I believe, standing at the beginning of my composition. Yet as I come to grips with my subject I shall be defeated by my adversary just like an inexperienced wrestler. And to many it may seem perhaps as though I have said something elegant about her, but as far as I am concerned this speech will not make even a small degree of progress toward describing her virtues, either because they are altogether beyond measure or because of the shortcomings of the measure imposed upon speeches. And indeed you, [21] O mother, were always educating me in them, not only as my skillful advisor, but by taking an active part yourself in my training and by inspiring me whenever you interrogated me as I returned from the school about what I had learned from the teachers, what I had contributed to my fellow students or what I had gleaned from them. And then you would instruct me how to remember those things that I had learned, pretending to listen with pleasure whenever I talked about orthography or poetry, or whence each element is derived and how it harmonizes with the whole, and what they all have in common and how, in addition, they are differentiated from one another.

---

64. Namely that women should accept a lower station than their husbands.

(b) I also remember this about you, which filled me with admiration, that you would stay up late at night with me when I was learning to read and you would lie on the same bed and inspire me with 'might and courage,' more than 'Athena inspired Diomedes.'[65] Nor did I fail to note this on the frequent occasions when I was going over my lessons, or sought to retain them in my soul, or whenever I was tracking down an elusive element of them. As though I were competing in a wrestling match, you evaluated me when I expounded the verses, stood by my side and defended me just as if we were in a battle line. Raising your hands up to God[66] and striking your chest with clenched fist— for this was your way in prayer—you would draw from above the definitive solution to my difficulties.

(c) Every child has some obligation towards its parents; rather, it owes them everything, since it has derived its very being from them. But this is an obligation that arises only through nature. My debt to my mother is twofold, since she both gave me being and also dazzled me with the beauty of discourse, not by ordering teachers to do this but by taking up the charge herself and sowing in me the seeds of learning. Yet this compulsory debt has not been entirely repaid, not because of any lack of gratitude on the part of the borrower, but because he lacks the means to satisfy the demands of the creditor. It is true in the case of my mother alone that although she has offered so many opportunities for praise, she has not yet benefited from a single one of them. For she did not build her roads in the valley nor can one approach her through a smooth and easy path, [22] but instead every step of the way is virtually untrodden, mountainous, and lies above the clouds.[67]

(d) I know that you have no need for the speeches that are produced down here, since you have attained the divine silence, mystical and ineffable.[68] Nevertheless, it would be terrible for me, who received the art of discourse from you, not to use it to contribute to your fame, just as shallow and barren earth

65. Homer, *Iliad* 5.1–2.

66. Cf. Deuteronomy 32:40.

67. The image alludes to the fable on "The Choice of Hercules" composed by the fifth-century sophist Prodikos, in which two paths are described, the rough and mountainous one leading to virtue and the easy one leading to vice (cf. Xenophon, *Memorabilia* 2.1.21–34). See Basileios of Kaisareia's reworking of this image in his *Address to Young Men on How They Might Profit from Greek Literature* 5; cf. Fortin (1996).

68. For the silence associated with mystical contemplation, see Criscuolo 257–258 n. 616.

contributes nothing to the farmer's sowing of the seed.[69] But my situation is different. For I have not spoiled the seed to such a degree and have yielded a crop. Still, the nourishment it produces is not at all suitable to you, who fare sumptuously on divine delicacies, which, even while you were alive, you offered to your soul in whatever degree was appropriate and beneficial, vigorously invigorating your most lofty aspirations.

11. My mother, in accordance with the law, was composed of flesh and blood.[70] I mean by 'law' the one that was instituted after the Fall from the original state of virtue. But as for the generic dignity of the soul and which part of it remains unmixed with the body and which is mixed, and what constitutes for it an inclination and movement toward worldly matters, and what, on the other hand, an ascent and a way up from them, from where and how it flies away and whither it travels and where it comes to rest, and what its fate is after this life, and who the elect are, what is given to them and what stored up for them, these things, then, and others she philosophized about on the basis of Holy Scripture, just like the most thirsty of all deer, rushing without restraint toward the springs of such pure streams.[71]

(b) And she desired to be separated from the world and to draw near to God, but it was not possible for her to act in this way since her husband was still alive and he also believed that a divorce from her was equivalent to an apostasy from God. Her thoughts on the matter became turbulent and she developed many winding arguments in her reflections on whether she would find the means to achieve her desired goal. She wanted both of them, as though they were two equal sections of the same road, to follow the same course and reach the same destination. She prayed, both day and night, for the most part in secret and undetected,[72] that she might attain [23] the monastic life and seek the state that is devoid of passions. For she had long loved the rags made of woven hair and the belt of the solitary and this was for her the chief object of meditation and philosophy: to cut her hair to the very root, make her body rough, her knees hard with calluses, to harden her fingers, and to live purely in the presence of the pure God.

(c) Thus she was unable to realize her intentions, but with regard to those who had attained that state, men as well as women, she submitted to the for-

69. Cf. Hebrews 11:11.
70. Cf. Galatians 1:16.
71. Cf. Psalm 41:2.
72. Cf. Matthew 6:6.

mer and associated with the latter, sleeping with them upon the same hide and resting her head upon the same rock. For she detested every soft bed and the luxury of superfluous clothing, and neither the blooming flower of beautiful skin, nor the softness of any fabric, nor the brilliance of any cloak, nor anything else of this kind could either win her over or attract her. Instead, her garment and delight, both sweet and beloved, were the roughness of the threadbare cloak, the sacred habit, the cross, the spiritual crest upon her head, and all the other symbols we have for the ineffable and most divine things.

(d) Yet she was still not permitted to enjoy these things, but only to suffer restrictions while surrounded by luxury and to be needy and poor amidst gold-gleaming and starry garments, and this only once a year, lest it seem to be an ill omen for her husband, at least for as long as she was not permitted to enjoy deprivation to the fullest. On that day she would mingle with those who had attained supreme contemplation, as though she were assisting them in the business transactions of virtue and sharing fairly in the profits. For she gave some things and received others: from them came the touch of hands, extended prayers,[73] and hope for the future, while from her came attendance, a sharing of material possessions, service and worship with her own hands. She would wash their feet, have them recline upon the bed and kiss their limbs, as many of them at any rate as were emaciated with disease or ulcerous.

12. But why should I not proclaim the dignity of her actions in a more grandiose way? Why [24] should I not add the color of rhetoric to the splendid images of virtue that she furnished? For she supported the poor not as the many do, who treat them like slaves and lean down over them and constantly reproach them for their misfortune. She did not act the part of the benefactor but instead derived some benefit from her actions, reverently giving her attention to those who for whatever reason were sick and suffering.

(b) Thus she would lead them by the hand up the stairs, giving them her hand and bowing reverentially before them, then washing and cleaning their every limb, anointing them with water as though it were myrrh.[74] She would not order a servant to do these things, but she herself would set the table and then fold her arms at her chest and serve them anxiously as though they were her lords (*despotais diakonêsamenê*). She would fill up the cup many times so that it gleamed and, holding it with her own fingers, courteously gave it back

73. Cf. Luke 22:44; Acts of the Apostles 12:5.
74. Cf. Matthew 26:6–12; Mark 14.3–7; John 12:3–8.

to her poor guest[75] after having skillfully mixed the drink so that it was both easy to imbibe and pleasant. In such a way was she skilled at helping the poor and she practiced each of the virtues with the same meticulous attention.

(c) In other respects she lived a quiet and untroubled life. She did not want to know something about everyone, nor about what was happening in the market-place, nor in the palace, nor if someone had been promoted to oversee and administer the grain supply, not even if it happened to be one of her neighbors. For she blocked out of her ears all superfluous speech and knew neither the crowded marketplace, nor whether any part of the city populace was in turmoil. Such things she entirely disregarded. But if some professed virtue, regardless of whether they were men or women, these she would indiscriminately gather and assemble around herself from afar, wherever they could be found, either inhabiting secluded bays and underground caverns, or standing elevated upon the air.[76]

(d) Yet the Lord of suppliants was not to defer her prayers for any long amount of time, but granted her request at the proper moment. Something of the following nature happened. But now it is necessary to bring this speech back to that chapter of the story from which it digressed above.

13. My mother's first child, that beautiful little girl, about whom I said some-thing earlier but then stopped, bloomed into maturity like the petal of a flower emerging from the calyx [25] and was soon near womanhood and ready to be given away in marriage. And, to leave out everything in between, regarding all those things which had accrued also to my mother on account of her beauty, namely fame, the convergence of suitors, the judgment over the best one and his selection, and those even greater things that stem from the graces of the soul, so much I will say, that we were a pair conspicuous and eminent, if not to others, at least to our parents and the rest of the family. She was beautiful without question, whereas I was only believed to be so. Her beauty presented itself immediately to all who looked upon her, both because of her external appearance and also by forming an image of its hidden counterpart. Mine was perhaps not so striking and so my account of it will be short, but in any case my parents, led astray by things that are not true, corrupted their verdicts in my favor.

75. Cf. Psalm 111:9.
76. Cf. the similar list in *Chronographia* 7:40, where Psellos evinces a very different attitude: Kaldellis (1999a) 88–89.

(**b**) And it is not the case that while our parents were so disposed toward us we were nevertheless disposed differently toward each another. Instead, as though we were two branches springing forth from the same stem, we were united to one another, at once separate and not separate, except insofar as her growth occurred much faster, while I came along more gently. Whereas she had a natural seniority of age, my inferiority to her was compensated by the superior quality of my gender. Whereas I simply took after my father, she grew up to resemble her mother, just as though she had detached those two aspects away from her, namely body and soul, and preserved the similarity in both respects. Hence she prevailed over every other woman in these respects, except of course her mother. For she was in no way different from her and thus victory was attainable for each through the other. When my mother seemed to prevail, my sister would carry off the victory, whereas when my sister was seen to be better than the others, it was my mother who received the beauty-prize. To such a degree were they similar that the only difference between them was a numerical one.[77] For if someone happened to see only one of them, he could be led astray into thinking that it was the other, whereas if he saw both, he would not immediately be able to discern their exact relationship.[78] So profound and complete was the similarity between them! For it was in the bloom [**26**] of life that my mother had given birth to her and thus was only a few years older. Hence, she did not differ from her offspring in the bloom of beauty and as a result they were differentiated from each another in no way.

(**c**) My sister ranked ahead of me in both age and the graces of her soul and excited respect in me for a long time, except that, unlike my mother, she did not have to maintain any reserve in her affection for reasons of prudent management,[79] nor to show her feelings secretly, but instead could kiss me frequently and hug me and tell me everything, about her desires, intentions, and actions. She directed me towards moderation and in other respects associated with me on a level of equal dignity, but on the need for moderation she was quite insistent, just as though she were issuing orders.

(**d**) But whereas she behaved in a sisterly and friendly manner, I submitted to her in all matters and treated her with reverence, even when she was hugging me. She was admired not only by the family from which she originated, but

77. I.e., that they were two, not one, or that their difference was only one of age.
78. I.e., who was the mother and who the daughter.
79. For the Byzantine notion of *oikonomia*, see Criscuolo 262 n. 754; cf. 8b above.

also by the one to which she was given in marriage. I will now recount a brief story about her, in order to indicate through it the abundance of her virtue.

14. In exchange for her youth, a certain woman from the neighborhood used to receive payments from those who desired it. Making a shameful living in this way, she would paint herself up in the manner of the courtesans and enchant the many with her artificial beauty. Well, those who were weakened by youth were emboldened to have her, while even the better and more noble men contended with the others over her. My sister censured her often, reproaching her licentiousness and condemning her obscene behavior, and finally ordered her to go and live far away. The other woman at first remained deaf to every accusation and exhortation and persisted without change in her chosen life. But since my sister did not desist from her barbs and reproaches, she said, "But if I renounce prostitution, where then will I obtain the necessities for life?" Replying abruptly and without hesitation, that girl so ardent in her love for the good or, rather, so philosophical in nature, swore awful oaths that she would furnish her not only with necessities but also with superfluous luxuries. This [27] persuaded her and the two were reconciled: the one no longer showed herself even to the eyes of men and entirely renounced her former haunts and habits, while the other shared with her all those things of which she had need: shelter, clothes, food, and, if she desired it, even luxury. She now rejoiced for having saved a soul from being devoured by the wicked beast.[80]

(b) In this way, then, she treated her respectfully and attended to her needs in abundance, to such a degree that she aroused jealousy in many women of the family who accused her, the savior, of preferring a stranger over her own kin. But she, knowing well the reasons why she favored that woman, did not suffer grievously from the reproaches and smiled calmly and gently in response to their extremely severe attacks against her, giving their words over to the winds. After some time, the woman, having kept the agreement, entirely abandoned her shameful life and was adorned with the beauties of temperance. And I myself regarded her as sincerely temperate and good, for she kept her eyes lowered and veiled her entire face with modesty. She attended the sacred temples and kept her head covered, and, if she happened to see someone all of a sudden, she would immediately blush. She was indifferent to her body, neither decorating her hands with a variety of rings nor binding her sandals with elaborate and flower-colored leather thongs. In this way did she turn her entire life around and move to the exact opposite disposition.

80. Cf. Ezekiel 34:8.

(c) But the conversion was limited by circumstance and, before her new habits could solidify, she lapsed back into her previous mode of life. O deceit! O sudden and new transformation! This event eluded my sister's attention and so while the one was guilty of prostitution the other loved her exceedingly and cared for her as though she had entirely changed her ways. But even she had to learn the secret eventually. And here my narrative becomes at once most sweet and highly painful, but my speech will arbitrate between the two.

(d) Being pregnant at the time, my sister went into labor. But she had a difficult delivery and the childbirth caused her great pain. The women [28] assisting in the delivery tended to her needs and comforted her, stimulating and relaxing the labor pains, and prepared lubrication for the infant. Participating with them in the delivery was also the woman who cloaked herself with the pretense of temperance and my sister took greater comfort in her presence than in that of the midwives. Because of this one of the latter became envious and said, "It's her fault your labor is difficult. For it is not permitted for pregnant women to help those in labor.[81] This is the law of the women's chambers." My sister replied, "And which one of you here is pregnant?" The midwife immediately pointed to the other woman and, pulling away her cloak, revealed her belly. At that point my sister came close to breathing her last and, forgetting all about her labor-pains, let her soul be torn apart by unspeakable pains upon this revelation. But she did not thereby deviate from the noble precept and ordered that woman to flee immediately to the ends of the earth. At that point her childbirth had a timely conclusion and the infant came forth from the womb. Nature had miraculously induced her to give birth in the prime beauty of her youth, but death took her away even more unexpectedly, even though it left untouched the image of her extraordinary comeliness and did not despoil her of it given that, as I believe, it could not.[82]

15. At the time of those events I was residing in the fields that lie before the city, having traveled a short distance in the company of a man who was highly experienced in rhetoric and who had been entrusted with the supervision of the judicial affairs of no small part of the western lands. That was the first time I had ever left the city and seen its surrounding wall, not to mention the open countryside. I was sixteen years old and tall for my age. I had just completed my study of poetry and had begun to apply myself to the art of rhetoric, not without grace. As my parents later told me, a terrible sickness had infected

81. For the beliefs and vocabulary of this section, see Plato, *Theaitetos* 149b–c.
82. For a (speculative) discussion of this episode, see Vergari (1987a) 410–414.

my sister's internal organs and her liver quickly began to fester within and then became swollen.[83] Her entire body was consumed by an inner fire and her nature finally succumbed, giving way before the more powerful forces. [**29**] Even though the wasting disease had not yet exhausted her strength, she died with her body still in full bloom and good condition. What the reaction of my parents was to this calamity the speech will reveal later. For now let it hold to the sequence of events.

(**b**) Since my sister died before her time, my parents, who could not undo the fact, were no less afraid on my account, lest I be struck down by the unexpected news and heap more grief upon their grief, no mean addition to an already enormous misfortune. For they knew how closely bound we had been to each other and that with one of us gone our united whole could hardly continue to exist. They wanted to take me in their arms, embrace me all around with words, and only then reveal the wound's painful sting. Therefore, they sent me a letter reproaching my long silence, playfully joking about my neglect in writing to them, and, so as not to end as I began — for, having set forth from the starting line at a sprint, my breath fails me quickly on this track — they added some ordinary news about my sister, of the kind that had often reeled me in previously. In this way they induced me to return to them. And they hoped that their device would go undetected, but I was besieged and conquered, as it were, from a different quarter and the truth fell upon me before the noble deceit. How this occurred the speech will presently relate.

(c) It happened that I had already entered the walls and found myself at that place where my sister's body had been buried. As it was the seventh day after the funeral, many relatives had assembled to mourn for the deceased and to console her mother. There I chanced upon one of them, a simple and good man who knew nothing of the fraud nor of the fact that I had been tricked into returning by my parents. I asked him about my father and all the others who were in some way related to me. And he, neither adulterating nor concealing the truth, said, "Your father is offering funeral laments to his daughter and your mother is at his side, unable to be consoled, as you know, over [**30**] this misfortune." Those were his words, but I know not what came over me. Just as though I were burned by holy fire, I was struck senseless and speechless. I slipped down from the horse's saddle and the news of my arrival reached the ears of my parents.

---

83. It is unclear whether this sickness was related to her pregnancy. See Volk (1990) 303–307.

(d) Whereupon a new lament was begun on my behalf and the wailing was now far more impassioned than before. For when a fire has been kindled, even a small bit of wood, if thrown in, can quicken the flame, rekindle the blast, and double the intensity of the conflagration. For as soon as they realized what had happened, like people possessed by madness they ran toward me, and then for the first time my mother displayed her beauty in public, indifferent to the gaze of men. They sank down over me as I lay on the ground and grasped me, one from one side, another from the other, recalling me to my senses with their laments. And then, even though I was half dead, they conveyed me to the tomb of my sister and gave me over to it. But O, how can I hold back the tears once again in order to relate these events, how will I be able to finish weaving my speech, seeing as my soul is shrouded by the mists sorrow? Yet I will speak, in whatever way I can, fortifying myself with the strength of the highest thoughts. As soon as I opened my eyes I beheld the tomb of my sister. I both grasped the extent of the misfortune and collected my wits, yet I was completely overcome with grief and poured out streams of tears for the deceased, just as though they were libations poured before a tomb. "O, my sweet one," I said, "not merely *my sister,* if only there were another name that denoted greater closeness and affection! O, extraordinary beauty, incomparable nature, unmatched virtue, living statue, spur of persuasion, Siren charm of speech, invincible grace! O, you who were everything to me, more even than my very soul! But how could you leave and abandon your brother, how were you sundered from your natural counterpart? How will you endure to live alone for such a long time? O, what abode has received you, what place of rest has been allotted to relieve you of care, what meadows, what graces? What paradise enchants you? What is that beauty that you have preferred over my company and sight? What flower draws you away, what rose-bed, what gushing rivulet? What nightingales, what cicadas casting their sweet voices? [31] As for the beauty of your body, has nature received, guarded and preserved it, or has the earth entirely destroyed it, extinguishing the blaze in your eyes, removing the bloom of your lips, dissolving the composition of the elements and breaking up their combination? Or is your beauty still intact, preserved in the grave as in a treasure-box? But if your spirit has departed from the body and has turned itself entirely toward God, having neither speech nor memory about the things that are down here, then hold tightly to the contemplation and illumination that exist there! I do not blame you for your lack of communication, nor do I reproach you for not sharing yourself with us, since fellowship with you transcends our nature. But if for a moment you should turn your attention to the visible world, do not begrudge us communion with yourself: take hold of me and give word to me of your destiny. And if here too I seem to fall short of your measure, still, this grave will not separate me from your body and when the dust of our bodies dissolves together, I will participate with you in their recomposition, even if to an inferior degree."

16. With these words and others even more heartrending did I lament over the grave of my sister. My parents wailed aloud, all but pouring out drops of blood from their eyes. The entire crowd that had gathered also mourned along with us and such was the excess of grief that everyone came close to passing out from the sorrow and thus silencing the chorus of lamentations. My parents barely managed to pull me away from the grave. "Have pity on us," they said,[84] "sweetest child, help us preserve the little bit of breath that remains to us: do not destroy us utterly! May no one have cause to blame you for our demise! Yes, upon the gray hairs of those who raised you, upon our souls, which are still held fast by these bodies because of our love for you!" Thus did they speak, but I could stop one lamentation only by beginning yet another. For as I saw my mother and recognized her, dressed as she was in a black threadbare cloak and having mortified herself in every way by the ragged and tattered garments she wore, I was beside myself and came close to dying right there and then. [32]

(b) Events had transpired for her in the following way. My sister lay dying and was taking her final breaths, her head resting in my mother's lap. Her soul had not fled, nor was her tongue moved to speak in delirium, nor had her breath abandoned her utterly. In a natural and unforced way, she then repaid the debt of nature to those to whom it is owed. My mother gathered her strength in whatever way she could and closed her daughter's eyelids, while her own eyes at once filled with tears or, rather, her entire being was consumed by an indescribable fire. She began a funeral lament and cried especially when she saw that her husband was also moved by the force of the misfortune—for he was easily affected, even on other occasions, by such calamities, and I recognize his character in the qualities of my own soul. So as she saw him affected in this way, she momentarily commanded her soul not to become clouded by grief. O, noble and resolute will, calm even amidst waves of such magnitude! She philosophically expounded some of the highest teachings, those which

---

84. There are some rather inappropriate allusions in this brief speech to Heliodoros, *Aithiopika* 1.12.

transcend circumstances and events, and expounded at great length to her husband about the passage to the better life. Using grief as her advocate in persuasion, she managed to win him over against expectation. And she refused to postpone her decision to another occasion but immediately offered the first fruits of her conversion to God by changing her attire, cutting her hair, and donning the monastic cloak while still in the prime of her youth. Not yet had she cast off her bloom, still her hair was full and luxuriant; not yet had her petal shriveled, still she sprouted forth a tender shoot, still she bore ripe fruit. My father assented to her words and so it was that they conveyed my sister to her grave, whose beauty still shone forth; the bright grace of her face was still visible.

(c) They said that once they had cut the curly locks of her hair and once those entrusted with the arrangement of the body had suspended them from the foot of the catafalque—for her hair was extraordinarily golden-blond and thick[85]—the funeral procession began with the bier raised high, visible even to those on the third floor. [**33**] Nor was there anyone who, after turning his eyes toward her, did not either dismount from his horse or come down from his third-story dwelling. All men and all women accompanied the procession and joined as one in the lamentations. Such was my mother's conversion to a higher life; this was the occasion for her to embrace the monastic life; this was the passion that led her toward the passionless life; this the death which introduced her to the deathless state.

(d) And then what happened? Once she had directed her footsteps toward the higher life and had entered upon the divine course and stepped down into the arena of the spirit, her soul was not confounded by seeing the audience full of angels[86] and people, which is something that happens even to the majority of men, some of whom turn back right from the very starting point, while others abandon the course and are dismissed without obtaining the crown. Yet with forethought she also arranged for the grave of my sister to be dug there, where she intended to retire from the world—indeed, there it still stands, and will continue to stand, a place where philosophical souls can practice virtue—she shut herself in there, immediately renouncing both home and livelihood, one could even say her flesh and blood, except insofar as she had disposed of

85. It was probably Theodote's hair that was suspended from her daughter's catafalque, as a sign of her intention to be tonsured.

86. "Angels" can refer to monks; see Criscuolo 271 n. 990.

her belongings in a virtuous way, equipping herself with the supplies necessary for the life upon which she had embarked. But since she had not yet been properly consecrated to God, nor had her conversion been performed by a spiritual guide, she once again took a more intelligent and wiser decision. She arranged for my father to be dedicated to God before her, yet again granting him precedence even in matters concerning the other life. And when she had witnessed the consecration of her counterpart, she rendered her own portion of the burnt offering to the Almighty and thus the first mystery rite of her initiation was completed.

17. As for subsequent events, I lack words with which to praise her.[87] Just as if a firm substance, rounded off into the shape of a sphere, is then set into motion upon a level surface and thereby reveals in accordance with its design how swiftly and easily it can roll, but when [**34**] it encounters an inclined or angled surface, it immediately rushes downhill with unstoppable force,[88] so too my mother, whose soul was easily led toward the better life from the beginning and through a natural tendency ran smoothly toward the good, when she entered the spiritual life, which is a slope leading conducively toward virtue, immediately and with irresistible force hastened toward the downward journey's end. For she was no longer divided between body and spirit, matter and immateriality, clay and holy ground,[89] nor was she separated from God, the ruler of the world, but her every desire, her every impulse inclined and directed her toward God; she was conveyed to Him by all the powers of her soul. Without hesitation she spurned the flesh, demolished its pretensions, and altogether deserted the body, that manacle of the soul;[90] she despised every expediency demanded by nature, gathered her soul into itself and removed it from her senses, subjecting every desire to it, and enslaving everything irrational within her; she eliminated foreign images from her imagination as well as unnatural thoughts, irrational opinions, worldly sensations, and transient notions; she lived by her mind alone and relied on it to effect her divine ascent.[91]

---

87. A conventional motif, but it can be taken literally to mean that Psellos is unwilling to praise his parents' decision to embrace the monastic life: J. Walker (2004) 80–81.

88. Cf. Aristotle, *Physics* 238a21, 248a22.

89. Cf. 1 Corinthians 5:3; Job 38:14.

90. Cf. Plato, *Phaidon* 67d; see Criscuolo 273–274 n. 1025.

91. The scientific comparison at the beginning of this paragraph casts Theodote's journey as a descent; here, in standard religious imagery, it is an ascent. For the possibly subversive intent of this reversal, see J. Walker (2004) 81.

(**b**) You should be the witnesses, not merely the audience, of her good qualities, for in this way both I may rid myself of suspicion and you may see the
truth. However, I cannot now tell you about *all* of her virtues, even briefly, and
so I will be doubted by the majority. For just as though she were ashamed of
having descended into the body, as has been rumored of one of the Greek philosophers,[92] she revealed only a small part of her face and hands and no part of
her was ever seen naked. She even conceived of human skin in a philosophical
manner, not only as something which clings directly to the body but also as
something added on to it from outside. At night she would sleep in nothing
more than it.

(**c**) She did not want to nourish the body at all but, rather, just as though it
were some shackle of the soul, to torment and weaken it. [**35**] Yet since nature
cannot be fought off entirely, she resisted nobly to whatever degree circumstances allowed and appropriated as much moderation for herself as immod-
eration itself lacks. She approached God, but whether she was immediately
seized in rapture I do not know, though it seemed so to all. Neither her head,
nor her hands, nor her feet, nor any other part of her bodily vesture was turned
or moved in any way; rather, she was like the shadow on a wooden board,
changing only as much as the eye may assume when it grows tired. One realized that she was alive only from her sighs and her posture.

(**d**) She would often philosophize to me about these matters, telling me
that prayer is a meeting with the Almighty and that it is necessary for one who
encounters Him not to be changed up to the point when he separates himself
from this encounter. She used to call this separation from God the deficiency of
the soul.[93] "For one must not say that," she said, "namely that He contracts or
expands; rather, the absence of procession or emanation is His unique quality
and everywhere He subsists as light, as air, as something else that is common
and open, as a sounding trumpet.[94] They see it and they perceive its sound
whose spiritual eye is well suited to sight and whose sense of hearing can listen
well to a ringing sound. Those, however, who 'while seeing do not see or while
hearing do not hear'[95] entirely lack intensity and discernment in their eyes
and ears. For through matter the mind perceives immateriality and, when it is

92. A clear reference to Porphyrios' *Life of Plotinos* 1.
93. For this view of prayer, see Criscuolo 276 n. 1055.
94. Cf. Exodus 19:16.
95. Matthew 13:13.

separated from the former, it can see the visible and hear the audible in a clear and pure way. But when it mixes itself with matter, it immediately loses its true utility. In this way, therefore, there are many who believe that they have heard voices and perceived sounds once their souls have attained a state of divine inspiration and of prudent bacchic frenzy. It is thus incumbent upon us to pray with our bodies unmoved and tranquil. The soul is not entirely submerged within its bodily vessel, but the part of it that has mingled with the flesh is dead with respect to perception, while the rest floats above, buoyant like the top part of a buoy cable or like a light cork that has not been dragged down by nets.[96] It is this part of the soul that [36] a different mind, an angelic one, turns toward itself from the outside and directs up to God." Such was her truly spiritual and divine wisdom, into which she was initiated from on high and into which she initiated us, who dwell down here.

18. I will speak more of my mother later. For now my speech will once again look to my father, who was in any case graceful both in his body and soul, but when he was dignified by initiation and ascent and elevation toward higher things he became even more beautiful and graceful. He seemed to have been liberated from his shackles, becoming, one could say with some precision, winged and free, as though he had become a living offering to God. He went around with his soul full of pure joy and would often say, "If some other heavenly kingdom has been set aside for those who are pleasing to God, that is for Him to know and the one who affirms it is without deceit. But even the life led by those who are turned toward Him does not at all seem to me to fall short of the other one which was first.[97] As for me, my soul is no longer 'submerged in the body'[98] as before, but is 'dancing'[99] and rejoicing as if it were within the grounds of sacred precincts. I do not now reason about its immortality, instead I contemplate it directly. For it has left the body behind and yet 'continues to subsist,' separate from that which was united to it, 'not only with respect to its activity, but also in its very being.'[100] The degree to which it is not released from the body depends on the will of the one who has bound it there. In the meantime it truly returns to itself and turns toward mind and through

96. For this Neoplatonic view of the soul, see Criscuolo 277–278 n. 1073ss.
97. A reference to life before the Fall or to those who are pleasing to God?
98. Plotinos 6.9.8.18–19.
99. Plotinos 6.9.8.45.
100. Plotinos 6.7.40.11 ff.

mind toward God." Philosophizing in this way,[101] he explained for me many syllogisms that could not be resolved through reasoning and also granted me unmediated intellection, basing himself on mind and drawing his conclusions from within its compass, as he had no need for any intermediate or stray steps. Thus I witnessed his complete transformation from one state to another, as he was elevated to the highest peak by uplifting forces, singing psalms for his escape from Babylon and ascent to Jerusalem.

(b) Not much time had passed when he summoned me to visit him. As I entered he said, "My child, joy is not now strong [37] within me to any great degree, but instead shadow has suddenly caused my soul to wander astray and I know that the source of that which has overtaken me lies in the worst of natures. For that part. . ."[102]—and he added on that topic a number of philosophical reflections, about how it ever acts, how it enters the soul, and other thoughts on the nature of those things and on the careful observation of experience. "I have no way to repel the siege, but my soul, just as though it were encircled by walls, lies hidden within and seeks refuge in its inner depths."

(c) Those were his words. I, however, relying to the necessary degree upon my eloquence, spoke of the ways by which spirits can attack and overrun us, but we turn ourselves around and ultimately prevail. Thus I removed his distress and restored the tranquillity of his soul. He then said, "O dear child, sweetest one, what gifts of hospitality would I not repay to you who have entertained me with such words? How pleasurable a thing it is for father and son to be together in a philosophical way and to partake of the common victuals." "But not upon one who is unwilling, O father, are you bestowing your hospitality. There is no way that I would have departed, even if it were not you yourself who invited me to be your guest." For a short while my father smiled gently at my words and then said, "If there are animals which again receive into their natural bosoms their offspring which have been shaken and disturbed, I have heard it from those who inquire into such matters. As for me, however, I would gladly even tear open my innards in order to shelter you within them."

(d) Well, I spent the day in my father's company and long after the sun had set I paid my respects to him with many embraces and, quitting the monastery, departed. I left him beaming with joy, but I was not in an entirely cheerful

---

101. The speech of Psellos' father is far less complex syntactically and rhetorically than that of his mother in the previous section.

102. Presumably, that part of nature that was afflicting him now.

mood. Hence I decided to visit my mother and use her as a medicine for the disturbances of my soul. She received me with joy as though I had returned from abroad and persuaded me to stay there for the night.

19. It was not yet the middle of the night when someone pounded on the courtyard door. The doorkeeper, seeing who it was, came to my mother and me in a state of some agitation. For it was already time for her to attend the early morning hymn. [**38**] She approached and said, "Your father, my most lovely child"—she nodded in my direction—"was struck down suddenly by a fierce fever yesterday evening and is now burning up." I at once set out for my father and she followed on foot. As we entered his cell we saw him absolutely consumed by the fire, afflicted by severe breathlessness and showing all the signs of an inflammation in his internal organs. When I sought to establish his pulse by placing my fingers on his arteries—I was long a student of this art[103]—I immediately lost all hope. For his pulse had abandoned most of his body, so that his blood showed faint signs of movement or, rather, it was agitated like the motions of an ant. I stood there trembling and dumbfounded, not knowing whether to lament him or to console my mother or, finally, to bewail my own condition. He realized my distress and grasped me with his right arm, saying, "O child, I am now departing on the path that was ordained for me, to which the Word has destined me. As for you, compel yourself not to mourn and become a sufficient consolation for your mother." He held out for a short time,[104] then suddenly opened his eyes widely, faintly whispered something indistinct, and finally shut his eyelids over his eyes and expired, giving his soul over to God[105] and delivering me over to the tyranny of mourning.

(**b**) Since none of his fellow monks was yet present, I 'fell upon his chest'[106] and kissed his heart all over, saying "O father." I did this many times but then stopped, for I had to catch my breath. Then, once I had composed myself and taken a deep and gasping breath, I renewed my cries, "O father, where have you gone so suddenly? How could you fly off and abandon your son? O sudden separation! O bitter parting! The echo of the words you spoke to me yesterday evening still reverberates in my ears. It is as though we are still philoso-

103. For Psellos' medical credentials (and pretensions), see also *Chronographia* 7.77; for a comprehensive survey, see Volk (1990), esp. 307–308 for the death of his father.

104. Cf. Plato, *Phaidon* 59e.

105. Cf. Luke 23:46. Through these allusions, Psellos implicitly compares the death of his father to those of Jesus and Sokrates.

106. John 13:25, 21:20; see previous note.

phizing and discoursing on the soul. What was that bolt which so suddenly wounded your soul? Who left that lance lodged within [**39**] your entrails? Who injected you with that deadly venom?[107] I thought I had removed the arrow, by somehow quickly opening the gash caused by the bolt, removing the sharp point, then quickly smoothing down the wound. You seemed to have changed your state and raised up your soul. O, those parting words which you spoke to me and your kisses of farewell! And it is possible that you, O father, gave to me your last woven discourse, just as you were about to lift off and depart on a long voyage abroad, while I believed that your conduct was an expression of natural generosity, which soon yields and becomes warm affection, as has often been the case. I do not know where to turn, how to contain the swelling in my soul. Shall I console my mother first or accept her consolations? You, O father, have departed on the path that is truly good or, rather, you rose up to the heavens, launching yourself into the air and ascending toward God, Who was always your highest concern. I, however, have been left behind in this life of false wandering and I do not know where I will end up or where I will come to anchor once I have crossed the great sea.[108] O father, for me a sweet and beloved name! If any memory of things down here remains in your holy soul, if the Almighty has granted you any recollection, then remember your son! For you will not interrupt your illumination nor will you deprive yourself of contemplation. Thus we hear even regarding the angels that they can take flight toward higher things at the same time as they supervise events down here. You have been dignified by the angelic state: now show us your new dignity, show us your unalterable transformation."

(**c**) These words did I wail aloud as I embraced my father tightly. When I lifted up my head slightly, then for the first time I realized that my mother was pulling me up and drawing me away with both of her hands. I turned around and saw her. O, what a soul! How could I describe the mixture of emotions she experienced, the manner in which she prevailed over the most oppressive one? Her innards suffered terrible pain and her very nature was overturned. Yet she seemed like a higher intelligence [**40**] in that she rebuked herself for her natural passions and was greatly troubled. Indeed, she restrained the flow of tears and held back the sigh which was drawn up from deep inside; her face, otherwise pallid, was turning red by the shame of the situation and a mixture of

---

107. Cf. Photios, *Letter* 234.13–17 (Laourdas and Westerink 150).
108. For this image in Psellos, see 5c above.

numerous oppositions raged in contest within her. Finally, however, the philosophical element prevailed. Her eyes then fixed upon me directly and she said, "So then profane wisdom has not benefited your piety? Has your education been in vain? Has the facility of your apprehension been lauded in vain? Have you not yet learned the philosophical message taught by the students of the evangelical way of life?[109] But this has ever been our pursuit, to weaken the body through self-control, 'to release' the soul from this natural union and 'be in the company of God.'[110] And that has been the goal of our calling and our many exertions in this world, which goal your father has now attained. Now his soul has been truly liberated for the first time.[111] What you see here is matter given shape by nature, composed of elements into which it will once again be dissolved. There was a time when even this body was beautiful and immersed in soul, but the serpent's poison has filled it with darkness and shadow. God now wants to purify it again and cast out the poison. For this reason He has dissolved the mixture, divided the compound, and poured out that potent venom, so that He may refashion and rebuild it anew and again install the soul in it. You will see your father again, if, of course, you want to, with the body to which he was once naturally united, when, according to our traditions, 'the trumpet will sound mightily,'[112] and the Creator will give form to matter[113] and shape to our dust; He will refashion man altogether.[114] These, my child, are the lessons that you must seek to learn; hold to the philosophy that is of the highest and, if you wish to mourn, then lament the fact that you are still bound by shackles, wandering aimlessly upon the sea of life without yet having found a safe harbor."[115]

(**d**) I felt ashamed—how else should one say it?—as my mother was expounding these things and, briefly halting my lament, I placed my father upon the ground [**41**] and turned to my mother, saying, "You now become my instructor in the higher learning and impart your wisdom to me, which you yourself have drawn in such great abundance from the celestial fountains."

20. Though I want to return this speech (*logos*) immediately to my mother, a different reason (*logos*) is pulling me in another direction and compelling me to dwell on my father or, rather, it is not a reason but a nocturnal vision, if, in-

109. This sentence has been emended to a question.
110. Philippians 1:23.
111. Cf. Plotinos 6.8.7.1.
112. Matthew 24:31 and 1 Corinthians 15:52.
113. Cf. Gregory of Nazianzos, *Or.* 44.4.
114. For the *anaplasis* of man, see Criscuolo 283 n. 1232.
115. For this image in Psellos, see 5c above.

deed, this also is not a reason, whether it is innate and produced from within the soul, which, through it, becomes aware of reality, or whether it comes from the outside and, being more divine, indicates the truth about things that really exist for the soul that has been separated from the body. I will briefly expound on this.

(**b**) My mind was struggling impatiently for I wanted to know what fate had overcome my father. Accordingly, during the evening before the vision I had offered many prayers to the Almighty concerning him and somehow I must have attracted even my father's soul to the same end; and, then, just as though I had constrained him to show me his current abode, I went off to partake of sleep. How much of the night I slept away I do not know, yet suddenly I thought that I could see him directly; perhaps I did not merely think this, but what I saw was quite real. At that time though, just as if I had opened my eyes, I saw my father wearing the habit in which he had been buried, only he was eminently more beautiful than before.

(**c**) He was absolutely joyful and his soul was elevated into a state of pure dance; his eyes shone forth like torches and their brightness surpassed all measure. Both of his aspects, namely the nooumenal and the visible, transcended my senses as well as my mind. He then approached me in an entirely human way and did not shun contact, but instead allowed me to touch him. He himself also took hold of me in return and addressed me in his usual voice. "Child," he said, "beloved to me then and now still more, take heart on my account. For at the very moment that I died I saw God"—in this way did he reveal his destiny to me—"and I have greatly beseeched and persistently entreated that ineffable Entity on your behalf."

(**d**) As for the rest of what you said, father, should I disclose it or keep it secret? I would prefer the former by far—for your words redound to my honor, [**42**] above all since they were divine and authorized by God—but I feel shame at having falsified His response. For God wanted all the most beautiful things for me, but I have always acted against His views, wherefore it is not God's voice which lacks veracity but instead the wrongdoing is all mine. For we are not constrained to pursue the better course, father, nor that which is worse, nor are we compelled to choose this or that way of life out of foreknowledge, nor can foreknowledge alter our habits, but rather it is our free moral agency[116] and our preferences and the inclination of our will which create variety in the

---

116. Literally, "that which is under our control." For this important Stoic concept, see, e.g., Epiktetos, *Encheiridion* 1.1.

conduct of our lives. God is in every way good or, rather, is the fountain of goodness and wants to make everything good, but my resolve is weak and I have willingly slid into evil. So if you are upset by the fact that the divine voice is greatly disturbed by my inclinations, then pray persistently and often to the Lord who is zealous on our behalf,[117] and raise me out of the sensible world and up to the realm of intellection.

21. Now that it has reached this point let the account of my father come to an end. I should now repay to my mother the remainder of my debt. For even before this time she had fallen in love with the blessed state that is devoted to God, but when my father died she wholeheartedly rose up to embrace that life. She held it to be a terrible thing for them, who had spent their bodily lives together without any division between them and who later had also been joined together spiritually, to follow now such different paths, the one dwelling with God while the other still lived in the world. Therefore, she again sought the more divine union and greatly cursed her prison because her soul was trapped by it,[118] a divine treasure held down by something inferior.

(b) She brought to bear on the loosing of her manacles all those things which she customarily conceived as conducive to her goal, a flood of flowing tears— for most of her material being had already been neutralized—abstinence not only from pleasurable things but even from the necessary ones, bodily deprivation, sleeping on the ground and every other kind of self-control. Hence she discarded everything earthly, dried her body of all fluids, and dispersed all airy thoughts, [43] granting ultimate authority to the elemental fire within us.[119] This element, when it is neither contested nor balanced against something else, burns ever brighter and sets our natural strength onto the path that leads beyond our nature; finally, it adapts the remainder of the body to the new conditions.[120]

(c) Henceforth her body was burned and consumed and gradually undermined; it no longer conflicted with her soul, but was easily conveyed and elevated by her toward God. I do not mean to imply that it is the actual weightiness or lightness of bodies which drag the soul down or lead it up, while it

117. Cf. Exodus 20:5, 34:14.

118. I.e., her body.

119. Psellos here describes his mother's asceticism in terms of the four elements of Greek physics.

120. For the connection between this fire and intelligence in some Stoic thinkers, see Criscuolo 287 nn. 1311–1312.

either is led down by them or leads them up, but instead that wherever the values of self-control are accepted and applied, neutralizing matter and exhausting the oppressiveness of its bulk, the body weighs lightly on the soul connected to it,[121] not in such a way that it rises along with it in a natural way—for ascension is not strictly in accordance with the natural lightness of matter—but in such a way that it does not resist the soul when the latter is rising toward the heavens or, even, so to speak, by changing itself along with the soul. In this way did her body become light, in fact even suspended in midair.

(**d**) She, then, as though just beginning to practice moderation, as though for the first time grasping self-control, sought one honor after another (*ephilotimeito*), and these things it is necessary to recount even though the majority of them she did not reveal even to me: she did not want anyone to know about them, except for one female attendant. For she completely shunned the love of distinction (*to philotimon*), even though she secretly[122] and ambitiously (*philotimôs*) practiced virtue, but if someone happened to take notice of what she was doing, she would stop and conceal her deed, pretending and alleging that she had really done something different. But I would do her an injustice if I were to suppress completely all of these contrivances of her virtue, especially now that she is dead, when the teller of them is free from the suspicion of flattery and the aspirations (*to philotimon*) of the narrative need not conceal in shadows the virtue of the one who has departed.

22. However, many and sundry reproached her for the untimeliness of her self-control, both those who were entrusted with the care of her body and who wanted her to regain her strength as well as those who philosophized about the measures and conditions of the [**44**] virtues, above all about the times at which we ought to either partake of or refrain from food, in particular the father who had caused her to be born again. This man was renowned for his illustrious life and the pedagogical quality of his discourse. He often reproved her for her lack of moderation. To be sure, he recognized the dignity of virtue, but nevertheless contrived through dissimulation to bring her down against her will and to change her regimen. On one occasion, when her soul was shaken by his threats, she instructed the maidservant who had been assigned to her to bring her a fat fish, expertly prepared. It was indeed prepared and placed before her and it was then for the first time that a dining table served up a course

---

121. Cf. *Letter to Keroularios* 2 (lines 35–37) for a different valorization.
122. Cf. Matthew 6:4.

of fish for her. But when she realized that she was now, at the end of her life, suddenly abandoning the philosophical life and introducing in its place luxuries to which she was not accustomed, breadbaskets and napkins and whatever else is found on dinner tables, streams of tears forced their way to her eyes and she sighed heavily and struck her chest with her hands as hard as she could, "Woe for my misfortunes!" she said, "If ever I had procured any provisions for my journey, now I have suddenly lost them all! How incompatible with me and my way of life are these preparations, dinner tables and wine bowls and fishes and drinking cups. Yet now these luxurious and superfluous things have intruded themselves into my life of philosophy! I do not recognize what has been set before me, I do not know this play, I am not familiar with the stage. I have rolled away from the life of self-control, been deprived of hopes, divested myself of the riches of virtue," and, raising her hands toward the heavens, said, "I have sinned before my Lord!"[123]

(b) When she finally stopped wailing mournfully, she instructed her maidservant to step outside the door of the monastery and to bring in the first needy person she happened to meet. So she went out and after a short while brought in a woman who was already old, even superannuated. My mother immediately rose up as quickly as she could and greeted her with unexpected strength. She then led her by the hand and made her sit upon the bed, [45] calling her mistress, benefactor, savior, and all the other most beautiful names. After the old woman had feasted on the fish, my mother clothed her with her own ragged garment and then sent her on her way. In this way did she benefit from the food that had been prepared for her, to such a degree did she enjoy the dinner table, to such a degree did she break away from the life of self-control!

(c) But when her entire body had collapsed and her hands could not move nor her feet perform their natural activity, did she then give up 'chanting while standing'?[124] Far from it. But someone might demand, "Where then did she find the strength to do what she wished?" Well, when the time came for the hymns she would lean against two of her maidservants or, rather, they would prop her up by her elbows, which were entwined around their own, and, then, easily supporting her, they would hold her in a standing position. And in this way, until the very end, she rendered her prayers to God.

123. 2 Kings 12:13.
124. 1 Kings 16:17.

(d) For a long time she passionately desired the more divine way of life,[125] but had feared its weighty consequences as though she were not yet prepared for them. Then she began to fear, in no less a measure, that she would fall short of this majestic and illustrious dignity. While she was wavering and in doubt over this issue a divine vision directed her aright on this serious matter. There was an elderly woman, who had grown old in the life of purity to which she had been consecrated while still in her very swaddling clothes, whose soul was carried off in a dream, but this rapture did not convey her high into the air; rather, it transported her to a kind of theater. But she was not led down into the stadium; instead, she was suspended up where the emperor's tribunal should be located. She looked around and saw a single golden throne, which would be very difficult to describe. For its material flashed so brightly that it allowed neither the eyes to look at it nor the woman to say anything about it. On either side many thrones had been prepared, some even made of gold but the majority of ivory, and in the middle of those on the right one stood out from the rest.[126] She had no way of knowing what material it was made from, except that it had been painted with a dark color. Yet its surface emitted some [46] brightness, which did not lack even rays. The old woman inquired about this and the one who had carried her away said that the throne was Theodote's—for this was my mother's name[127]—and added the following, word for word: "The emperor says that he had this throne prepared for her as she will soon arrive here." At this point the dreamer awoke and, swiftly going to my mother, recounted the vision. My mother understood its significance and—O soul surpassing all the heights of knowledge and virtue!—explained the dream differently to the other woman, thereby allowing her to leave without having exalted ideas about herself.[128]

23. Now that she knew about her impending departure, lest she arrive there uninitiated she ordered that the mystery be performed for her on a certain day.[129] When everything had been prepared, the cross, the belt, and, above all,

125. I.e., the monastic habit.
126. Cf. Revelation 4:2–4.
127. This is the only place where Psellos refers to his mother by name.
128. The interpretation of the final clause of this paragraph depends on how the elderly woman interpreted her dream: if she woke up believing that Theodote would be exalted in heaven, then Theodote would have explained the dream away in such a way as to maintain her humility. If, on the other hand, she was worried that Theodote would soon die, then she "allowed her to leave without any great worries on her behalf."
129. I.e., consecration into the monastic life.

grace, 'the fattened calf was sacrificed'[130] and 'the table was set,'[131] the candle was lit and 'the daughters of Jerusalem'[132] were arranged in order, ready to escort the Queen. We thought that she would be carried in a litter—what else were we to expect?—but she . . . O, how could I describe the miracle, how could I persuade with mere words? For if I who saw the events scarcely believed them, how could others be convinced by mere words? But God knows and angels are witnesses to the veracity of my account.

(b) That was what we thought at the time, but she appeared all of a sudden as though from a royal bedchamber, conveying herself to her bridegroom and King, blooming in beauty,[133] bright of face, at the peak of her strength, bearing bride-gifts to her bridegroom like no other woman: squalid hair, calluses on her knees, withered bones, and rough skin. But He gave her more honorable gifts in return: 'on her finger a ring,' its golden 'band' flashing brightly,[134] 'sandals for her feet,'[135] that they may 'tread upon scorpions and snakes,'[136] the victorious sign of the cross, 'the helmet of salvation, and the sharp sword of the spirit.'[137] O those gifts! Just by recounting them [47] my soul is vexed, since I have failed to attain those things which I had desired so ardently. Finally, the groom sacrificed Himself and allowed His bride to eat of the sacrificial offering. Once she had partaken of all the nuptial gifts, the only thing remaining was the victim. She was then commanded to go forth in the company of the cherubim and so she followed them and took flight alongside them. I saw that indescribable sight and immediately fell down, flattening and leveling myself against the ground; I clasped her feet and entreated her to grant me her blessing and prayers. With a gentle voice she nodded slightly in my direction and said, "O child, may you obtain these good things!" and as she said this she flew off on her seraphic wings and joined the higher powers. Since it was necessary for her to see and to eat 'the sacrificial calf,'[138] that which she saw or that which she tasted her soul alone knows, because by partaking of it she was transformed

130. Luke 15:23.
131. Cf. Exodus 38:9.
132. Song of Songs 1:5.
133. Cf. Joel 2:16; Song of Songs 6:4.
134. Luke 15:22.
135. Luke 15:22.
136. Luke 10:19.
137. Isaiah 49:2, 59:17; Ephesians 6:17.
138. Luke 15:23.

and her visage beamed brightly. None of those present failed to see this or to marvel at the sight. From that moment on she never again so much as set foot outside church grounds.

(c) But I—this too was perhaps an aspect of divine economy and the Almighty decreed from above that I not witness my mother's transposition, since I had not been at all purified in preparation for that mystery—but I, then, seeing my mother become changed all of a sudden and not in any way suspecting that she would soon die, brought my visit there to an end. However, since the time of her death was at hand and she was presently to lay her body to rest,[139] as indeed her maidservants told me, she sat upon a low bench and then reclined upon her left side, offering many thanks to the Word. Suddenly, as though something had appeared on her other side, she turned around in a highly startling way.

(d) But how can I again lament my own fate, how can I, O mother, indicate to so many the affection that you had for me? She stared ahead intently as though in a trance, then came to [48] herself and said, "Let my dearest son come forward." O, that divine voice! O, my unlucky life and soul! O, how can I bear the misfortune, even if only to recount it? And then she said, "But where is he?" At this, one person after another stepped forward—but allow me to delay the account of what I did for a while. When she again uttered the same words and no winged messenger relayed them to me, nor did the wind convey me to her, as happened to Habakkuk,[140] she again saw what she had seen earlier and, as though she had an equally strong desire for that, lifted herself up from the ground as much as she was able and folded her arms over her chest. Then, pleasantly and serenely, she released her soul into the hands of those who lead it away, for the time of life allotted to her had expired and the chains of nature had been broken. Her soul departed gently, as if it had just melted into the light that appeared before her and returned to that to which it was akin, flying up to God.

24. So much for what happened to her. When I heard the news I raced back in a wild rush to see her while she was still alive and hear her parting words and perhaps even to benefit in some small way from her transition. Yet as my desires were not to be entirely granted and she was already dead when I saw her, I was immediately filled with indescribable tears and afflicted with a keen pain in my

---

139. An expression that occurs in many hagiographical texts. For Theodote's death, see Volk (1990) 326–328.

140. Cf. Habakkuk 1:11.

soul, as though stricken by Korybantic frenzy, so to speak, and bacchic enthu-siasm. I fell upon the sacred and divine body itself, the truly living one—for whoever says *that* does not lie—and I lay there as though I were dead, with no awareness of what I was doing or suffering, until those who were present took pity on me and, pulling me away, raised me to my feet and sprinkled cold water on me.[141] Then they placed their fingers, sprinkled with perfume, under my nos-trils, bringing me to my senses and reviving my strength.

(**b**) But when I again realized the extent of my misfortune, I lamented bit-terly and cried out loudly, "O mother, you were that by nature alone, but by the dignity of your soul you were my ruler and benefactor. O mother, sweet name!—I am constrained to use it, even though the word transcends my worth—O being who alone [**49**] of all terrestrial things was most divine, es-pecially for me, for it was not only in a bodily way that you conceived and gave birth to me, but you brought me forth spiritually as well, adorning me with learning, beautifying me with pious manners and allowing me to be proud and even boastful of you, thereby showing yourself and being recog-nized as greater than all the others. O living fountain; O intelligible radiance, you who poured forth the rivers of all your good things for my sake and dazzled me with the light of your virtues,[142] but now, unexpectedly, you have blocked those streams and hidden the light away! How did death ever prevail over you? But if that at least was only natural, how is it that you did not ask the angels carrying you away to postpone their task for a moment until you could see your son and give him words of farewell? Instead, this: your eyes shut sud-denly, those eyes so full of modesty, your mouth, always speaking of God, was closed, and your inspired voice fell silent! What part of you shall I embrace first? I do not know if this is something you would want, but my passion dares to yearn even for that which cannot be touched! Shall I kiss your heart all over, that fountain, flowing with life, of the revelations of the Spirit, embrace your bosom, which was fit to receive and contain the illumination that is sent down from above, hold your head lovingly, that sacred shrine of God? Shall I bring my lips to your mouth, in the hopes of drawing forth from there some divine stream? Shall I take my fill of every part of you, in the hopes of somehow sa-tiating my longing in that way? But where now is that part which reasoned,

---

141. Note the contrast between Psellos' deathlike state and his mother's "truly living" corpse.

142. Cf. Acts of the Apostles 9:3.

which spoke? Where the sacred mind and the most radiant soul? Are you enrolled in the order of the angels or have the archangels received you into their
ranks? And is the fate you have obtained an ethereal one or an even higher and
heavenly one? Or have you transcended bodily existence altogether and are
now dancing far beyond the great enclosure of the universe, where exist the
undefiled brilliance and the blessed visions and everything that is intangible
and invisible? Will you even there, where you are near to God, continue to
watch over me? Or has one of your longings prevailed over the other, namely
the one for God over the one for me? My father, [**50**] when he departed, immediately asked God about my destiny and received a response. Don't show yourself inferior to him, but rather pose the same questions, propitiate even God on
my behalf and now more than ever take care of your son. By departing you
have deprived me of your words and you did not grant me a farewell. Now that
you are there, compensate me for your oversight and allow me to see you in my
dreams along with signs of your affection. But O, again, my sweet mother! and
this often and forever!" And here I cut my speech short. Such things and more
like them did I say in my lament, and I then accompanied the funeral procession, pronouncing words of farewell, as circumstance demanded. I myself
picked up that divine and holy body and, holding it up with my own hands,
placed it in the temple.

(**c**) And then what happened? The event was miraculous. How so? The news
regarding her spread, so to speak, to every part of the city, and from each quarter they assembled to her side at a run, one after another.[143] For they had already been greatly impressed by what they had heard about her sanctity. Nor
was it possible to push the crowd back; they rushed together, men as well as
women, the old and the young, differing in origin and age but animated by the
single desire to touch every part of her. Some placed their hands on her,[144] others their face, others still a different part of the body. In the end they even tore
the very garment in which they saw that she was wrapped, dividing it among
themselves, but not in an equitable way, for each was eager to obtain the greater
portion.[145] Yet honor (*philotimia*) was bestowed through this avarice.

---

143. Cf. the description of Basileios' funeral in Gregorios of Nazianzos, *Or.* 43.79–80
(*Funeral Oration in Honor of Basileios the Great*).

144. Cf. Mark 10:16.

145. Cf. Matthew 27:35; Mark 15:24; Luke 23:34; John 19:23–24, on the garments of
Jesus divided by the soldiers at the crucifixion. Similar scenes occur in hagiographic texts.

(**d**) In addition to these people, her spiritual father also came and paid his proper respects. He then looked around at the crowd and disregarded the majority, but seeing the mother of the deceased standing there by the side of the catafalque[146]—for she was still alive—he spoke freely and openly, in such a way that he would be heard, "You, O woman, know that you have been the mother of a martyr and a saint. I am certain of both of these facts and [**51**] bear witness to your daughter." That was what he said. His words excited the crowd and had not a few resisted the onrush of newcomers in order to lay the body to rest in the ground, the assembled crowd would not have dispersed even on the third day.

25. Thus it happened that she who had lived the divine life in an incomparable way also obtained a sacred funeral when she died. Dissimilar things were established in her alongside each other and their opposition was reconciled for her alone, or else contrary things were seen in one and the same nature—how should I say it?—to have become conformable. She 'blotted out the sin'[147] even for the first mother of our race,[148] not only because she became a councilor for the good to her husband, driving out the words of the serpent, but also because she procured immortality, not by burying the soul along with the body nor by submitting to nature, but in a different way, by making nature obey her and by being the only one to submerge the body within a higher nature.

(**b**) She became an ornament to her kind and a paragon of virtue for those who come afterwards. She passed judgment from both sides on the feminine and the masculine and did not give one gender the advantage, leaving the other with an inferior lot—that would be a sign of a thoughtless arbiter and a careless arbitration—but granted an equal measure to both. And if the two genders differ in the tenor of their bodies, nevertheless they possess reason equally and indistinguishably, and reason is not weakened through association with weaker elements, but rather the latter are strengthened by the better element.

(**c**) Anyone who considered her life would number her among the holy women and enroll her among the martyrs. For she too struggled against a terrible tyrant,[149] whose brow was always heavy with anger, and she was less fright-

146. Cf. John 19:25, on Mary, the mother of Jesus, standing by the cross.

147. Psalm 31:1.

148. I.e., Eve.

149. Cf. 4 Maccabees 17:14. Psellos alludes in this paragraph to the martyrs under Antiochos IV Epiphanes, but the motif is common in hagiography. The tyrant in this case is bodily desire, or, more broadly, materiality.

ened of him than he was of her, as she steadfastly withstood his cruelty and refused to cower before his punishments. She even sanctified the earth with blood, though not from where nature furnishes an outpouring for it but, rather, from where tears usually flow. And her body was cut into pieces, not with sword thrusts, but instead the continuity of her being was broken by genuflections, by straining and bending her limbs upon the ground. She even 'passed through fire,'[150] burned by the desire for necessary things, but she did not partake of them, [**52**] holding out even against things that were offered to her. No less did she 'pass through water,'[151] refusing the use of wine and satisfying the needs of her body with the ancient draught.[152] In these ways did she 'find relief.'[153]

(**d**) She took the prize for holiness from each and every woman by causing her flesh to waste away through self-control, neutralizing her body, subjecting dust to spirit, treating nature as a slave,[154] and through her practical impulses ably cultivating her practical virtue. She advanced steadily in the contemplative life through the illumination given by contemplation and became a model for both kinds of life to all men and women, wisely arbitrating between matter and immateriality and distributing whatever is suitable to each part or, rather, mixing immateriality into matter, rendering it more sublime and splendid through its participation in the higher element.

26. Yet, O mother, although I can admire and regard you with amazement, I am not entirely capable of emulating you.[155] To the contrary, I alone have disappointed your prayers and have not turned out according to your hopes. Or perhaps your advice has not failed even on this point, for I have fulfilled that part of your goals which concerned the outward habit: my devotion to philosophy is limited to its cloak. This too was your doing, done even after your death. I am induced to say this by a certain dream-vision.

(**b**) For when you departed from this world, I concealed the seed of your prayer in the furrows of my soul. One time, when I had fallen asleep for the night, it seemed to me that I saw some hierophants clad in white who told me

---

150. Isaiah 43:2; Psalm 65:12.
151. Isaiah 43:2; Psalm 65:12.
152. I.e., water.
153. Psalm 65:12.
154. Cf. 1 Corinthians 9:27, regarding the body; cf. Gregorios of Nyssa, *Life of Makrina* 1 on overcoming nature.
155. The theme of emulating a morally superior life recurs in Psellos' *Letter to Keroularios*, where it is treated sarcastically.

that they had come—so they had been commanded—to lead me before the holy monks. No sooner had they spoken than I immediately rose up and followed them as though they were superior beings. They went before me. The path, which was wide, contracted and somehow collapsed in on itself, nearly crowding us together as we were leaving. They said to me, "The constriction here is great, O child, as you see, and few can proceed any further; hence, we are in fear [**53**] for you. Yet you must not thereby shrink back, but instead take heart and follow along."[156]

(**c**) That is what they said, when both our discussion and the path came to an end, for a barrier blocked our progress. This barrier was of hewn stone, not too white and not of the opposite color either, but sort of yellowish, thin, certainly, yet not entirely translucent. At its exact center a kind of navel was imprinted upon it, which lay open in the form of an uneven and not very wide circle. It was as though needles were suspended all around its circumference, further narrowing the small aperture in the stone. Those escorting me said that I had to pass through this very hole—for there was no other way for me to move beyond that place—and they suggested that I put my head in first and then let the rest of my body slip through. I followed their advice and the stone yielded before me as I moved forward; it fell apart as though it were made of the softest material. And when I reached the other side, the first thing that I found was a stairway leading into the depths. I gathered my courage and began to descend.[157] At the bottom a temple stood open before me, its left side adorned by an icon of the Mother of God, but its other side was not yet entirely visible to me.[158]

(**d**) Then I saw my mother standing by the icon, virtually hanging from it in her devotion, and I rushed to embrace her as quickly as I could. But with a brief sign of the hand, you ordered me to stand still. Alarmed, I suddenly froze. And without turning about, instead as though you wanted to deprive me of the opportunity to speak, you said, "Turn your eyes to the right side of the temple." I did so and saw a monk. He was not standing but, rather, bowing on his knees. There was in his hands a scroll on which he had fastened his eyes. He seemed to be surpassingly great, his visage was austere, his brow was sullen:

156. This is perhaps an allusion to the narrow path of the Christian life according to the Gospels or to Byzantine monasticism.

157. For the imagery of this vision, see Graf (2004).

158. J. Walker (2004) 66, 93 suggests that Psellos may have had the monastery of *ta Narsou* in mind here, and see 92–94 for a reading of the vision as a whole.

he was the perfect embodiment of the ascetic life.[159] "And who is this?" I asked my mother. Still without turning around, she replied, "O child, that is the great Basileios. Go and do homage before him." When I drew near and looked at him, he threw his head back.[160] Then he suddenly rolled up his scroll[161] and vanished with a clap of thunder. I could no longer see my mother, [54] but found myself in another place. Then those who had led me there appeared out of nowhere and it seemed to me that they adorned me with a new outfit and whispered some words to me, which, however, I could not remember when I awoke.

27. That you, O mother, have diligently watched over your son even after your death I am absolutely convinced and I have come to this conclusion after many proofs. However, as though resisting your righteous advice and bending against the rule, I do not entirely philosophize according to that philosophy which is so dear to you, and I do not know what fate took hold of me from the very beginning and fixated me onto the study of books, from which I cannot break away.

(b) For I am attracted by the art of words[162] and, along with the arrangement of premises, I also exceedingly love its flowery beauty. Like the bees I fly over the meadows of discourse, plucking some of the flowers, while from the others I suck up the dew of style and make honey in my own hive.[163] The circular revolution of the sphere[164] does not allow me to rest, but forces me to inquire closely into what its motion is; what the source of its rolling; what its nature;

159. Cf. Basileios of Kaisareia, *Ascetic Oration* 1 (= *PG* 31.881b); *Letter* 119. Basileios is here presented as the founder of Byzantine monasticism and not as the (lukewarm) defender of Hellenic literature. The qualities ascribed to him here are exactly those that Psellos condemns as signs of arrogance and inflexibility when writing about monks and the ascetic life in other works, particularly in his *Letter to Keroularios* and Book 6.A of the *Chronographia*; cf. Kaldellis (1999a) c. 23. Cf. the description of Basileios by Elpios (or Oulpios) the Roman, *Ecclesiastical Antiquities: On the Physical Appearance of the Saints* (Chatzidakis 412; Winkelmann 122).

160. *ananeuô* ordinarily means to throw one's head up in denial. It is not clear if Psellos intends to signify that Basileios did not accept him as a monk or that he merely lifted his head and looked up (as in 19c above); see (independently) J. Walker (2004) 94.

161. Cf. Luke 4:20.

162. I.e., rhetoric; cf. Plato, *Phaidon* 90b.

163. A standard image of literary and philosophical ecclecticism, endorsed by Basileios of Kaisareia in his *Address to Young Men on How They Might Profit from Greek Literature* 4, and used elsewhere by Psellos (e.g., *Letter to Xiphilinos* 7).

164. Perhaps not merely a reference to the movement of the stars, but to the movement of all spherical bodies in general (cf. 17a above).

what its rotations; how they overlap and how they are separate; how great the sections of straight lines are; what angles are and what simultaneous ascensions, equalities, and obliquities;[165] what extensions are and of what nature; how movements are produced and how many of them there are; and whether everything comes from fire or from some other element. I am also moved by the static science[166] and am unable not to reflect upon the continuity of extension[167] or not to contemplate the exactitude of logical demonstration; how axioms are derived from mind and how propositions that require no middle term are derived directly from axioms; how everything is established and how it is specified exactly; what proportion is; what the incommensurable; what the rational magnitude; what the disproportionate; what the commensurable; what kinds of lengths and powers there are,[168] and what rotations of solids. That first element, which is also immaterial, gives me no rest. I am fascinated by its relation to everything and by the relation of everything to it, by its limitedness and unlimitedness, and by how all other things derive from these two; by how idea, soul, and nature are referred back to numbers,[169] [55] the first to that which is congenital to mind, the second to that which follows close upon reason, and the third to that which corresponds to the natural order; by the varieties of physical discourse; by what is perfect in it, what symmetrical, regular, beautiful, self-sufficient, equal, identical, pure, simple, paradigmatic, principle; by that which generates life and that which is spiritual; by the natural properties of the numbers up to ten;[170] by how the triad is produced; what procession is,[171] and how it extends throughout all the divine generations.

(c) Music has attracted me to itself through its indescribable charms and, in a sense, I grew up with it and have appropriated it as my own. I do not, however, stand on the surface of that discipline, nor have I examined only the types of words, meters, and technical motions, but I have also inquired into its functions, operations, causes, and the essence of its rhythms, namely which of them are straightforward and which cannot be characterized in that way, what is the source of their beauty and what part of them is adapted to the life of the soul.

165. These are technical astronomical terms.

166. I.e., the science of bodies at rest.

167. Cf. Aristotle, *Physics* 219a11.

168. I.e., roots; cf. Plato, *Theaitetos* 147d.

169. For the science and theology of numbers in ancient philosophy, see Criscuolo 300–303 n. 1714.

170. Cf. Aristotle, *Metaphysics* 1084a12, 15, 32.

171. Or, "emanation."

(d) I do not investigate the genus of the various sciences alone, but also whether any currents flow out from them. Nor do I merely investigate the supreme science,[172] the one which presides over the others, 'gives them their basic principles,'[173] interprets their premises, is absolutely immaterial, and comes after physics (*meta tên physikên*), I also honor it and revere it, whether one wants to call it dialectic, that which supervises logical activity from above,[174] or just simply wisdom. For the first name has been appropriated by some of the more recent wise men for a particular branch of logic.[175]

28. I also admire proofs that employ syllogisms, not only those which draw conclusions from within their own terms but also those which employ induction and consequent clauses. I study sophistries only insofar as is necessary to avoid being caught by them, lest I conclude that knowledge and wisdom are the same thing or that wise men know by virtue of their knowledge and that knowledgeable men are wise by virtue of their wisdom,[176] or that man is the only animal, given that he is the only one that laughs and everything [56] that laughs is an animal.[177] These things attract me, but still more does the apprehension of things that are hidden, such as what providence and fate are, and whether that which is posterior completely participates in being, what the immobile is and what the automotive, and whether the soul receives anything into itself at the moment of birth or nothing whatsoever.[178]

(b) I have also raised questions about living beings in general, whether they are always aware of this very knowledge and whether immortality is an essential quality of the soul or whether it supervenes in some other way. For the most part I have philosophized that it is essentially immortal, from its assimilation to the divine, from the fact that it does not admit of opposites, from its return, from its movement during sleep, and from its illumination. I am also seeking to discover whether it is bonded to the body, in which it has embarked for the first time upon a second life;[179] how the irrational is mixed with it; what its ultimate

172. I.e., metaphysics.

173. Plotinos 1.3.5.2.

174. Plotinos 1.3.4.19.

175. Probably the Stoics; cf. Diogenes Laertios, *Lives and Opinions of the Eminent Philosophers* 7.42–43.

176. This example is taken from Plato, *Theaitetos* 145d–e.

177. Aristotle, *Parts of Animals* 673a8; cf. Sextos Empirikos, *Outlines of Pyrrhonism* 2.211. For similar sophistries, see Lucian, *Auction of Lives* 26; Clement of Alexandria, *Paidagogos* 2.5.

178. Cf. Plato, *Phaidon* 61c.

179. Alluding, perhaps, to the doctrine of the preexistence of the soul.

fate will be in the restoration;[180] what the judgment is;[181] what its final lot; whence it comes; what it is; what its capacities are; how many activities it carries out; how it is mixed with mind; what its return is; and, lest I enumerate every-thing about it, I am entirely consumed by the questions that surround it.

(c) But I am not about to limit my natural inquisitiveness to that, for I have also studied the practitioners of astrology, who treat some of the stars with, as it were, violence and insolence, while to others they nearly offer sacrifices. I really do not understand whence arises the difference in the way each group is treated or how birth is regulated and determined in accordance with their configuration. I therefore repudiated these speculations as neither clear nor true and benefited from my curiosity as much as is necessary to denounce them on the basis of my knowledge of them.[182] I have also rejected the idea that some people are modeled and remodeled by the stars[183] and attacked the predetermined characters and signs, the admissions and the descents of the divine bodies. The power to make accurate predictions about the future I grant to neither stellar configurations and conformations; nor to the voice of the birds, to their flight, cries, and movement; nor to meaningless sounds, to "for-eign" doctrines, or to anything by which Hellenic thought was led astray. [57] And if I have inquired into the precise rules which regulate the sphere stud-ied by astronomy, this is indicative of my love of beauty and wisdom.[184] And even if I search after origins and sources,[185] this too is desired by contempla-tive souls.

(d) As for the hieratic art, I know what it is,[186] but after 'crowning it with wool' I banished it altogether.[187] I have learned well the ineffable powers as-cribed to rocks and herbs,[188] but have utterly repudiated the needless employ-

180. A term which can refer to the Christian doctrine of the resurrection of the dead.
181. The Last Judgment?
182. A typical excuse made by those delving into officially forbidden realms of knowl-edge; cf. *Chronographia* 6A.11.
183. Cf. Plato, *Timaios* 50a.
184. Cf. Plato, *Phaidros* 248d, a curious context.
185. Cf. Plato, *Phaidros* 245c.
186. Practitioners of the hieratic art sought to manipulate the material world by using the "sympathy" that existed between its elements and components, visible and in-visible. Cf. Proklos, *On the Hieratic Art according to the Hellenes (De sacrificio et magia),* on which see Bidez (1936).
187. This is how false poets are treated as they are banished from the true city of Plato's *Republic* 398a.
188. Cf. Proklos, *On the Hieratic Art according to the Hellenes* (Bidez 151, line 5).

ment of such things. I loathe amulets, both diamonds and coral rocks,[189] and laugh at Zeus-sent images. I hold it to be a monstrous thing to claim that one can alter the order of the universe, given that everything is ordered well by the providence of God. I rail against propitiations,[190] purifications, engraved sigils, names,[191] the so-called inspired motions, the ethereal connector[192] and the empyrean one,[193] the leonine fountain,[194] the First Father,[195] the Second,[196] the Iynges,[197] the world-guides,[198] Hekate and the Hekatesians,[199] the undergirding one,[200] all so much nonsense and mere verbiage.[201] But as for eternity and

189. For Psellos' knowledge of the powers ascribed to these rocks, see treatises 19 (lines 167–169) and 34 (lines 13–15) of his *Phil. Min. I.*

190. Yet in 24b, above, Psellos begs his departed mother to propitiate God on his behalf. The word used in both cases is the same.

191. Referring probably to the mystical names used to invoke supernatural beings. The remainder of the sentence refers to the philosophy of the *Chaldaean Oracles.*

192. This was "a class of noetic entities whose primary function is to conjoin the various parts of the universe" (Majercik [1989] 154; cf. also 10–11). They are mentioned in a number of fragments from the *Oracles* (see ibid. 240 [index]).

193. Cf. the "empyrean channels" in *Chaldaean Oracles* fr. 2.4; for a text and translation of the *Oracles,* see Majercik (1989); cf. ibid. 141: "the mystical rays of the sun on which the soul makes its ascent." In his *Summary Exposition under Headings of the Doctrines of the Chaldeans,* Psellos distinguishes three kinds of connectors: empyrean, ethereal, and material: *Phil. Min. II* 39, p. 146, lines 15–16.

194. This concept derives from Psellos' interpretation of *Chaldaean Oracles* fr. 147 as a zodiacal reference: see his *Exegesis of the Chaldaean Oracles* in his *Phil. Min. II* 38, p. 134, lines 3–16, and cf. the commentary in Majercik (1989) 196.

195. The First Father was the supreme principle of Chaldaean theology; see Majercik (1989) 5–6.

196. The function of the Second Father was "to fashion the intelligible (or empyrean) world on the model of [the] Ideas," which were created by the thoughts of the First Father: Majercik (1989) 6.

197. The Iynges performed a number of functions in the Chaldaean system, chiefly as "the 'binding' force between men and the gods" (Majercik [1989] 9). Psellos discusses them in a number of his works on the *Oracles*: see *Phil. Min. II,* p. 203 (index).

198. In his commentary on *Oracles* fr. 79, Psellos notes that "the Chaldaeans postulate powers in the world and call them world-guides as they guide the world through providential motions": *Exegesis of the Chaldean Oracles* in *Phil. Min. II* 38, p. 133, lines 7–9.

199. "According to the Chaldaeans, Hekate is a goddess, holding in her right hand the fountain of virtues and in her left that of souls": *Phil. Min. II* 38, pp. 133–134, lines 24–2; cf. also p. 135, lines 11–14.

200. For the rank of this entity in the chain of Chaldaean theology, see Psellos' *Summary Exposition under Headings of the Doctrines of the Chaldeans* in *Phil. Min. II* 39, p. 146, line 19; for a modern discussion, see Majercik (1989) 143–144.

201. Psellos wrote a number of treatises on this "nonsense."

time;[202] 'nature, contemplation, and the One';[203] as for 'sense perception and memory'[204] and the mixture and blending of opposites;[205] as for whether the intelligibles exist in the mind or whether they exist outside of it;[206] if, then, I inquire into these matters, I consider it necessary to proceed philosophically.

29. I must, of course, devote myself to God alone, especially now that I have renounced the world; but my way of living, the unquenchable love for every kind of knowledge of the soul and the demands of my students, have induced me to indulge in all those fields.[207] However, anything that I might wish to say in this regard, you would already know, O mother, since you are now a pure soul; my speech is therefore addressed to the others, and I am speaking not only to men, but also to God and the angels. Having read all the Hellenic books, and even the barbarian ones,[208] those written by Orpheus, Zoroaster, and Ammon the Egyptian; those composed in verse by the Parmenideses and the Empedokleses—for I pass by the Platos and the Aristotles and all their contemporaries [58] and successors who toiled in philosophical discourse— who wrote on both communicable and ineffable matters; and, having read their entire theology and their treatises on nature and demonstrations, I admired the profundity of their thought and marveled at the inquisitiveness of their discussions. But if I observed anything that lay outside of our doctrines, even if were supported by the most rigorous arguments, even if it were saturated with every wisdom and grace, I despised it as a completely meaningless piece of utter nonsense. I pay no attention to their better teachings, yet the ambition of my soul does move me to be at least aware of their doctrines.

202. Cf. Plato, *Timaios* 37d; for the problems of infinity and time, see Plotinos 3.7 ("On Eternity and Time"); Proklos, *The Elements of Theology* 52–55. For Psellos' treatises on these topics, see his *Phil. Min. I* 41 and *Theol. II* 32.

203. This is the title of Plotinos 3.8.

204. This is the title of Plotinos 4.6.

205. Cf. Plotinos 2.7: "On the Blending of the Whole."

206. Cf. Plotinos 5.5: "That the Intelligibles Are Not Outside the Mind."

207. Psellos uses a similar justification for his eccentric intellectual interests in *Chronographia* 6A.11 (cf. also 30a below).

208. This extravagant claim contains a subtle point of attack: Psellos accused his detractors of ignorance of the books they condemned him for reading (cf. the roughly contemporary *Letter to Xiphilinos* 5, line 157). In section 1, lines 11–19, of that letter Psellos produces a similar list of Hellenic and barbarian texts and again claims that they fell short of the purity of the Scriptures.

(b) For there are 'unfailing treasures'[209] of wisdom on our side as well and profundities of doctrine and beauties of thought, if anyone should want them, and even a spontaneous flowering of speech, though not an overwrought one. And should one inquire what divine revelation is; what the intelligible and what the intellectual; what that which flows from the universal source, and which of the latter's hypostases proceeds from the One; what the name God is and what is designated by it;[210] what the whole is and what the part and which of the two we should identify with God, or perhaps neither; what the intelligible things are and which the intellectual; what kinds of symbols are interpreted theologically and what each one of them is individually,[211] for example what the wheel is, what the elektron, what the gold that has been refined, the vapor, the advent of the cloud, the throne, the river, what the flying sickle, the ax, the tree, and the cutting, the frankincense tree, and the oak; what the proper names of the angels, what the rites that we celebrate, what communion, the ointment, the lamp, the ladder, the small pillars, the uplifting love, the essence of virtue and the beautiful, from which all other things proceed and to which they ascend; what the perfumed maiden is, the door, the net, the burning heat, the sun, the vineyard, the prison,[212] and the escape from there.

(c) And if someone, giving up on these things as too sublime and lofty, approached our leather-cutters or tent-sewers and net-weavers[213] and decided to understand their words with precision, he would then [59] recognize that those other things impress the many like the emissions of the visible sun, while these things are like a hazy and obscure star, which only the mind may see, for sense perception cannot approach it.[214] For there is not a single one of them that is not full of mystery and ineffable initiation.[215]

(d) For not one of them is incapable of being theorized, not even the smallest detail: not the furnished upper room, not the water jar, not the closing of

209. Luke 12:33; cf. Wisdom of Solomon 7:14.
210. For various attempts to explain the word, see Criscuolo 321 n. 1830.
211. For the list of symbols in 29b and 29d, see Kaldellis (2005). For a literary and philosophical interpretation of the list of Christian symbols, see J. Walker (2004) 95–98.
212. Or "the guard."
213. A reference to the Apostles and Evangelists.
214. The contrast between the different suns, the one material and the other intellectual, stemming from Plato's *Republic*, was a metaphor employed by the Neoplatonists and adapted by some Christian authors.
215. In other words, neither of the two kinds of teaching, Hellenic or scriptural, is unambiguous and therefore intelligible to the common man: cf. the end of 29d.

the doors and the recognition of the Word; even the disciple Didymos, as a doubter, has become an object of contemplation, as has the pair which ran together and those who ran ahead.[216] The hook is not without an explanation, nor the fish that was drawn up from the sea, nor the stater, nor the number of the fish. Neither are the names of the Apostles without symbolic significance, nor the girdle of the Prodromos, nor the camel hairs, but rather, to put it in brief, every single passage of the Gospels is imbued with an implanted significance which the many cannot easily grasp. It is with these that I anoint my head and cleanse my soul, and thus have no need for Hellenic purifications.

30. But since a mode of life has been assigned to me such that it does not suffice for me alone but lies at the disposal of others as well and allows them to draw up water for themselves as though it were some kind of basin overflowing with fresh water,[217] for this reason I have also engaged in secular learning, not only its theoretical branches, but also in those which come down to the level of history and poetry.[218] And so I lecture[219] to some of my students on matters of poetry, on Homer, Menandros, and Archilochos, on Orpheus and Mousaios, and also on the verses sung by women, Sibyls and 'Sappho the poetess,'[220] Theano[221] and the wise Egyptian woman.[222]

(b) Many also entreated me earnestly about the terms that occur in those works, in order to know what the *akratisma* is, what the *ariston,* what the *hesperisma,* what the *dorpis* and the dinner-time *isaia;*[223] which authors wrote in verse and which made use of prose composition; what the dance is in Homer,

216. The disciple Thomas (the Doubter); for this passage, see J. Walker (2004) 96.
217. For this image, see Kaldellis (1999a) 15–16.
218. Note that history and poetry constitute a "descent" from the level of contemplative metaphysics and theology (cf. *Letter to Xiphilinos* 7, line 227). Psellos, one of the best Byzantine historians, has nothing more to say about historiography in this summary of his intellectual interests, but we should keep in mind that he had not yet written the *Chronographia* or his more modest *Historia Syntomos.*
219. The present tense implies that Psellos had been lecturing in the recent past or even during the time of the composition of this speech.
220. Herodotos 2.135.1.
221. Wife, daughter, or disciple of Pythagoras.
222. The Alexandrian philosopher Hypatia (ca. 400), famous for being murdered by fanatical monks.
223. Respectively: breakfast, luncheon, supper; *dorpis* is some kind of supper time meal (see Criscuolo 326, n. 1877); *isaia* (sc. *moira*): "equal portions." For some of these terms see Philemon in Athenaios, *Dinner-Sophists* 1.11d.

and, in general, what the heroic life is in the poet's view; what dainty living is and what luxury, what use [60] do fruit grown on the upper branches have;[224] what the most ancient of the Trojan events was; what *nektar, ambrosia,* and the *propoma* are;[225] what the 'geranium under the earth' and what 'the generation that occurs within the earth.'[226] I leave aside all the issues that I am asked to clarify, such as who Alexis was and who Menandros;[227] who Krobylos, 'who brought his own provisions,'[228] Klesaphos,[229] and any other who may be known for his poetic compositions.

(c) Many also compel me to care for their bodies and demand treatments and diagnoses on their behalf. For this reason I have investigated the art concerning such matters in its entirety, so that I do not have to tackle each case from the beginning.[230] Many, not limiting themselves to pleas, have used even their very hands in order to drag me down to the Italian science, and I do not mean the philosophical one of the Pythagoreans, but simply that other which seeks the common weal and is entirely devoted to material things.[231] Here I have to discuss private and public lawsuits, laborious procedural arguments, slavery and freedom,[232] legal and illegal marriages, and the gifts and benefits that they involve; degrees of kinship and contracts, both military and civil; what a surety is and what the surety is entitled to in legal procedures; why a kicking horse or a goring bull or a biting dog passes the responsibility for its own crime onto its master;[233] what the legally binding rule is; why false names are used; inheritance, ascendants and descendants, natural offspring and illegitimate; what the scope of each concept is; what assault is and into how many

224. For this topic, see the sources cited by Criscuolo 326 n. 1881–1882.

225. *Propoma* is a drink taken before a meal to stimulate the appetite.

226. Theophrastos in Athenaios, *Dinner-Sophists* 2.62a; possibly these are truffles.

227. Alexis was a comic poet (ca. 375–275) who lived in Athens and may have been the teacher of Menandros (quoted in Athenaios, *Dinner-Sophists* 1.47c–e).

228. Krobylos was a fourth-century poet of the New Comedy. Psellos seems to have attributed one of his verses to the poet himself (Krobylos in Athenaios, *Dinner-Sophists* 1.47e).

229. This poet is unknown.

230. For Psellos' medical pretensions, see 19a above.

231. I.e., law, known in Byzantium as "the Italian science" or "the wisdom of the Italians" (i.e., those who speak Latin).

232. Or, possibly in a legal sense, "duties and rights."

233. Cf. Plato, *Gorgias* 516a, and Exodus 21:28–29 on the responsibility incurred by goring bulls.

parts it is divided; and how much time is allotted to each kind of lawsuit. Having induced me to engage in these discussions, therefore, as in the field of philosophy, they exact from me an account of what has been legislated.

(**d**) Nor do they neglect to question me about the measurements of the earth, how much of it is uninhabited and how large that fifth zone is which human beings inhabit.[234] It is therefore necessary for me to explain the geography of the entire earth to them, to correct for them the geographical tablet or to fill in what has been left out of it, and to discuss whatever Apelles, Bion, and [**61**] Eratosthenes expounded accurately on these issues.[235] I never stopped interpreting the Hellenic myths to them in an allegorical manner,[236] and in this way also did they drag me out and tear me to pieces, since they were uniquely captivated by my tongue and soul, which was imbued with knowledge far more than that of anyone else.[237]

31. O mother, this mode of life has been consecrated for me, while the other has been stored up as treasure, to which I have urged myself to hasten for so long. Even though I am still constrained by many hooks, the emperor has taken a firm hold of me and is disputing with my superiors[238] over me and winning through his extraordinary dignity and splendor and by the fact that he prefers me to all the others and over all the others, all who have both now and in the past partaken of the same culture or come into communion with it. And if indeed my monastic habit and cloak appear to be irreconcilable in some way to the emperor and his court, this is no innovation of mine alone, but is believed to be for the best not only by those who remain in public life but also by the majority of those who live separate from it.[239] If my character adapted itself to changing circumstances, let others philosophize about it; for me it was a spontaneous reaction. Be gracious from on high to these twists and turns of

234. For the division of the earth into five zones, see Strabon 2.2.1 ff.

235. Cf. Strabon 1.2.2.

236. For Psellos' allegorical works, see his *Phil. Min.* I 40–48.

237. Psellos describes his students' enthusiasm and admiration for his knowledge in his *Letter to Keroularios* 3, lines 102–106. For the almost magical effect of his speech on others, see the description of his meetings with the emperor Konstantinos IX Monomachos in the *Chronographia* 6.44–46, 6.161.

238. Presumably Psellos' monastic superiors.

239. Alluding to monks who continued to engage in public affairs, as Psellos himself would do after the death of Konstantinos IX Monomachos. For Ioannes Orphanotrophos, see *Chronographia* 4.14; for Leon Paraspondylos, 6A.6–7; in general, see Weiss (1977) 277–282. Psellos discusses such political monks in *Letter S* 54 (Sathas 285).

mine or, rather, change my direction and restore me to the path which leads to God, and grant that I may delight purely in the evangelical life, in the life hidden within God. Then provide me with the fountain of virtue so that I may drink as much from its streams as I am allowed and able; afterwards, when I have changed for the better, accept me and, through your free speech before God and your entreaties, fill me from the first and divine 'spring of the intelligibles.'[240]

240. *Chaldaean Oracles* 56.

Funeral Oration for his daughter Styliane, who died before the age of marriage

Introduction

It is impossible to assign precise dates to the short life of Psellos' only biological child, his daughter Styliane, yet it is likely that she was born in the early 1040s and died in the early 1050s, during the years, therefore, that her father was working at the court of Konstantinos IX Monomachos.[1] Her final sickness, which Psellos describes in some detail,[2] lasted for thirty days (79). A letter is preserved that seems to have been written during that month: addressed to a *prôtovestiarios*, Psellos mentions the grave sickness of one close to him and harps on one of the themes that he would soon develop in the *Funeral Oration* for his daughter, namely his inability to maintain a philosophical disposition when grief strikes close to home (*Letter S* 177; see p. 176 below). In the *Oration*, Psellos ascribes his daughter's illness to a "pestilential disease (*loimikê nosos*)" for which there was no known cure (77), possibly smallpox, and states that others had been or were being infected with it and surviving, "snatched from the noose of death" at the last moment (81). The late eleventh-century historian Ioannes Skylitzes mentions an outbreak of a "pestilential disease (*loimikê*

---

1. See the general introduction above, p. 13. For the basic information, see Sideras (1994) 119–121; for a summary of the oration, Leroy-Molinghen (1969a); for various aspects, Vergari (1985), who is sometimes needlessly skeptical.

2. For a useful and detailed medical analysis, see Volk (1990) 309–325; for a rhetorical analysis, Jouanno (1994). Lascaratos and Tsiamis (2002) claim that it was smallpox.

111

nosos)" in Constantinople in 1054,[3] the last date to which we may assign Styliane's death.

The following is an outline of the contents of the *Funeral Oration*:

62–63:   exordium
63–65:   Styliane's ancestry and beauty in infancy
65–66:   her early education in letters and weaving
66–68:   her virtues and conduct
68–73:   her physical description (*ekphrasis*)
73–76:   her prospects for marriage and moral qualities
76–79:   her illness and death
79–82:   her parents' lament, and her burial
82–85:   her visions during the illness
85–87:   Psellos' lament and final farewell

Psellos here follows the rules for funeral orations: biographical information is used to demonstrate and illustrate the subject's moral qualities; attention is paid to her final days, death, and burial; a lament highlights the grief of her relatives; and, finally, there are aspects of a consolation. Funeral orations were one of the most highly developed and frequently practiced genres in Byzantium, and were facilitated by both manuals and acknowledged models (e.g., among the writings of the Church Fathers).[4] But the text to which Psellos' *Oration* is probably closest, indeed one with which it shares tight thematic and linguistic affinities, is the letter of consolation written by the exiled patriarch Photios in ca. 870 to his brother Tarasios after the death of the latter's daughter at about the age that she would have been married (*Letter* 234).

Compared to other funeral orations, the distinctive features of this one are largely due to Styliane's early death, which meant that Psellos had to make the most of comparatively little material. But the result was highly successful; indeed, the *Funeral Oration for Styliane* is one of the most interesting and moving works of Byzantine literature, testifying to Psellos' literary genius and his

---

3. Ioannes Skylitzes, *Historical Synopsis: Konstantinos IX Monomachos* 30 (Thurn 477).

4. For a preliminary catalogue, see Sideras (1994); for the genres of the literature of death, see Agapitos (2003); for rhetorical strategy, Mullett (2003) 156–157; for the consolation letter in antiquity and the early Christian period, see Scourfield (1993) 15–33; in patristic writings, Mitchell (1968) and Pizzolato (1985); in the middle Byzantine period, Littlewood (1999); for literary treatments of the deaths of children, Jouanno (1994) 99–101.

eagerness, attested in many of his works, to go beyond convention in an effort to capture the nuances of love and grief. To be sure, there are many passages that strike a modern reader as excessively rhetorical, and the translation has aimed to reproduce this quality. But, for the following reasons, the synthesis must be judged skillful and original.

First, even more so than in the *Encomium for his mother* Psellos deliberately elevates the physical aspects of human life to virtual parity with the intellectual and the spiritual (for the *Encomium,* see p. 39, 43–44, above). The emphasis on his daughter's beauty is pervasive and sometimes overplayed, leading one scholar to speculate on his need to fashion a symbolic substitute for his lost daughter (rhetoric acts here as psychotherapy);[5] still, the theme is redeemed from a literary point of view by the extended and detailed *ekphrasis* of Styliane's face and body, the longest single passage in the *Oration.* We have little in Byzantine literature to rival this, at any rate not until the romances and humanist literature of the twelfth century which, to be fair, were possible only in the literary and philosophical context that Psellos himself did so much to bring about.[6] The *ekphrasis* of Styliane should become a major source for the convergence of modern aesthetic and literary criticism. There are no signs of physiognomic analysis, except in the general sense that Styliane's bodily beauty reflected and complemented her inner beauty. In other words, Psellos deploys *autonomous* aesthetic criteria, such as contrast (the black of her eyebrows and the red of her lips with the whiteness of her skin), a preference for natural over artificial beauty, and the avoidance of excess in any direction (except that of beauty itself). Moreover, the *ekphrasis* contributes to one of the main themes of the *Oration,* namely the contrast between Styliane's early splendor and the hideous wreck to which she was reduced by the ravages of the disease (a theme prominent also in Photios' letter).[7] Psellos does not play down either condition, and the result is a transformation that effectively deepens our grief and mobilizes our sympathy.

Second, most Byzantine funeral orations tend to be formal and abstract and, because they were written by trained professionals, vacillate between stiffness

5. Jouanno (1994) 101 for the extraordinary emphasis on beauty and 101–104 for psychology.

6. For a detailed and voluptuous description of a woman's body, see Konstantinos Manasses, Ekphrasis *of the Earth in the Form of a Woman.* Manasses wrote one of the four learned romance novels of the twelfth century, and clearly used the same descriptive arts in writing this brief text (which describes a palace mosaic) that he did in his novel.

7. Photios, *Letter* 234.17–30 (Laourdas and Westerink 150–151).

and hyperbole. These qualities are readily apparent in this work as well. But there are also moments when Psellos' grief surges to the surface and breaks through the rules of formal prose. This does not happen in works that he wrote for others, even for his own mother (possibly because she had died many years earlier). Especially toward the end of the oration, a number of brutally direct sentences allow us to almost hear his sobs and experience his heartwrenching sense of loss. Rather than quote them here, I will allow the reader to experience them in context. Granted, this effect is the product of art, as is the rest of the oration, but it is art in the service of a unique moment in the life of its master. Psellos was painfully sincere when he wrote, twice within the oration itself (63, 86) and once in the letter that he wrote during Styliane's illness, that philosophy had utterly failed him. The oration accordingly makes use of Christian symbols, concepts, and hopes. Particularly felicitous are the visions that Styliane experiences shortly before her death. In one, her soul takes the form of an infant cradled by a gigantic God in the midst of paradise; in the other, the mother of God, cradling the infant Christ, comes to her room and reclines upon her bed, as Styliane's mother had during the illness. Thus does the girl pass from the loving hands of her earthly parents into those of God and His mother.[8]

But deep down, when he had no need to console himself and an assembly of relatives — there is *always* an audience, these works are never personal confessions — Psellos almost certainly did not believe in the Christian version of heaven or even in God's providence, as a close reading of his other works reveals. Consider Photios' letter of consolation mentioned above. It begins with a not altogether convincing outburst of lamentation and grief, but swiftly adopts a rather strident Christian tone. Photios declares, as a point of fact that all true Christians must accept, that Tarasios' daughter is in a better place and concludes from this that it is "slander" against God to suggest that she was somehow taken before her time. Moreover,

> Christ proclaims that grieving over those who die is characteristic of unbelievers who have extinguished the hope of resurrection because they refuse to believe the power of Christ's mystery. . . . It is fitting, then, to give thanks for what He has arranged, to accept what has been done, and not to insult the judgment of the Creator with lamentation and bewailing.[9]

8. An astute observation by Nardi (2002) 117.

9. Photios, *Letter* 234.99–114, 201–203, 229–231 (Laourdas and Westerink 153, 156–157; tr. from White 122–123).

Now, Photios could be a cold and manipulative man (as his biography and letters indicate), and we do not have to accept his strictures for what constitutes proper Christian behavior. But he is right that believing Christians can, indeed must, find solace in their faith, even if he somewhat overplays his hand here. For the Fathers, "the central feature of their letters of consolation is the comfort to be derived from the assurances of a faith that holds out the prospect of a future happiness unalloyed with sorrow."[10] The Church, moreover, made a concerted effort to curb excessive lamentation and wailing at funerals and did so on the basis of Christian doctrine. By contrast, Psellos' oration follows an exact opposite trajectory to that of Photios' letter. It begins with abstractions (nature and truth) and a rather formal declaration of grief (62–63), talks about Styliane's childhood as though this were an encomium of some imperial princess, but then, especially with the onset of her disease, gradually collapses into lamentation. Psellos mentions Christian beliefs regarding the afterlife and the resurrection (esp. in 84–86), but they are apparently unable to comfort him at all. It is significant that he uses his favorite image of the ship finding refuge in a harbor not for Styliane's ascent to heaven but for the brief moment when it seemed that she would recover from the disease (78). The oration ends in utter misery and despair, mitigated only by the pathetic hope that Styliane might appear in her parents' dreams as she was before her illness.

The reader of this oration is left with a powerful impression that Styliane *was* in fact taken before her time. "Who reaped the harvest of your youth before the summer?" (80) The answer is, of course, God, but Psellos clearly cannot explain His actions. The one explanation that he offers is that God wanted to preserve Styliane's purity and so took her away before she could be stained by the filth of this world, i.e., by sexual intercourse in marriage (77–78), a suggestion that is also made by Photios in his letter. And it is entirely possible that this was one way by which Psellos could feel better about what had happened. But it was far from satisfactory even as a self-imposed delusion: theologically it was weak and, besides, Psellos was an avowedly worldly man who in principle did not accept such a Manichaean view of the world. Hence he has recourse to the inaccessibility of God's mind and the inexplicability of His decisions, which is, of course, a perfectly unsatisfactory explanation. In fact, at one point Psellos hints at an alternative that he would probably have preferred to develop further, but no doubt only before a suitable audience and once his

10. Mitchell (1968) 318.

pain had subsided: "Who caused your sunny beauty to darken and made it no different than the dead in their tombs? If this is due to the disorderliness of matter, then we must not lose heart, for it is in its nature to produce many kinds of maladies" (80).[11] But the time was not yet right for this. He goes on to question God's decision. Granted, this occurs in the lamentation that he puts into his own and his wife's mouths after Styliane's death, so these are the rash words of anger and bereavement. But it is significant that Psellos later quoted these words in producing the finished oration. They are among the most moving in the entire work and, paradoxically, they are perhaps truer expressions of Orthodox spirituality than all the priests' sermons and theologians' disquisitions.

> But if it is due to divine providence, which governs everything to advantage, well, it is not for us to contest divine decisions . . . . But, still, it is possible to see others who reached their very last breath after being wasted and exhausted by some such disease, yet snatched from the very noose of death and given an extension of their life—and this even though they lived for the most part in wickedness and evil . . . . Why then did you not too, child, obtain a similar reprieve, given that you were so pure and without blemish . . . ? Why was the Creator not moved to pity by your sores . . . ? Why was He not constrained by the entreaties of all the saints, whom we sent as envoys to plead before Him, but decided instead upon your death? He knew the great love that parents bear for their children . . . . He too partook of human nature once, shared in its qualities, became all that we are, except a sinner.[12] Why, then, did He not take pity on our suffering? (80–81)

Editions and translations. For a list of manuscripts and all studies referring to this text, see Moore (2005) 387–388. There is as yet only one edition of this text, in Sathas (1876) 62–87. The new edition announced by Vergari (1985) 69 never materialized, but in (1985), (1986), and (1988) she offers various notes on the text, both critical and interpretive, some of which I have followed (only the

11. Other Byzantine authors insinuate their less-than-orthodox explanations in a similar manner: for one instance in Prokopios, see Kaldellis (2004) 211; in Agathias, Kaldellis (1999b) 212–213, 217.

12. Hebrews 4:15.

most important are mentioned in the notes). A new edition is currently being prepared by P. Agapitos and I. Polemis for the Teubner series. They have announced that it will be numbered as *Or.* 19 in the corpus of Psellos' *Funeral Orations*: Agapitos and Polemis (2002) 152. Two translations have been published: a good albeit extremely inaccessible one in Italian in Vergari (1988), and a very poor English one in Kyriakis (1976–1977) 3.2, 82–99. The division and numbering of the text into paragraphs are from the forthcoming new edition (I thank Prof. Agapitos for showing me where to place them). The bold numbers in brackets correspond to the page numbers of the Sathas edition, which is cited in all discussions of the text so far.

Funeral Oration for his daughter Styliane, who died before the age of marriage

1. [62] By honoring my daughter in speech, I am convinced that I am honoring truth itself; by honoring truth I am honoring the common nature of us all, and this with good reason. For as nature brings forth species in their pure and unmixed state and, following God's instructions, gives shape to derivatives by modeling them on their prototypes, and, moreover, does this in accordance with truth and infallibility; the truth, likewise, repulses all that deviates and distorts, revealing all things bare and pure as they are by nature; so one would not be wrong to say that the two are in perfect harmony with each other and characterized by equivalence and an incapacity to deviate from each other even slightly. Hence it seems to me that one may clearly observe even in the books of the ancient sages that they say nature when they mean truth, by transferring the sense of one to the other, given that neither differs in its meaning from the other.

2. For this reason, then, it seems just to me to ascribe to nature that which belongs to her and to assign to truth that which is hers, and to employ both of them for the present purpose. And so, an attentive and impartial judge of our words will not be able to take hold of us and convict us, because we have not betrayed the truth through the partiality of affection, but rather honored it without falsehood despite being bound in this instance by the ties of nature. Therefore, even though I fear this too, namely that I will insult and belittle nature with my words, which, intimidated and fearful on all sides as they are, are unable to reach up to what is higher; nevertheless, this other thing drives the fear away from me, namely that I will deal with the matters at hand truthfully.

On account of truth, then, both [63] nature will be praised and the truth itself will be revealed in all its greatness and magnitude.

3. Therefore, given that our speech has been prefaced appropriately for a child, and a child, moreover, whose equal one would not dare to claim to have encountered or heard of, even if he is acknowledged to be superior to the others in experience and knowledge of history; come, then, let us attempt to give an account of her and, if our tears should give us even a slight respite, to speak these words of farewell. My innards are all twisted up, my heart is rent asunder, and I am everywhere falling to pieces, pushed deeper into depression by the memory of her. Not even if one were made of iron and had a soul harder than rock would he be able to philosophize under such grief, but would leave aside speaking in a proper manner about her and turn to melancholy and lament,[1] even though no one is capable of making the tears equal to the suffering. For only Jeremiah made his lament to work alongside ours, causing, if indeed it were possible, the font of our tears to flow without end from our eyes.

4. But because our nature has been activated and we have made a demonstration of tears, to the small degree called for by the rules of our speech, we will give an account of the deceased girl to whatever extent memory serves. We will, then, give an account of her family descent, her upbringing, education, conduct, her decorous and dignified character, and all the other aspects in which the child surpassed other women, gaining the advantage through the gifts of nature. I will not be rejected for admiring things dear to me, but will rather be accepted as one writing the truth by those who have beheld our lives with eyes free of envy and who do not cause trouble in this matter with their reproaches and accusations.

5. She was descended from high nobility on her mother's side; drops of imperial blood flowed in her veins or, rather, of ancestors who were closely related to emperors and registered as the fathers of emperors and joined to them by marriage; it was from them that she received the brilliance of her ancestry, deriving it through natural participation.[2] And then, having been swaddled and weaned, even as an infant she straightaway [64] revealed the first signs of the woman that she would become. From then on she conversed with her wet nurses, she made friends with girls her age, played with her maidservants, and

---

1. This is precisely what happens at the end of the oration, where the sentiment is repeated.
2. For the ancestry of Psellos' wife, see the general introduction above, p. 13.

found an outlet for the incomplete state of her development in childish pleasures. You would say if you saw her that she was like a rose bursting out from calyxes that had just broken open and that she surpassed in the beauty of her visage all others of her age.

6. Her parents rejoiced at the sight of her and celebrated because of her as though they had suddenly discovered a great treasure. It was not possible for one gazing upon her to be devoid of enchantment, as the surpassing extent of her beauty drove the pleasure deep down into one. She was raised by a decorous mother who took thought as to how she would always be exposed to decency and did not allow our worst aspects to be imprinted upon the softness of her nature. She ensured that the girl would, by gradual influences, be led in her progress from infancy to a more steady and decorous character. Even though she never attained maturity and full development, still she did not behave in all ways as children do, prevented from doing this on the one hand by [. . .] while, on the other, she was drawn in a contrary direction by her innate instincts and her mother's lessons. The capacities of the growing child had imperceptibly formed and developed, drawing her away from infancy and distancing her from it.

7. Such, then, was her infancy; thus was it adorable and decorous and free, on the surface, of the immaturity shown by others of her age. And when she passed beyond the stage of infancy and moved toward that of maturity, not only did her beauty increase in proportion to her bodily growth, but both her manners and her decorum were radiant and she felt the stirrings of modesty. As her mind developed, it became more steadfast and reliable, and then she devoted herself to good deeds to the degree that nature prompted her. For her behavior was honest and decorous and revealed her inner state, by degrees changing toward the better and floating above lowly things. Like newborn sparrows, which, while they still lack feathers, skim the ground [65] in their flight, but, when they begin to grow feathers, take flight to the heights and remain aloft, so too was she trained at first in the earthbound flights of children, but later flew aloft upon the virtues of a proper maiden. She lay exactly between infancy and maturity and occupied a middle position through the distance that separated her from either extreme; or rather, she was nearer to the more mature side, for she approached it to the degree that she moved away from the other, even if in reality she belonged to both. And that it was truly so, I bring forth as a reliable witness my own experience of her progress.

8. It was now the sixth year of her life, when she immediately began to speak with great facility, articulating her words clearly and without impediment, which

it was possible to see in only a few. For if, according to the prophet, 'faltering tongues spoke out and proclaimed the peace,'[3] but she greatly surpassed a childish mode of speech, it is nothing to be surprised at that she would have been able to proclaim that peace in an articulate and clear voice.

9. Thus she came to elementary instruction and the conjunction of syllables and the composition of words. With this as her mental preparation, she embarked upon the Davidic Psalms. Studying them through the keenness and sharpness of her nature, she easily stored them away in her mind and could recite them faultlessly. You have to admire the magnificence of my child and her docility and willingness to be led to those things that are good by nature. For other children to be initiated into these things is an uphill struggle that they do not undertake willingly, given that the softness of their minds is resistant to the imprint of solid reason; in her, however, the capacity to learn these things was so far developed that she even went to her teachers on her own initiative and satiated herself on the sweet honey of divine discourse. Whereas other children have to be dragged to learning through fear, small threats [66], and the switch, for this most beautiful child a natural love for these things alone sufficed. Giving in to this love, she learned easily, to such a degree that she was the first and best among her classmates, enriching by the ambition of her nature the inimitability of her education.

10. But can one say that she was naturally inclined to learn the rudiments of a literary education, but found it difficult to master the techniques of weaving? One could not say this either. She herself ordered the times of each day in the most prudent manner, setting aside one portion for education and another for weaving, while occupying herself with both. So at one time she would be learning her letters and at another she would be performing the women's work and the careful labors of the loom. Presently her mother introduced her to the art of embroidering garments; initiated and instructed in this art, she did not require many days, or the passage of much time, or many instructors, or experienced guides, but rather absorbed what she was taught by the keenness of her nature. It seemed as though this was imprinted in her mind and so she did not require much hard work to master it, that is, if we may trust the most wise Plato, who proclaimed that the learning of the soul is recollection.[4] In time, she was using the shuttle and weaving fine linens, and the complex

3. A slightly inaccurate recollection of Isaiah 29:24.
4. Plato, *Phaidon* 72e.

patterns and designs of silken threads were expertly brought to perfection by her ivory fingers. Who could ever admire these things enough?

11. Who else so loved her parents, or was so inseparable from them, or so revered their visages, or never had her fill of such an abundant love for them? I know this, its truth is shown to me through experience, for the proofs and signs of her affection toward me were many: hugging [67] me around the neck often, rushing to embrace me, spending long days together, lying together upon our bed, sitting on my knees, passing from one bosom to another, eating the same delicacies, sharing the same drinks, in sum, wanting to share everything that was offered and set before her on account of the boundless sea of love that she felt for me.

12. Do you suppose, listener, that her physical qualities were excellent and lacked nothing, but that the same was not true with regard to her soul? Or that she was not as one would have expected her to be? In no way! For concerning the hymns sung by lamplight and the nighttime praising of God, she was more eager than all others going to the temple, spontaneously racing there as though in flight. She revealed her reverence for God by standing without leaning and by paying close attention to the hymns. She chanted the psalms at vespers that she had learned all by herself and memorized the Davidic sayings immediately upon hearing them. She sang along with the choir and, by listening to those who quietly chanted the divine hymns, neglected none of those things that are necessary for praising God.

13. What then? Did she have such an eager disposition in ecclesiastical rites but no interest in the mystical and sacred rituals? Or did she pay close attention here too and show zeal for these as well? Did she not partake of the sacraments as a pure and undefiled maiden or, perhaps, did partake of them but not reverently and decorously and in an honorable manner suitable for a lady? Or did she do this too, but without adorning her head with a veil, as befits a maiden especially? But will anyone be found who partook of the mysteries in as immaculate and undefiled a manner as she? And will anyone else be spied among the maidens so devoted to divine things that she attends the matins and joins in the choir of chanters and is recognized as a chanter in her own right among the others? I, at any rate, do not think so. And if one does boast that she has risen up to such a degree of grace that she equals this girl's superiority, only the crows will be convinced.[5] [68] But the crow will quickly lose

---

5. An allusion to one of Aesop's fables.

its wings and will shed all that has been added to it from the outside, and then it will be known how great the difference is between one who has attained the most beautiful things naturally and one who has grown wings and takes flight artificially and by pretense.

14. Where did her upbringing take her from there? Like a noble flower sprouting up from the earth and sending up shoots, which reveals as it rises gradually the signs of its nobility, which previously it held within itself as potential but which it now actively brings forth in full bloom, so too, in the case of this altogether exceedingly comely maiden, the qualities of her extraordinary beauty were laid bare and brought to light in the transformation of her body as it passed from one age to another. Entering her ninth year, her features became more expressive and revealed an even more perfect beauty. Not only that, but whatever else about her used to be imperfect was now imperceptibly transformed to being simply perfect.

15. From then on I was again rekindled inside and the affection in my heart for my child burned ever brightly. I was not able to endure the boundless joy that I felt for my daughter. For the signs of her beauty, which were gradually being revealed as though they were coming out from some hidden treasury and showing themselves, bound me like a prisoner to my paternal love for her. It was not possible for me not to be seized by this passion and to remain impassive and loveless. It would be good to give some sense of her beauty, so that my listeners might have an idea of her extraordinary comeliness and her more-than-august appearance, of those qualities that astonished anyone who looked at her.

16. That blameless Creator fashioned a head that was neither oblong nor wide on either side, nor a forehead that was too broad. The one is proper for a Skythian while the other is unseemly, and neither is to be admired. Instead, he adorned her with roundness on all sides and made her head fit to receive all the graces and beauties of a maiden. Her eyebrows did not form arcs with too great a curvature, [**69**] nor were they laid out in too straight a line, for then they would have lacked measure;[6] rather, they were bent slightly toward their ends and gently curved in the middle, thus enhancing beauty with symmetry. The ends of each eyebrow, where they met from either side at the bridge of the

---

6. But in *Chronographia* 1.35 straight eyebrows are deemed more appropriate for a woman. For eyebrows similar to the ones described here, see ibid. 7C.12 (Konstantinos, the son of Michael VII Doukas).

nose, did not quite reach the same point, but were separated from each other by enough space so that the sharpness of the nose could be highlighted in the distance between them, showing its point of origin to complement the perception of where it came down to an end. At the conjunction of their ends, her eyebrows did not thin out too much, for that it is unattractive and inelegant; rather, they began at a certain point and grew wider by the thickness of the hairs, graced by a slender arc, then gradually became thinner and came to a sharp end. Their color was a deep black, which magnified the bright whiteness of her forehead, enhancing her charm.

17. Her eyes were bright like stars, but not on account of the roundness of their shape; rather, they were beautiful on account of their size. They were not equally wide at all points, but slightly extended on either side. Where they approached the nose, they resembled, in the delight that they gave, buds that had just opened, the very image of inimitable grace. The eyelids rested just above them like pomegranate peels, protecting the exceptional beauty of the eyes, which, under their cover, shone brightly with the splendor of virginal maidens kept safe at home. The center of the eyes shone purely white, while the pupils that surrounded them were black, elevating through the purity of their color the beauty of each part to an incomparable level.

18. And what of the nose? Its shape was on the whole straight and unwavering, neither spoiled by a snub nor, on the contrary, by being turned up, but rather raised up sufficiently to act as a border between her cheeks, to separate naturally the colors of her face and to delineate the various spaces on it. Her nostrils rivaled the symmetry of her other features, neither opening too widely, which would have been very unshapely, nor closed together tightly, which would have been mean [70], but spread open in an intermediate manner, allowing her to breathe the air as freely as is healthy and in good measure. Being so artfully crafted, they were admired more than on the noses of ancient statuary.

19. Her mouth too was symmetrical and dignified by her lips, lips which were so red that they seemed to be alight, not a little like the color of a pomegranate that has been cut open and confers comeliness through sheer redness—which indeed Solomon praised well in his Songs, granting it a good reputation.[7] It seemed to me that even rubies, when the sunlight falls upon them and forces red rays of light to beam out, could not compete with such glowing radiance. And whenever those lips opened in the maiden's magnificent smile, they re-

---

7. Song of Songs 4:3.

vealed the whitest teeth that we may liken to brilliant pearls arranged in a row
or like a necklace made of the most shining crystals and polished to be worn as
an ornament around the neck. These teeth, being covered by the torch-bright
lips, let fall much delight when she smiled, as the pearly whiteness mixed together with the redness, achieving a multicolored and composite grace.

20. Her cheeks were somewhat rounded out by well-nourished flesh of the
softest kind and their whiteness shone brightly, being at once brilliant and
charming. Buds like red roses blossomed at their center which, conveyed by
the blood from around the heart and making their way to the cheeks through
unknown channels, lent to her beauty a sweetness of which one could never
have enough; they continually enriched her blooming appearance, neither
withering in winter nor shedding their foliage in the fall, but at all times sav-
ing and preserving their luxuriant freshness. To such a degree did this rose
garden bloom and thrive that those who beheld her were convinced that they
could pluck the beauty and ripeness of natural flowers with their hands.

21. The head rested upon a neck that was proportionate to it [71], lest it
detract from her beauty; it was not too slender and thin, which would have
disgraced such perfect beauty, but rather like some crystal worked in relief, or
gleaming plates of ivory, or the tower of David at Thalphioth, the one mentioned in the Songs,[8] it held up the maiden's head, the seat of her perceptions
and the receptacle of an intelligence beyond her years.

22. And what could you say about her hair? It sprang from the peak of her
head and flowed down to her ankles, just as thriving stalks of wheat take root
and shoot up from well-watered and fertile land. It stretched out and unfolded
over her back, covering it like a bed of flowers, adorning it with curls and twists,
and causing it to shine with a striking blond color that was just a shade shy of
golden.[9] Above her forehead, it was parted in two and streched away on either
side in orderly curves, where it was bound together and shaped by inserted hair-
pins, gushing forth insatiate delight. From her temples too it cascaded down like
a bunch of grapes or tassels painted to seem real, framing the jaws, appearing like streams flowing from the same spring. But its color was not entirely
blond, nor, on the other hand, did it shade over into pitch black; rather, it

---

8. Song of Songs 4:4.

9. Yet Styliane's eyebrows were earlier described as deep black in color (69). Prof.
P. Agapitos (pers. comm.) informs me that "blond hair and black eyebrows was the ideal
combination for feminine beauty." Cf. Theodoros Prodromos, *Rhodanthe and Dosikles*
1.42–48; Niketas Eugenianos, *Drosilla and Charikles* 1.120–158.

was mildly blond, approaching the color of gold, not as the latter is by its nature, but just as it occurs mixed together with other elements, casting a dimmer and deeper glow.

23. Her arms, too, were appropriate for her body and were fashioned not in a masculine way but rather in an appropriately feminine one. Their skin was smooth and soft, qualities that they preserved all the way down to her wrists. One would not miss the truth by far to call her 'white-armed.'[10] From her palms grew fingers which seemed like newly budding twigs. Wider at the base [72] and polished smooth, they gradually became thinner before reaching the nails. Seeing them, you might compare them to newly cut ivory tusks fashioned into the fingers of a hand.

24. Her breasts were still undeveloped and unripe, jutting forward only a little or not at all, and were not yet recognizable in their softness, contracted as they were by their immaturity and hidden along with her internal organs, like undefiled treasures whose worth lay solely in their inviolability. Her waist: this too was not fashioned in an uncomely way, but was slender and thin, bound and restrained by a belt. Her flanks converged toward the middle, given that they were hollow and not defined by bony protrusions. Her thighs, next, widened out on either side, inferior in no way to the statue of Aphrodite of Knidos, with which, the myths say, a certain man fell in love and embraced sexually, so taken was he by the beauty of the statue.[11] As for her legs and the harmony of her knees, the former were adorned by smoothness, the latter provided perfect dexterity in movement. Nor were her ankles devoid of grace, for those too were white and, like a flash of lightning, struck the man who saw them and knocked him out.

25. Such, then, was her entire body, being thin wherever that was necessary and broader wherever that was more appropriate, possessing no limbs that were not symmetrical and beautiful. Nor was the entire complexion of her body unpleasant and empty of charm. She was fashioned from whiteness so genuine and pure that you would think that snow had just then fallen and whitened her. Redness bloomed in her cheeks and in any other place where it was fitting, which enriched her appearance and caused her to stand out, but those other places which had to be covered up more than these were white.

10. I.e., like Hera in the poems of Homer.

11. Lucian, *Amores* 13–16; *Essays in Portraiture* 4; *Hermotimos or Concerning the Sects* 51. For Lucian's tale and the original context of the statue, see Spivey (1996) 178–183. The statue was moved to Constantinople and destroyed in 476: Bassett (2004) 233.

26. I recall these things not to make her seem, through the power of my speech, more beautiful than she was. For even before then a meadow of natural flowers was planted in her body and a rose bed [73] of flawless beauty bloomed and flourished in her. No, I did this in order to demonstrate to you her superlative beauty and what great order and symmetry of limbs she carried with her. Indeed, she would win and prevail by far in any comparison with respect to the sum of beauty and splendor, even against those women who were greatly admired in the past, who would be ranked beneath her in beauty, in fact they would not even come close; still, she succumbed to the noose of death and fulfilled the common destiny of human beings.[12]

27. These things first aroused and encouraged and then excited high hopes for her marriage: her stature, like that of a palm tree,[13] the sprightly motion of her feet, the way her tunic was lifted by the wind when she walked, the gathering up and binding of her thin and even transparent linen clothes about her waist, the open movement of her fluttering legs and ankles, the way her mantle was draped and arranged around her shoulders and neck, as well as the way it clung to and enveloped all areas of her chest and back; these things, then, persuaded me that I was not wrong to expect that her name would be on everyone's lips, that she would be praised and admired by many of those in high station, and that her hand would be sought in marriage. For this reason pearls and precious stones and gold laboriously woven into expensive cloaks paled in comparison to her beauty, overwhelmed by the lightning-flash of her appearance; they even became indignant, as they were unable to adorn her anymore than she was already. For these things are meant to correct the deformities and artificial appearance of those who in truth are graceless and ugly, but when they are placed upon natural forms and beauties they can only be defeated. Necklaces and collars, or earrings, or diaphanous ornaments for the breasts, or elaborate veils and clasps, or blends and godless mixtures of enchanted potions, or contrivances and inventions of exotic hair-braids, were unable to add anything to such beauty, as natural advantages push artificial ones [74] to the side and show up their ephemeral "creators" as vain and false.

28. Had he been able to see her, Homer would have called her 'robe-trailing,' or 'beautiful-ankled,' or 'silver-footed,' or by whatever name he used to exalt the goddesses of the Greeks,[14] taking their praise to such heights. But how can

12. The last is a conventional formula.
13. Cf. Song of Songs 7:8.
14. These compound adjectives are used by Homer to characterize various goddesses.

she not be praised more then they were? Where they lapsed through their passions into shameful unions, they revealed the praise of their beauty to be false and the appellation of divinity to be a matter of mere time or tyrannical imposition. She, however, who both was and was recognized as the most beautiful of women; who preserved the beauty of virginity undefiled; whose mind was unpolluted by thoughts of passion; could she not, then, elbow aside those myths and in all truth offer her natural and faultless beauty, which immaculate hands fashioned, to those wishing to praise it?

29. I rejoiced at these things and was full of joy at the good fortune of my child, indeed I was quite beside myself.[15] My high hopes for her were constantly surpassing themselves and becoming ever brighter. She kindled an inner flame in her parents and my soul was captivated by her ever greater growth and progress and delivered over to hope. Who, beholding her and entranced by that beauty, that beauty which seemed almost not to have taken shape from elements coming together but to have been fashioned by that Pure Hand; who, I say, would not be noticed turning around to look again, as the poet says?[16] Who, hearing of her character and the propriety and honesty of her condition, would not convert to a better life? Who, pondering the formation of her body, observing the symmetry and harmony of her limbs and parts, and keeping in mind the tribute paid to her by her Creator, would not be stunned after her death? Who, seeing her practicing the words of the Lord, would not[17] suppose her to be a swallow or a nightingale with a rich voice among the best? Who, hearing her sing in the temple of the Lord and mixing her halting whispers in with the strains of the chanters [75], would not praise the Creator of nature and admire the piety of the singer? Who, seeing her compassion for the needy and her generosity with all goods at hand, would not yield to pity, even if he were otherwise harder than iron? Who, knowing her fiery love for her parents, as well as how she depended completely upon their love, and this even while her body was still immature, would not admire this maiden's affectionate nature? Who, knowing how she divided herself between the art of weaving and the discourses of education and how well versed she was in each, in fact lacking nothing in either, would not boast of her to the others?

15. This phrase is repeated later (85), effecting a pointed contrast.
16. Cf. Homer, *Iliad* 6.496.
17. I agree with Vergari that "not" must be added to this sentence.

30. Who else brought maturity into its fullness before the time of maturity by possessing a nature that was superior to the laws that govern the lives of human beings? Who else tolerated the games of children so long as they did not slide over into indecorous behavior, and rejected even these when she advanced to a more orderly disposition? Who had a mind so firm in a body so gentle and revealed an intellect so greatly superior to her age? Who was so dutiful toward her parents and remained obedient to them, educating actual servants by offering herself as a model of submission? Who served the sick and shared their pain and urged her parents to become more compassionate toward them? Who broke bread for the poor and gave away morsels from the table in such abundance? Who observed a love of goodness and beauty in all circumstances and tightly embraced that which is praiseworthy and orderly, while driving away that which is vulgar and affected? From whom did there come such hugs for her parents and constant embraces and little arms wrapped around their necks, by which she fired up their love for their child? Who was for me a consolation, a comfort in misfortune, a cure of the incurable, a transformation of grief, and a release from cares? Who, carried in my bosom like a newborn chick, soft and tiny, caressing me by fluttering its wings, so thoroughly delighted me with bridal hopes? Who so revered and embraced the immaculate and divine icons [76] and displayed her ardent passion for God by lighting candles and offering incense?

31. But what? Did she possess all these adornments in such abundance, but did not have a body more beautiful than that of all the maidens in the city of Byzantium? Or perhaps, enjoying *that* advantage, did many of those from noble and wealthy families not hasten to secure a marriage arrangement, captivated as though by a charm at the mere description of her? Or perhaps, while surpassing others in beauty and the affection of her suitors, she nevertheless lapsed from her duty and was tempted by the amorous contrivances of the young? Not at all! For whatever rumors reached her ears of such dealings failed to compromise her virginal modesty. Nor, as someone affected by the passions of youth, was she made nervous by the bridegrooms or was overly curious about their habits. She did not welcome matchmakers and intermediaries or those who exhort the sentimental to have recourse to such things. She did not most shamefully disgrace her noble visage by a flow of colors and powders. She did not consort with other girls well versed in such things, but allowed them to see freely her blameless and sunny beauty. Nor did she accept or use any other ornament of those that are of concern to women. For she knew,

O yes, she knew, that if she used these things and dared to fashion a beauty contrary to that bestowed by her Maker, if she should desire to correct the things that He had not perfected in contravention of nature,[18] she would have provoked deep laughter against Him among those of unsound mind and intolerable blasphemy. But, as it was, she remained within the boundaries of modesty and proper behavior, preserving the work of the Creator without blemish and preserving the beauty that He had given her undefiled. On this account, one would be all the more inclined to admire the Creator and exalt Him for having planted in that body of earth and clay[19] such a vast meadow of beauty.

32. Such was my child's conduct, even when she drew the eyes of everyone upon herself. Hopes were aroused within us and bridal expectations and all the other things that life promises for young maidens [77], and we went about watching for the right moment for their fulfillment. But what did He do who governs and regulates all things in wisdom and providence, what did He decree for her and to what end did He carry this decree? He believed it to be most inappropriate for this inimitable beauty, which He Himself had fashioned with His divine hands, to be defiled by the passions of intercourse and for a virgin so beautiful, so decorous, and so adorable (as Homer would say),[20] to succumb to marital pollutions; besides, He knew in advance about other things that would happen to her, things both secret and inexpressible, which are unknown to us but known to Him alone, and so, forestalling events and cutting the future short in advance, He infected her with a pestilential disease that was grievous to bear and physically repulsive and understood only by those who suffer it.

33. As for other diseases, regardless of whether they are caused by harmful food, or by contaminated fluids, or by the excess accumulation of one of the elements within us, or by the outbreak of sores on various places, they torment the body terribly but may be turned aside by medical care and the patient is restored to health. This disease, however, is not caused by any of those factors, but is churned out from the very marrow and the bones themselves and originates in every part of our bodily constitution. At first it produces a fever in the patient and then breaks out all over the surface of the body in grape-like clusters and grows into suppurating bubbles. It causes the harmony of the entire body to collapse, making shapeless and repulsive the former beauty of the

18. This clause is problematic.
19. Cf. Job 13:12.
20. *erateinê:* a word common in the *Iliad* and *Odyssey*.

flesh, flesh that now swells and is inflated by the sheer multitude of sores, striking fear even into those who witness its effects.

34. There are no arts among doctors nor strength in medicine that can cure it nor does any other human remedy avail. And this is to our advantage, lest in our boldness we assume that all is under our control whenever we are ill and entrust our health to the ephemeral power of doctors, who more often fail than not; rather, we should turn our gaze upon Him and entreat Him for aid. [78] Moreover, we should learn from this disease just how vulnerable and corruptible we are, we who may rot and waste away even before being buried, and just how powerful and inexplicable His judgments are; also, that, through both disease and grief, in His forethought He governs our lives according to what He determines is good for each of us, removing some of us from this place who He knows will fall into worse evils, or in order that their purity and innocence not be polluted and stained by the filth of our lives. Others, after allowing them to endure in illness, He restored to health, knowing in advance that they would return and convert to a better life. But our daughter, however, did not succumb to these causes: the sole reason for her death was so that her purity and freedom from passions not be defiled by bodily human intercourse, her youth stained by filth of the flesh.

35. So she lay, afflicted all over by numerous sores; so many and so great were they that one could not count them. Clustering around the apertures of her ears, her nostrils, above her mouth, and all over her neck, what pain they must have inflicted upon the miserable girl! At the dawn of the twentieth day our hopes revived as the sores dried up and dropped from her body like scales. But O, what happened to her then! She was shipwrecked, she who had just found refuge in a harbor.[21] A violent fever, kindled where and how I know not, ravaged what remained of her flesh. Wasted though she was by her earlier torments, indeed almost withered, still she endured the fever's irresistible flame and uttered nothing bitter during the passage of so many days. She did not wail or cry out inarticulately or make the plaintive sounds that those who fall into such illness tend to emit. Rather, she demonstrated a strength like adamant [79] in fighting against both the fever and the sores. What happened then? Weakened as she was by lack of nourishment, her vital strength slowly sapped away, she was not able to resist the fever's flame, given that she had been exhausted earlier and consumed by the sores.

---

21. One of Psellos' favorite images: see Littlewood (2006).

36. At that point we burst out in tears and expected the end; her departure was understood to be imminent. When she realized that her death was upon her, she made some indistinct and inarticulate sounds calling for her mother, and was never again able to either speak or make any sound at all. For all activity had ceased in her vocal cords. She raised her hands ever so slightly, though these too were burdened and ravaged by sores and had almost no bone or skin left in them, and with them she clasped the hands of her mother. Thus did she grant what I now know was her last embrace, which she formed by giving her hands in this way. And this gesture burned and rent the heart of her mother, whom the girl had called to her aid, and reduced all who were present to uncontrollable tears. For, as loving parents of their own children, they grieved along with us, understanding the depth of our sorrow from their own experiences.

37. And then what? The day of her passing had arrived. It was the thirty-first from the day in which she was first bedridden. And she lay silent, eager to depart. The crowd standing around was weeping and striking their chests, wishing to die along with the dying girl, until she who suffered so much finally gave up her spirit[22] to the luminous angels standing about her. At that point a wail swelled up and lamentations could be heard along with groans and sighs; friends, relatives, slaves, slave women, free men and women, all fell upon her body, also her wet nurses and caretakers, who more than the others, like mothers really, were naturally attached to the body that lay there, enveloping it in an embrace and calling upon their mistress, their lady, the one whom, apart from giving birth to her, they had swaddled and breast-fed and nourished [**80**] and raised to such an age. When there had been enough mourning for the moment, she was given her last bath, adorned with funerary garments, and placed on a bed. She had cast off the majority of the sores on her face but carried the rest on her body, displaying them as a testimonial of the disease with which she had wrestled. There was no way for those who wanted to embrace her to satisfy their desire, as her entire body appeared to be one large sore and an open wound.

38. Her parents, seeing her laid out like that with her original features so disfigured, retaining no sign or remnant of her natural form but all shapeless and unrecognizable and covered in sores, were overcome with grief and fell in confusion upon her together. If they found any part of her body free of sores, they insatiably attached themselves to it. "Dear child," they said, "beloved and sweet child, the first and only one granted to us by God, what do we see here? What has happened against all hope? What is this bestial and barbaric disease

22. Though rooted in Scripture, this expression had become a conventional formula.

that covered you with sores and filled you with pus and then swiftly sent you to your death? For what purpose did it brand you with so many wounds and devour you with torments, only to snatch you away from here? For it visited many others as well, producing sores on them too and attacking them with blisters, but brought death to none of them. Who bore you malice, who put the Eye on you, who wished you harm, who contrived a deadly lot and betrothed you to death before your time?[23] Who reaped the harvest of your youth before the summer? Who caused your sunny beauty to darken and made you no different from the dead in their tombs?

39. If this is due to the disorderliness of matter, then we must not lose heart, for it is in its nature to produce many kinds of maladies. But if it is due to divine providence, which governs everything to advantage, well, it is not for us to contest divine decisions, to wag our tongues against the Creator [81] and to be rebellious and impatient just because we cannot always understand His decisions. But, still, it is possible to see others who reached their very last breath after being wasted and exhausted by such a disease, yet snatched from the very noose of death and given an extension of their life—and this even though they lived for the most part in wickedness and evil—so that they reached an old age. Why then did you not too, child, obtain a similar reprieve, given that you were so pure and without blemish and had not sullied your purity with the stain of any reproach? Why was the Creator not moved to pity by your sores and why did He not acknowledge your patience and endurance under their assault by returning you to life? Why was He not constrained by the entreaties of all the saints, whom we sent as envoys to plead before Him, but decided instead upon your death? He knew the innate love that parents bear for their children, how brightly they burn with affection for them, and our natural and innate tenderness for our offspring. He too partook of human nature once, shared in its qualities, became all that we are, except a sinner.[24] Why, then, did He not take pity on our suffering? Why did He not show compassion for the sick girl, devoured as she was by the pain of so many sores? Why did He overlook the agony and turmoil of your parents but instead took you away too, who were their only consolation?

40. O my child, you who were once beautiful, but are now hideous and unsightly, how did you endure the savagery of those sores? How did you endure the stench of festering wounds and pus? How did this lethal disease, like a wild

---

23. Cf. Photios, *Letter* 234.31 (Laourdas and Westerink 151).
24. Hebrews 4:15.

beast, sink its teeth into you and cause your death? Where are the signs of your superhuman form? Where the blush in your cheeks, the healthy complexion and symmetry of limbs that shone brightly like a rose amidst the lilies, where the unhindered motion of the feet, by which you amazed not only your parents but anyone who saw you by the purity of your beauty? [82] Since God, Who governs our lives according to what seems good to Him through the inaccessible decisions of His forethought, has taken you from this place and prepared a pleasant meadow for your repose, as was indeed revealed to you in advance, go forth, then, upon that good and eternal path and take your rest in those heavenly places, rejoicing in the company of the spirits of the prudent virgins.[25] As for us, who burn hotly with love for you, show yourself in our dreams as you were before your sickness, giving strength and hope to our failing spirits. Grant to your parents this one favor, that they might obtain some relief from their sorrow on your behalf!"

41. After her parents had uttered these words in lamentation and other things even more miserable and heartwrenching, the maiden was placed upon a stretcher and conveyed toward the exit, given that the time had come for that, indeed it was now necessary that she be buried. When we reached the dwelling of her repose and the tomb was made ready, she was honored with divine hymns while a holy and bloodless sacrifice was performed on her behalf. Thus she was given over to the grave and the slab was placed above her. She moved many to tears, caused us to moan repeatedly, and was pronounced blessed by all present. Nor was there anyone so stony and steely in his heart[26] that he was not moved by our grief for her so as to shed tears and wail aloud.

42. As for that which is the most dear to us of her blessings, namely that she did not effect her transition from here without the consent of God, we bring her forth as a witness, she who saw the vision and relayed it to her mother. About ten days prior to her final departure, her mother, who watched over her by night—for she lay on the floor near to her daughter's bed—asked her how she was feeling and whether she had slept well at all. She replied, "O mother, though I often begged the man whom I saw [83] to open the garden gate for me, he did not yield, even though he had the keys in his hand. Then I insisted in my request, following him as he went along, urging him to open it. After we had traveled upon a long and stretched-out road, I was worn out, drenched in

25. Cf. Matthew 25:1–13.
26. Cf. Euripides, *Medeia* 1279–1280.

sweat, and, believing that the length of the road would finish me off, gasping my last. But when we reached a certain spot, the entrance to which was barred, that man who had appeared to me opened it with the keys that he had with him. We both went inside and beheld a shady garden with trees ripe with fruit, thickly planted with all the other varieties of flora and exceedingly delightful. Neither roses nor lilies nor any species of fragrant flower was missing.

43. Pleased by the garden's delights, we had moved inside a short way when I saw the tallest and most enormous man seated near the middle, indeed he reached to the very sky.[27] Servants clad in white stood around him, all of them clasping their hands and full of fear and trembling. The sight of him made my knees weak and I was filled with fear and awe at his size, indeed I felt faint and trembled. So, as those who were standing in a circle around him paid homage to this man, I too paid homage to him along with them and behaved as though I were one of them. After our proskynesis, when everyone was standing by with their hands folded in fear, behold, two young men arrived, dressed in white and carrying in their arms a tiny infant, very thin and lean and extremely weak. Drawing near to the huge man, they placed it in his bosom. Taking it up in his own hands, he rocked it this way and that. And as it was being rocked it regained its health and strength and seemed to be reborn. Then, he placed it on the ground beside him on a spot graced by every kind of flower. When I saw this, my innards were all twisted up, my hair stood up on end at the strangeness of the sight, and I was no longer able [84] to bear looking. With sobs and tears I turned to the man who had the keys and, clasping his knees, begged and pleaded with him to take me back. My heart stopped as I did this and I woke up just now from the vision that I was seeing all drenched in sweat."[28]

44. When the maiden had finished her account, we immediately suspected that she was about to die: the man who had appeared to her was one of those saints who guard the entrance into paradise or, as I believe, the first and chief of the Apostles, to whom Christ gave the keys of the kingdom of heaven.[29] The one whom she saw who was greater and taller than all the rest was, it seems to

---

27. Cf. Isaiah 66:1; Jeremiah 23:24.

28. It is noteworthy that the syntax and vocabulary of Styliane's account are simpler than in the rest of the oration. Nevertheless, her dream bears striking similarities to a vision seen by a certain Syrian monk named Hesychios, reported in a book on Ioannes Chrysostomos by a certain Georgios of Alexandria and summarized by Photios in his *Bibliotheke* 96 (Henry vol. 2, 51).

29. Matthew 16:19.

me, the Maker and Creator of the world, the Ancient of Days,[30] the One revealed as taller and vaster in His very substance. Those standing around Him
were angels, performing their obeisance to Him, their Creator. The young men,
who conveyed the infant in their arms, were angels sent out to serve Him; they
brought the child's soul in the form of an infant to the Maker of the world, withered and sickly as it was, on the one hand, because of the persistence and viru-
lence of the disease, but returned to health and convalescent on the other because of its patience and endurance in the face of the disease, which prepared
her soul to regain its strength in the presence of God.

45. But we should not overlook that dream-vision which she saw even before this one, for that one too was somehow divine and believed to have been
sent to her by God. She believed that she saw a certain woman cradling in her
arms an infant on whose head the sign of the cross appeared; holding a
branch in each hand, she drew near to her bed and lay down upon it beside her,
then rose up again and moved as though to depart. My daughter asked for one
of the branches and the woman gave her the smaller and shorter one. The child
pleaded and begged to receive the larger one as well, but the woman in the vision did not grant that but left the room and departed.

46. Having seen these things, the child awoke and [85] recounted the vision
to those who were waiting upon her. It seems to me that this woman was truly
the mother of our Lord and God herself, bearing her divine Son in her arms as
she approached the bed of the sick girl. And why did she lie down? She wanted
to observe and examine matters for a little while. By giving her the shorter
branch she indicated the brevity of her life and its sudden cessation. These matters, even if they should seem unlikely in themselves, are made even more bi-
zarre by the fact that they were seen and recounted in detail by a nine-year-old
child, given that Providence does not consent to appear to other girls of this
age. It is no great thing for them to see such things because sometimes they
turn what they see into what they expect to see, so that clarity and receptivity
to such visions is worthy of wonder in those who are young and immature, in
fact far from being mature.

47. But she had drawn upon herself none of the stains and the filth of this
world; she entered that intelligible paradise stainless and pure, as the vision
indicated. As for me, I now go about life dejected and sullen and, hardly differing from a dead man, lament the loss of one so dear to me. I go to her grave

---

30. Daniel 7:9.

and call upon the one who lies there. Then I return, striking my chest, and am quite beside myself.[31] I don't know where to turn or what medicine to take to rid me of this sorrow. Jacob cried when he believed that Joseph was devoured by a beast, even if only briefly; but his joy was magnified when he later heard that he was alive.[32] Jeremiah lamented for Jerusalem, foreseeing its capture, even if only [. . . .] But my grief is not of this kind, it is not bounded in time, it will not end at a certain deadline, it will not relent even for a little while, but will last for the rest of eternity and press upon me until we are all resurrected at the very end.

48. Because of this, the mist that darkens my eyes dims my sight and the groans that come straight from my heart [**86**] cause my tear-ducts to open wide. I am delirious with pain and I don't know how to make this suffering end. All my comforters are good men, but to the same degree that they seek to comfort me they fuel the fires of my grief. Yes, most of us are good at maintaining a philosophical disposition at the misfortunes of others and affecting steadfastness and magnanimity. But when grief comes upon *us,* then our natural reactions overcome magnanimity along with all reasoned discourse, proving that nothing is more powerful than nature and nothing is more painful than the loss of a child. For other misfortunes come upon us from the outside and, even if they inflict pain on our soul, in the end they are only superficial and do not strike down deep into us. But as for our children, because they are our flesh and bones, as Scripture says, born from our own essence, it is not possible for the lament over their deaths to be conditional or for the soul to ever cease being wounded by the barbs and red-hot nails of that pain.

49. But you, dearest and most beautiful of children, the adornment of your parents, the pride of your relatives, the ornament of our household, the splendor of all those your age, and the blessing of your siblings,[33] as God's majestic and ineffable providence has decreed that you should roam the heavenly bridal chambers, that you be filled with everlasting delight, and that you consort with the spirits of the just, accepting you as untouched and undefiled by the filth of the world, may you now cause the flow of our tears to stop, check

31. This phrase was used once before (74), in the exact opposite context. A contrast is apparently intended.

32. Genesis 37:31–35.

33. Note above (80), Psellos claimed that Styliane was his only child. These siblings probably have only a rhetorical existence; see Sideras (1994) 119–120 n. 86.

the distress of our groans, and extinguish the furnaces of grief that you lit. You will do this by appearing to us at night, in our sleep, speaking to me and addressing me in that most sweet voice of yours, clinging to me as you did in life by putting your arms around my neck and fueling my love for you through your embraces; even so, now that you are far from us, don't forget to appear to us in our dreams and don't ever leave off enfolding me in your dearest arms, drench with your kisses [87] my dry and withered mouth, and relieve us of this sorrow and despondency that we feel on your account. Even though we have been separated from each other by God's command, still, our ties of closeness and union will endure forever.

50. Yes child, come to me, the man whom you called father for so brief a time but who will now remain childless for so long. Remember your father's misfortune, your mother's love. You know all the labors that we underwent for you,[34] all the troubles, you know how many vigils we made for you, how we struggled with fasting and weeping, how often we entreated God on your behalf that we might see you reach adulthood. Remembering these things, pay us back for educating you, for nourishing you, for giving birth to you. How? With your attendance, your apparitions, your visitation in our dreams, so that in the sight of you we might find some relief from most of our sorrows and be henceforth only a little troubled and distraught on your account. To be sure, only in death will we ever be entirely free of this grief for you, or else if we should drink that potion which, according to the mythic tale, causes forgetfulness, since, for sure, words of consolation are scattered to the winds and dispersed and overcome by the magnitude of our sorrow.

34. This sentence refers to the days of Styliane's illness.

The Court Memorandum (hypomnêma) regarding the engagement of his daughter

Translated with introduction by David Jenkins

Introduction

Among the texts related to the family of Michael Psellos is a curious court memorandum involving his adopted daughter. Found in two of the most important and extensive manuscript collections of his works (Parisinus graecus 1182 and Laurentianus graecus 57, 40), the report details the facts, testimony, and decision of a case in which Psellos himself appears to have been one of the parties. In addition, the title of one of these manuscript versions seems not only to identify him as a party but to attribute the work to him as well, and there are stylistic reasons to believe that he was in fact its author.[1] Nevertheless, the text is not written as a first-person account of the proceedings, but as if emanating from the judges themselves, who refer to the father of the girl in the third person as the "*vestarchês* Michael." So while the text provides us with a wealth of information about Byzantine society in the eleventh century, its very

---

1. The title is found in Laurentianus graecus 57, 40. The stylistic argument is suggestive at best, based on several expressions that occur here and in other works of Psellos but rarely if ever in other eleventh-century authors. One idiom in particular is common to this and to the other surviving legal memorandum written by Psellos (namely "he fled to the ultimate anchor"): see, below, *Hypomnêma* 148, as well as the *Hypomnêma regarding Ioannes Iveritzes* (*OFA* 6 [A 3]; Dennis p. 166, line 144).

nature is immediately problematic. If Psellos wrote the report, why would he write it as if the judges themselves had done so? And if he was a party in the case, how could he be the author of its report?

The contents of the memorandum are as follows. In an attempt to insure the future of his adopted (and unnamed) daughter while he was still in the good graces of the emperor Konstantinos IX Monomachos, the *vestarchês* Michael (at the time still named Konstantinos, or Konstas) betrothed her to a certain Elpidios Kenchres, the son of a high official. A prenuptial contract was drawn up that included a penalty clause and the payment of earnest money by Elpidios in order to discourage the dissolution of the engagement until the girl could be legally married at twelve (she was probably nine years old at the time of the engagement; Elpidios was eighteen). Michael then immediately put his future son-in-law in full possession of his daughter's dowry and used his influence at court to have him promoted with honorific titles that the *vestarchês* himself purchased. All went well until it became clear to Michael that Elpidios Kenchres was a malicious lowlife. He was openly hostile to the *vestarchês'* attempts to improve his education and character and preferred instead to spend his time with mimes and charioteers while completely ignoring his future bride. Michael was at a loss about what to do, but he continued to hold out hope that Elpidios would turn around and respond to his influence.

Nevertheless, at some point the *vestarchês* reached his limit and broke off the engagement. He appealed directly to the empress Theodora (Monomachos had died the previous year, 1055) in hopes that she might revoke the honors that he had acquired for Elpidios, with the exception of the office of *prôtospatharios,* whose value was part of his daughter's dowry. The empress granted his request but remitted the case to a civil court in order to determine the resolution of the engagement contract (the memorandum is written as if emanating from this court). A tribunal of four judges then heard testimony and decided that Elpidios' conduct was not egregious enough to void the penal clause. They also determined that Elpidios was liable for the value of the honorific title that he had retained since it was part of the dowry, which he was now obligated to return. The amount of the penal clause was less than the value of the honor, but the judges said they would forgive Elpidios the difference if he agreed to forego his right to sue for twice the amount of his earnest money (which was obviously less than the difference). The case was then settled, and the decision made public in August 1056.

As is clear from this short summary of its contents, the memorandum is an important witness to several features of Byzantine society in the eleventh century. First of all, the report documents an instance of both adoption and engagement and then proceeds to give a detailed account of a prenuptial contract and dowry. It also documents the sale of honorific titles and provides an example of the salaries that these titles often drew from the imperial treasury. Evidence for the procedure, jurisdiction, and identity of a civil court is also apparent, as well as information regarding the creation and form of legal documents. Finally, if the "*vestarchês* Michael" is Michael Psellos, the report not only provides us with much of what we know about his adopted daughter, but it also contributes to our knowledge of his career and chronology and to our judgments regarding his character and ambitions.

The circumstances of the *vestarchês'* life that are described in the memorandum square remarkably well with what we know about Michael Psellos: he was a *vestarchês* in 1056; he was a close advisor of Konstantinos IX Monomachos; he was the first "Consul of Philosophers"; and he fled to a monastery on Mt. Olympos precisely at the time and under the circumstances mentioned in the memorandum. It is not surprising then that Konstantinos Sathas, who published the report's first edition in 1876, assumed that Psellos was a party in the case, as did Albert Vogt a generation later.[2] However, in 1959, Rudolph Guilland wrote the first of two extended articles on the memorandum (including a French translation) and suggested that the "*vestarchês* Michael" was not Psellos, but that he had been one of the judges present at the case and wrote the memorandum.[3] Having based his argument on the edition of Sathas, who used only one of the two manuscripts that contain the text, Guilland softened his position a short time later when Franz Dölger pointed out the title of the work in its other manuscript version, which seems both to attribute it to Psellos and to identify him as a party.[4] Alice Leroy-Molinghen argued in 1969 that the report was a copy of the official memorandum, written by the tribunal concerning a case in which Psellos was a party.[5] She later admitted that her position was "less nuanced" than that of Paul Lemerle,[6] who had maintained in a 1967 footnote that Psellos both wrote the report and was a party in the case. He also suggested

---

2. Sathas (1876) 203–212; Vogt (1908) 65 n. 4.

3. Guilland (1959) and (1960); this view was endorsed by the text's English translator, Kyriakis (1976–1977) 4.1:80 n. 53.

4. Guilland later reprinted these papers in (1967); his original text is emendated at 92–93 in order to accommodate Dölger's notice, which appeared in *Byzantinische Zeitschrift* 53 (1960) 169–170.

5. Leroy-Molinghen (1969b) 288.

6. Leroy-Molinghen (1971).

the first plausible explanation for this concurrence: Psellos had written the memorandum, "shortly before the death of the Empress Theodora, upon whom the case depended and who had decided in his favor (the work is dated August 1056, and Theodora died on the twenty-first of this month), but he presented it more or less adroitly as if emanating from the tribunal in hopes of recording to his advantage the outcome of the case so that its decision could not be challenged."[7] In 1994, George Dennis remarked that the *vestarchês* Michael was "clearly Psellos himself; at any rate, it was Psellos who drew up the memorandum, supposedly emanating from the court, which gave an account of the case."[8]

If Psellos wrote the memorandum as if emanating from the tribunal, we can assume that he did so in order to protect his interests. But what was the context of this "adroit presentation"? Lemerle's suggestion that Psellos wrote a version of the case in hopes of passing it off as an official copy of the proceedings implies that Psellos believed, first, that there was no official version of the memorandum (or that he had little confidence in its permanence), and second, that this "adroitly presented" copy could somehow pass the test of authenticity required in order to be admitted as legitimate. While, granted, we have much to learn about the documentary practice of the Byzantine courts, both of these assumptions seem implausible. First of all, it is hard to imagine that a case which was tried before the state's highest civil court and involved someone of Psellos' stature would have failed to produce an official memorandum. Copies of this official memorandum could have been provided for the parties, but these would have carried official notary statements attesting to their authenticity, statements which our present memorandum lacks.[9] Second, we know from a collection of excerpted memoranda written in the first quarter of the eleventh century, and more than likely emanating from the same court which heard this case, that the authenticity of copies was in fact rigorously tested and that forgers were prosecuted.[10] Finally, the alleged advantage that this document purports to establish is nothing more than the *vestarchês'* moral indignation. While the failings of El-

---

7. Lemerle (1967) 84 n. 14: ". . . mais plus ou moins adroitement présenté comme émanant du tribunal, et par lequel Psellos, peu avant la mort de l'impératrice Théodora, de qui l'affaire avait dépendu et qui se prononça pour lui (la pièce est datée d'août 1056, et Théodora mourut le 21 de ce mois), voulut consigner à son avantage le déroulement de l'affaire, afin que l'issue n'en fût pas remise en cause."

8. Dennis (1994) 193.

9. Dölger and Karayannopoulos (1968) 129–134.

10. Eustathios Romaios, *Peira* (here Zepos pp. 193–194, 237–239).

pidios are repeatedly documented, and the *vestarchês* often appears as the innocent and sometimes heroic victim of his maliciousness, the decision of the court remains clear: the *vestarchês* must pay the amount of the penal clause. This seemed clear to Sathas as well, who in his printed edition provided the memorandum with the title, "A judicial decision against Psellos."

Moreover, the title of the report that is found in one of its manuscript versions makes no attempt to conceal the fact that Psellos wrote it *in the person* of the judges. The judges themselves are not named in the title, but their offices are specifically identified. The specificity of these offices, all of which we know to have existed in this period, suggests that the title was written by a contemporary who knew the details of the case and not by a later scribe. The phrase in which these offices are mentioned was translated by Guilland as, "written by Michael Psellos, a *vestarchês,* concerning the action which he (Psellos) brought before the *prôtoasekretis,* the *epi tôn kriseôn,* the *nomophylax,* and the *skribas.*"[11] However, it is far more likely that the Greek words which Guilland translated simply as "before," *prosôpôi dêthen,* actually mean, "written by Michael Psellos, a *vestarchês, assuming the persona* of the *prôtoasekretis,*" etc. Psellos himself used the word *prosôpôi* in the sense of "assuming the persona of" more than thirty times in his verse *Commentary on the Psalms.*[12] He also frequently employed the particle *dêthen* for its nuance of obviousness, which, depending on his intention, could stretch from an honest "obviously" to an ironic or indignant "evidently."[13] If we assume that Psellos wrote at least this part of the title, the meaning might be "obviously"; if we assume a scribe wrote it, he might be using the particle to distance himself from Psellos' actual or perceived intention, in the sense of "evidently" or "supposedly." In either case, the author of the title is consciously acknowledging that Psellos wrote the memorandum *as if* he were the judges.

So if the document is not an attempted forgery, what could it be? A satirical dialogue written some seventy years after this case makes an interesting

---

11. Guilland (1967) 92: "rédigé également par Michel Psellos, vestarque, sur le procès qu'il intenta devant le protasecretis, le Président du Tribunal, le nomophylax et le greffier."

12. Psellos, *Commentary on the Psalms* (= *Poem* 54; Westerink pp. 327–390). Psellos also composed official documents in the person of the emperor; see the three extant chrysobulls in *OFA* 5, 7–8 (A 2, 4–5; Dennis pp. 155–160, 169–181). Other Byzantine authors assumed the persona of someone else, including Ioannes Geometres, *Lament on a judge as if spoken by his wife;* the epigrams and poems of Manuel Straboromanos; and Gregorios of Cyprus, *Concerning his own Life.*

13. Denniston (1959) 264–266.

suggestion. The anonymous work, known as the *Timarion,* chronicles the descent into the afterworld of the soul of its eponymous hero. In the course of this adventure in which various Byzantine institutions and personalities are lampooned, Timarion eventually reaches a tribunal that is to decide whether or not his soul should be reunited with his body. The judges hear the evidence and proclaim that it should, since it had been mistakenly rent from the body in the first place. At this point they summon a writing tablet and the "Byzantine sophist," who stands ready nearby on account of his "ability and speed at improvisation" (41). The sophist then dictates to a scribe the details of the decision, although mumbling (*hypopsellizôn*) his way through. When he finishes, the scribe reads his transcription to the court, and the proceeding comes to a close. The "Byzantine sophist" appears later in the dialogue and in such a way that, combined with the punning reference to mumbling (*psellos* means mumbler), it is clear that he is none other than Michael Psellos.

While the conclusions we draw from this source should be tentative, other references in the works of Psellos suggest that extemporaneous composition was consistently involved in the creation of court documents.[14] This is understandable if we assume that the volume of cases not only demanded the fastest means of producing reports but also required rhetorically trained compositors since the language of these documents had to be elevated from the everyday speech of the proceeding to the learned imitation of ancient Greek that was required by Byzantine tastes. While the execution of these extended extemporaneous compositions in an unspoken dialect is difficult for us to fathom, its techniques were long the basis of classical and Byzantine literacy, which was fundamentally dependent on memory, recall, and declamation. Byzantine jurisprudence itself reflects the dominance of this sensibility, preferring a rhetorically crafted argument to one based on consistent legal reasoning.[15] In fact, this forensic improvisation is a perfect example of the paradoxical nature of Byzantine literacy in general, which was somehow fated to seek the illusion of spontaneous expression in the rhetorical compositions of a dead language.[16]

14. The present author (D. Jenkins) is planning on addressing this issue further in a future study of "Michael Psellos and the Extemporaneous Composition of Court Documents."

15. Dennis (1994); Simon (1973).

16. Hermogenes (third century A.D.), the father of Byzantine rhetoric, had this to say to lawyers in his treatise *On the Method of Forcefulness* (*Peri methodou deinotêtos*) 17

It was precisely Psellos' talent for this kind of extemporizing that so endeared him to the emperor Konstantinos IX Monomachos.[17] He was arguably the greatest orator of his time and an authority on all aspects of learning and culture, including law.[18] In 1056, he was at the height of his powers, the so-called "Consul of Philosophers" and the center of the court's intellectual circle. It is perhaps not implausible to suggest that at the trial regarding his adopted daughter's engagement contract he was permitted by the judges, all of whom he undoubtedly knew personally, to extemporize a draft of the proceedings in their presence or under their supervision. The title of the memorandum does not explicitly say that Psellos *wrote* the document; it simply relates that he *created* it at the trial.[19] Such a scenario might explain why the memorandum appears to be a draft without notary statements and signatures, which would have been added later by a scribe, and why the *vestarchês* Michael is represented as the unwitting victim of Elpidios' astounding wickedness but is nonetheless responsible for paying the contract's penalty. Perhaps the empress Theodora herself, who was fond of Psellos and had initially ruled in his favor, directed the judges to grant him this extraordinary privilege, thinking no real harm could come from giving her wounded favorite the opportunity to spin things as best he could.

But regardless of the nature of the document itself, we cannot help but comment on the Psellos represented here, especially if this representation is autobiographical. The adoption would have occurred shortly after the death

(Rabe p. 433): "In court, even if you have prepared your remarks, try to appear to speak spontaneously like the ancients did. For although they had written out their speeches, they all pretended to be improvising. Why? Because the judge is suspicious of the orator and fears that he might be deceived by the force of rhetoric."

17. Cf. Psellos, *Chronographia* 6.44–46.

18. Psellos had served in Anatolia in a judicial capacity before his rhetorical talents brought him to the attention of the court: see his biography above, p. 4. He tells us that he was tutored in law by his friend Ioannes Xiphilinos in exchange for his own tutoring of him in philosophy: see his *Funeral Oration for Ioannes Xiphilinos* (*Hist. Byz. et alia*, pp. 427–429). At the request of Michael VII Doukas, he also composed a didactic poem on law drawn from a variety of Roman and Byzantine legal sources: *Poem* 8 (Westerink pp. 123–177).

19. Byzantine notary statements distinguish between the creation of a document and its release or promulgation as a legally binding artifact. The creation of a document is often further distinguished by being either written (*graphen*) or created (*gegone*). Since "written" usually designates the scribe who actually wrote the document and "created" the activity of the judges, the distinction might be one of transcription and dictation. See Dölger's review of H. Steinacker in *Byzantinische Zeitschrift* 29 (1929–1930) 324–329.

of his beloved Styliane, and we see that Psellos expresses the same kind of affection for his new daughter. While he tried to carefully provide for her future, he has to admit that he badly misjudged the character of her fiancé and was forced to break off the engagement after his attempts to reform him failed. He portrays himself as simply responding to such moral depravity as anyone would, and his attempts to protect the value of his daughter's dowry and avoid paying the penalty for breaking the engagement as following naturally from his concern for his daughter. On the other hand, he portrays Elpidios as willfully malicious; if he was in fact permitted to compose the memorandum, Psellos made the best of the opportunity by relentlessly assailing the character of his opponent. He even implies that he could have avoided paying the penalty altogether if he had been willing to shame himself in front of the court by describing in even greater detail the baseness of Elpidios' conduct. Nevertheless, in the end, his initial blindness to a character so blatantly wicked more than qualifies the concern for his daughter that apparently motivated the engagement and the attempt to protect her assets following its dissolution. This blindness only ends up suggesting that for Psellos, like so many before and after him, affection and concern sometimes took a back seat to ambition.

Editions and translations. For a list of manuscripts and all studies referring to this text, see Moore (2005) 382–383. The text was first published by Sathas (1876) 203–212. The latest edition is that of G. Dennis, *Michaelis Pselli Orationes, Forenses et Acta* (Stuttgart and Leipzig: Teubner, 1994) 143–155. Two small corrections to this edition are proposed by I. Polemis (1994) 502 and the reader has to correct for himself a few minor typos. The work was translated into French by Guilland (1959) 205–211; reprinted in (1967) 84–90. There is also an English translation (not always reliable) by Kyriakis (1976–1977) 4.1:70–80. The bold numbers in brackets correspond to the page numbers of the Dennis edition.

The Court Memorandum (hypomnêma) *regarding the engagement of his daughter*

[143] The copy of the memorandum[1] created by this same monk Michael Psellos (who was a *vestarchês* at that time[2]) assuming the persona of the *prôtoasekretis,* the *epi tôn kriseôn,* the *nomophylax,* and the *skribas,*[3] at his trial regarding the dissolution of the engagement of his son-in-law, Elpidios Kenchres.

    1. Byzantine courts produced a number of official documents. As opposed to a *sêmeioma,* which usually contained only a case's decision and rationale, a memorandum (*hypomnêma*) included the relevant facts, testimony and argumentation: see Oikonomides (1986) 177. Copies (*isa*) of these documents could be admitted as evidence if they were properly notarized and authenticated.

    2. Honorific titles were an important aspect of Byzantine court life and established the ceremonial precedence of its members. Titles (*axiômata*) should be distinguished from offices (*ophphikia*), whose holders performed actual administrative functions, though this distinction is often difficult to make in any given case and period. Psellos obtained the honorific title of *vestarchês* from the emperor Konstantinos Monomachos, most likely in 1054. This honor was superseded by that of *proedros,* which he obtained from the emperor Isaakios Komnenos in September 1057. See Gautier (1976) 95–97.

    3. The composition of this tribunal of judges suggests that the case was heard in the court of the Hippodrome (which met not in the great circus, but in the "covered" Hippodrome just west of the imperial palace). As opposed to the metropolitan and criminal courts of the *quaestor* and *eparchos,* the court of the Hippodrome was concerned primarily with matters of civil law. Among the judges assigned to this court, twelve judges under the leadership of the *droungarios tês viglas* were considered judges of the Velum. There is some question whether these judges made up an elite tribunal within the court or whether they were simply privileged members who sat behind a "velum" (or curtain). In any event, cases were tried by one or more judges depending on the content and prominence of the dispute, or more importantly, at the pleasure of the emperor, who referred cases directly

It is indeed wise and to some degree near to the Divine to foresee the future so that we experience it as present and make good use of our circumstances. [144] But being human and not possessing the knowledge of future events, we miscalculate and stumble into many unintentional situations. Often in ways we could have never imagined, the invisibility of the outcome overturns the certainty and precision of our intention. The circumstances of this case will make these introductory remarks clear.

The most pious monk Michael was a man of considerable learning, who had obtained from the emperor the honor of *vestarchês* and also the Consulship of Philosophy, this both from the emperor and on account of his own merit as well.[4] This man, then, cared a great deal for the good name of his adoptive daughter and transformed their relationship into a natural one, displaying the affection of a birth parent towards her. Since he had no other children, he was extremely generous with this child, not only providing well for her every present need but planning far ahead so that she might enjoy the best possible future. He did not wait for the time of puberty when marriages and sexual relations are legally contracted, but when she was still a child and not yet old enough to marry, he betrothed her to Elpidios, the son of the *prôtospatharios*[5] Ioannes Kenchres, a boy who had just passed the age of puberty and was twice the age of his fiancée.[6] This sort of engagement was and still is practiced by many oth-

---

to it, often at the request of the Imperial Chancery. The judges listed here, in the order of their honorary precedence, suggest such an instance, since the tribunal was both directly commanded by the empress Theodora and included the *prôtoasekretis,* the head of the Imperial Chancery (judges not directly connected to the court of the Hippodrome often took part in its proceedings). The *epi tôn kriseôn,* the judge who heard provincial appeals, and the *nomophylax,* who presided over legal education, were both high judicial officials and undoubtedly members of the Velum. The office of *skribas* was originally attached to the *quaestor,* but by the eleventh century its duties had extended to the court of the Hippodrome. See Simon (1973) 7–8; Oikonomides (1972) 322–323; and idem (1976) 133–135.

4. For the office of "Consul of the Philosophers," see the brief biography of Psellos in the introduction. The use of the present infinitive to express the holding of this office (*to de philosophian hypateuein*) suggests that Psellos was still the Consul of Philosophers at the time that this memorandum was drawn up (the present infinitive carries the sense of duration, of an action that is going on or repeated, as opposed to the aorist, which expresses simple occurrence).

5. An honorific title of significant status at the court. By the eleventh century it bore few if any actual administrative duties.

6. Psellos' adopted daughter was probably nine years old when she was betrothed and eleven and a half when the engagement was dissolved. Elpidios, twice her age, would

ers, and the law permits it and [145] sanctions the agreement of the two parties. Since none of us knows how long we will live and whether we will be alive when our children mature, it soon dawns on us to take heed of this natural fact and to arrange their marriages in advance. In the case of the *vestarchês* something else was of concern. Since he was close to the emperor who was reigning at the time, Konstantinos Monomachos, and was a leading member of the Senate, he decided that he should provide for his daughter when he possessed what many call good fortune, lest, should his luck change, he fall on hard times and regret his negligence. Being a man of intelligence, he was well aware that human affairs are not static and that what appears to be stable is really in motion and evolving, which is something many do not realize. Just as the helmsman should grab the rudder before his ship completely overturns, so too should a responsible man arrange his affairs to his apparent advantage. Such a man should be defended for doing so and acquitted of any guilt.

Therefore, after turning down many who held offices and not a few whose families were of ancient and noble lineage, he betrothed his adoptive daughter to Elpidios and straight off, as they say,[7] began to make arrangements on his behalf. First, he enrolled him among the *prôtospatharioi* and, then, among the lower imperial notaries of the bureau at the Church of the Antiphonetes;[8] finally, he went so far as to have him admitted among the judges of the Hippodrome. The office of *prôtospatharios* was accounted as part of Elpidios' dowry, but the other offices [146] were considered tokens of the *vestarchês'* generosity. Having promised his daughter a dowry of fifty pounds, he distributed the amount in the following way: ten pounds in minted gold coins, twenty in various kinds of goods, and the remaining twenty in the office of *prôtospatharios.*[9] Before he received these gifts, Elpidios drew a salary of twelve *nomismata* as a

then have been eighteen at the time of the betrothal, or just past the age of puberty (*ephêbos*), which the Byzantines considered to last from the age of fourteen to seventeen for boys. Children could be betrothed as young as seven years old, but they could not marry (or have sexual relations) until puberty (twelve years old for girls, fourteen for boys). See Guilland (1960) 1–2, 22–26.

7. The works of Psellos are sprinkled with common proverbs and sayings, as he made good use of the several alphabetical compilations that circulated in Byzantium. One of these collections is even attributed to him. For this expression, see *Corpus paroemiographorum graecorum*, vol. 2:145,18.

8. For the location and history of the Church of the Antiphonetes, see Janin (1969) 522.

9. Although the legitimacy of a dowry presupposed marriage, by this period the fiancé often came into its full possession at the time of the engagement contract.

spatharios, but the *vestarchês* now multiplied that amount by adding to it another sixty.[10]

Nevertheless, the *vestarchês* should not have immediately decorated him with external ornaments nor adorned him with jewelry, but instead he should have demonstrated his affection for him by starting, as they say, from the foundation of the temple of his soul, first laying down the keel before attaching the ribs on either side. I don't know why, but he began with the body instead of the soul, making what should have come first come second. Elpidios, enthralled by exterior brilliance and in love with the beauty of superficial splendor, shut his eyes to the light of learning. The *vestarchês* labored to cultivate his soul, but Elpidios labored hard not to accept what was given to him. The former gave him the opportunity to read books and develop his mind, but what the latter demanded instead was a good horse, and he spent his time with mimes and charioteers. Each of them strove against the other, the one so that the other might become good, the other so that he might become good for nothing. And so they struggled with one another on account of their different values and habits. The clash of their battle was brilliant, but the victory of Elpidios was even more brilliant, and he left the field crowned by his complete ignorance, having bested every influence of the *vestarchês.*

[**147**] These things grieved the *vestarchês;* how could they not? Nevertheless, although he often cursed the suitor with the vilest of oaths, he did not immediately demand the dissolution of the engagement, making an allowance for the future and still hoping for a change in his character. But when even time could not change Elpidios, but only deepened his willful rejection of learning, making him even more keen and vehement for a life diametrically opposed to it, it became despairingly clear to the *vestarchês* that his attempts to lead him in the other direction should be abandoned. In the meantime, he continued to try to rein him in, urging him to stay away from buffoons and mimes and to converse

10. The sale of honorific titles was common in Byzantium and was a significant source of revenue for the imperial treasury. The initial cost of each title was determined by (1) a set asking price relative to the status of the title, (2) an additional sum that allowed the buyer to draw a salary (*roga*) at a set rate of return, and (3) any additional amount that returned an "augmented" salary at more than twice the normal rate. In this particular instance, the initial "investment" in the office of *prôtospatharios* (20 pounds) returned an overall salary of 60 *nomismata,* or about a 4% return (there were 72 *nomismata* to a pound). Since the salaries of different titles could be accumulated, Elpidios now drew an annual salary of 72 *nomismata* (12 as a *spatharios* plus 60 as a *prôtospatharios*). See Lemerle (1967); Guilland (1960) 26–32.

with intelligent men, from whom he might glean a little dignity. But Elpidios closed his ears to these admonitions as well and instead did only what his heart desired. In spite of this, the *vestarchês* did not repay him with malice nor try to seek revenge; he continued to promote him with honors and make him more prestigious in hope that he might subsequently embrace a better life. He first petitioned the emperor and acquired for him a judgeship at the Velum; then he honored him with the office of *thesmographos,* and, after that, of *mystographos,* and finally had him promoted to an *exaktôr.*[11] In truth he was unequal to these honors and an unsuitable choice, but his attitude remained the same and never fell out of tune with itself.

Not a short time later the *vestarchês* was seized by an illness that brought him to the brink of death. He immediately became mindful of his conversion and fled to the life he had long ago chosen.[12] Disdaining the emperor's alternating threats and appeasements, as well as his own family's needs and accustomed life, [**148**] he divested himself of his secular tunic along with his worldly life in exchange for the monastic cloak and the ascetic life. When he had somewhat recovered from his illness, the emperor offered to grant him whatever he wanted. The *vestarchês* requested only one thing: that Elpidios be promoted to the rank of *patrikios.*[13] The emperor reluctantly granted this wish thanks to the persistent urging of our empress and queen.[14] After the promotion took place,

11. The offices of *thesmographos, mystographos,* and *exaktôr* were associated with a judicial career. Since judges often assumed administrative and financial responsibilities in addition to their legal activities, judicial experience did much to promote a bureaucratic career. See Oikonomides (1972) 323–326; Magdalino (1994).

12. Among the many autobiographical digressions in Psellos' famous history, the *Chronographia,* few are more detailed than his explanation of this episode. However, the account of the events leading to his monastic conversion that we read there (6.191–200) differs in a critical way from the one we read here: in the *Chronographia,* Psellos admits that the "illness that brought him to the brink of death" was actually feigned and that his flight to the monastery was not so much the result of religious conviction as of fear of the emperor's unpredictability.

13. In his account in the *Chronographia,* Psellos makes no mention of requesting the rank of *patrikios* for Elpidios. However, he does perhaps allude to it, saying that the emperor promised him a great future upon his recovery.

14. The empress Theodora ruled with her sister Zoe for three months in 1042 before the ascension of Monomachos. At the time of Psellos' conversion (sometime during 1054), she was effectively retired though obviously still of some influence. She managed to assume the throne again on Monomachos' death in January 1055 and reigned until her own death on August 31, 1056.

the *vestarchês* set off immediately for the holy mountain of Olympos,[15] intending to join the ascetics who lived there and take up some of the vows of the ascetic life. After drawing as much as he could from this fount, he again returned to the city in order to visit his own people and to settle a few minor affairs so that he could spend the rest of his life without cares.

Then an Iliad of evils descended upon him.[16] Having seized the authority to do whatever he wanted with his life, Elpidios no longer merely stumbled towards a character completely at odds with virtue; he was now running headlong after it. He talked to his fiancée about as much as he conversed with philosophy and literature. The *vestarchês,* at a loss about what to do, abandoned options that were near at hand and fled to the chief and ultimate anchor, I mean the empress of the Romans, the ruler of almost the entire world. He submitted to her a petition, which did not instruct her as much as remind her [**149**] how much he had originally given to Elpidios; how, after she had later assumed the throne and given these gifts to him a second time, he had again passed them on to Elpidios;[17] how the *vestarchês* had arranged all of this for him but had received the very opposite in return, enmity and disobedience to himself and hatred for his daughter; how Elpidios was unwilling to heed his wishes; how he carelessly tossed books aside and chose instead of these a life among the most shameful characters; and, finally, how he had disowned Elpidios and broken off the engagement. Concerning the honors Elpidios had received, the petition stated that the *vestarchês* did not want them returned to him now that the contract was dissolved, since, as has already been mentioned, they had already been bestowed twice. But if he ever extended the offer of marriage to another, he would be grateful if the best of these[18] were granted to him again; but if not, he would still be content.[19]

15. Mount Olympos in Bithynia (modern Ulu Dağ, just southeast of Bursa, Turkey) was an important center of Byzantine monasticism, the home of some fifty monasteries.

16. Another well-known proverb: see *Corpus paroemiographorum graecorum,* vol. 1:96,43.

17. Honorific titles were entirely dependent on the will of the emperor. The titles that Psellos acquired for Elpidios were the gifts of Konstantinos Monomachos; when Theodora assumed the throne, Psellos was no doubt quick to have them reconfirmed by the new ruler.

18. I.e., the title of *patrikios.*

19. While honorific titles were in theory nontransferable, exceptional "substitutions" were made at the whim of the emperor. That Psellos would ask that the rank of *patrikios,* one of Byzantium's highest honors, be held for him indefinitely for an unknown future recipient is probably evidence of both his ambition and the extent to which these exceptional substitutions were made.

When the most sympathetic soul heard this petition, since she was well aware both of the *vestarchês'* situation and that these honors had been granted to him many years ago and then confirmed again by her, she was immediately moved by compassion and reached an absolute decision that the belt[20] should be removed from Elpidios. This decision was absolutely binding and recorded, possessing the force of law in itself and liable to no retrial or appeal. Nevertheless, it was entrusted to us, not to reach a second decision concerning the issues on which the empress had already judged and proclaimed, but to arbitrate the conditions of the dissolution of the engagement.

Therefore, charged with holding such [**150**] a trial and gathered together for this purpose, we summoned the parties for judgment. They were led in, on the one hand, the monk and *vestarchês* Michael, and on the other, the former *patrikios* Elpidios represented by the *spatharios* Ioannes Kordakas.[21] When the *vestarchês* was asked why he dissolved the engagement, he appeared distressed that he was now compelled to make public in a court of law the extent of his complaint. Nevertheless, he began at the beginning and described in the time he was allotted all that he had done for Elpidios on every occasion that he was able and what he had then received in return (which our report has already mentioned above). He included in his testimony descriptions of his malicious character, his inattention to and hatred for learning, the unseemliness of his conduct, his unwillingness to obey him, his refusal to live like someone of senatorial rank, preferring instead to embrace the company of mimes and to associate with fools, his refusal to heed as he should the *vestarchês'* admonitions and criticisms, the vehemence and harshness of his opinions, his stubbornness about everything that he said and did, his hatred for his fiancée, and his opposition to the very man on whose account he had received such wealth and honor. He not only stated these things himself, but he also brought forth witnesses who were obviously trustworthy and were believed on the spot: they were the consul and *epi tês katastaseôs* Theodoros Myralides, the *mystographos* Euphrosynos Xeritas, the *thesmographos* Gabriel Xeritas, and the [**151**] *thesmographos* and *exarchos* of the *vestiopratai* Michael.[22] The consul Theodoros

---

20. The title of *patrikios* was displayed by the wearing of a particular belt (*zônê*).

21. Psellos was apparently representing himself.

22. The office of *epi tês katastaseôs*, the master of ceremonies, was most likely charged with the order and execution of palace ceremonies (this is history's last mention of this title). The *exarchos* of the *vestiopratai* supervised the sale of garments.

Myralides testified about the harshness of his attitude, his hatred for the *vestarchês,* and his rejection of his fiancée. The two Xeritai also mentioned these things and added his refusal to live according to the *vestarchês'* directives and his preference for a lifestyle and embrace of a manner that were at odds with what the *vestarchês* would have chosen. The *thesmographos* Michael repeated what the other witnesses had said and pointed out in addition his ungratefulness towards the *vestarchês,* his shamelessness and stubbornness, and his complete unwillingness to obey his benefactor.

This testimony was consistent with what the *vestarchês* had charged in his written petition to our great empress and proved the trustworthiness of his account presented to her, in response to which that marvelous soul, in her imperial wisdom, reached that marvelous decision, casting Elpidios as a living statue of maliciousness. But a few details in the dissolution of the engagement remained if the letter of the law was to be followed. The judges directed the *vestarchês* to do one of two things: he should either produce additional evidence, if he had any, that might support a dissolution without penalty to himself, or he should pay the penalty and settle the complaint if he did not wish to maintain the engagement.[23] The *vestarchês* then fell silent for a while and appeared to be considering his decision. He finally responded by saying, "O laws and judges and all of you here present, [152] I would never shame these gray hairs"—as he pointed to them—"nor impose an alien character on my previous way of life, nor for the sake of 15 pounds of gold[24] defend forbidden courses of action. In the first place, I will feel ashamed to describe such infamous and reprehensible conduct, and then I will also become a scandal to many others and reveal actions that should remain secret. This is something I would never do, as you are my witnesses. Therefore, I will gladly pay the penalty and incur a loss so that many others are not insulted and harmed."

At this point, the entire court fell silent, and the parties rested their cases. What was the use of more or even conflicting testimony if he agreed to pay the penalty? Indeed, the contract of engagement was drawn up for this reason alone, and the law supports this action, and the action is in agreement with the

23. An engagement could be dissolved by the simple desire of one of the parties. Nevertheless, the written contract of the engagement often included a penalty (*prostimon*) that discouraged such dissolution. Although there were legitimate causes for breaking an engagement without liability for this penalty, the judges apparently felt that, in spite of the testimony they had already heard, Elpidios' conduct did not qualify as one.

24. The amount of the penalty agreed upon in the engagement contract.

law. Furthermore, the testimony and the paying of the penalty both strongly corroborated one another: the testimony argued for the paying of the penalty, and the paying of the penalty required the testimony of witnesses. So the bond of engagement was broken. May the *vestarchês* enjoy his honor, since for its sake he paid the penalty and saved both of their reputations. This part of the case was therefore settled. But while the *vestarchês* agreed to pay the penalty, he presented an additional complication regarding the dowry of his adopted daughter. He said that Elpidios still owed him twenty of the dowry's fifty pounds [153] since Elpidios had retained the office of *prôtospatharios*, which had been given to him in lieu of twenty pounds, as the engagement contract specifies. When he submitted his written petition regarding Elpidios to the empress, he argued that he should be stripped of his other offices but allowed to retain the *protospathariate*, which, he said, was given to him as a portion of the dowry.[25] We have reviewed this petition and indeed it so stipulates. The writ of confirmation regarding his demotion, which was filed with the Bureau of the Imperial Treasury,[26] mandated that Elpidios be enrolled among the *prôtospatharioi*, a condition that the *vestarchês* says he requested. Furthermore, the answer to his petition begins with the words, "Your request will be granted." It is implied that the dowry would be preserved at fifty pounds without removing the office of *prôtospatharios* from Elpidios, an action not of compassion but in order that the dowry of his daughter might not be diminished. For if she allowed Elpidios to keep his many gifts, she would be robbed of what the *vestarchês* had given to him on her account, and while he was the cause of his own demotion, she would be cut off from her dowry and condemned to both disgrace and poverty.

When Elpidios began to contest this claim and to reject the honor of the *protospathariate,* he seemed to be ashamed to be saying this, since he knew how far he had fallen. Nevertheless, this meant no harm to the *vestarchês.* For if [154] Elpidios rejects the office, let him exchange it for another if he can; if he cannot, what would the *vestarchês* care when he is still owed twenty pounds for the cost of it as their initial agreement makes clear? But why are we debating

---

25. In all likelihood, Psellos was adamant that Elpidios retain the office of *prôtospatharios* because he wanted to make sure that there was no confusion about Elpidios' liability for its portion of the dowry (20 pounds).

26. *Sekreton tou idikou.* Since the imperial treasury was responsible for the accounting and payment of court salaries, it was important that it be notified about any decision that might affect these. Although Elpidios retained the rank of *prôtospatharios,* he was apparently stripped of his rank as *spatharios,* which drew a salary of 12 *nomismata.*

this issue anyway? There is no need to discuss it any further since our great empress has somehow already decided this and all other points as well. For just as he argued in court, in his written petition the *vestarchês* preferred that Elpidios retain the *protospathariate,* but since the office was part of the dowry, he should be liable for its cost. The empress accepted this argument and rendered her decision, recording in the writ that was sent to the Treasury the reason why Elpidios should retain the *protospathariate.* Since a verdict has already been reached in this matter as well, and both the dignity of the judge and the laws confirm it, we decree that the *vestarchês* owes Elpidios the penalty of fifteen pounds and that Elpidios owes the *vestarchês* twenty in recompense for the office of *prôtospatharios.* These amounts will be credited against each other, the penalty against the cost of the *protospathariate* in the case of Elpidios, and the cost of the *protospathariate* against the penalty in the case of the *vestarchês.* The required compensation will be paid to both parties. But since the amounts of the penalty and the *protospathariate* are unequal, the former being [155] fifteen pounds, the latter twenty, as their initial agreement makes clear, Elpidios should pay the *vestarchês* the difference of five pounds so that the recompense might be equal. The court then appended a compassionate clause on behalf of Elpidios, releasing him from the obligation to pay the five pounds on condition that he not seek to claim double the amount of his *arrha sponsalicia* (whatever that amount might be), which he said that he had given to his fiancée at the time of their initial agreement.[27]

The present memorandum was issued in order that the decision reached by our holy mistress and empress and confirmed and proclaimed by us might be made public, the month of August, of the ninth indiction, 6564.[28] Lord Jesus Christ, remember the soul of your servant.

27. In addition to the penalty for breaking the engagement (*prostimon*), the *arrha sponsalicia* also served to discourage dissolution. Paid as earnest money to his future bride, Elpidios could legally claim twice the amount if she broke the engagement without good cause (she simply kept it if he broke the engagement). Although the amount of the *arrha* is not mentioned here, we can assume that the "compassionate" forgiving of the five-pound difference meant that it was not more than half of that.

28. I.e., 1056 A.D. The Byzantines counted time from the date of the world's creation, which they calculated to have occurred 5508 years B.C. The indiction refers to the fifteen-year cycle of tax assessment that was established by the emperor Constantine I in 312 and used as a chronological indicator throughout the Byzantine period. The year 1056 falls on the ninth year of this cycle (subtract 312 from 1056 and then divide by 15; the remainder, in this case 9, is the indiction).

To his grandson, who was still an infant

Introduction

The following piece needs little by way of introduction. It is one of the sweetest works of literature to survive from antiquity and the Middle Ages, rivaling in that respect the meeting of Hektor, Andromache, and Astyanax in Book 6 of the *Iliad*. If the latter is superior in nuance, majesty, and tragedy, it falls short in observed personal detail and affect. In the last line, Psellos admits that he composed it while holding his infant grandson in his arms. He senses his own death drawing near (152, lines 2–3) and wishes to leave behind a memorial to his grandson, by which the latter may know "what skills your grandfather had in life and how proficient he was in the use of language" (lines 14–15). Hence it is written in the past tense: his grandson is meant to read it many years later in order to learn about his own infancy. To my knowledge, this is an exercise without precedent and therefore an additional tribute to Psellos' literary imagination. It is also a superb example of what we may call his "humanism," namely his willingness to explore all the facets of human life, especially emotional ones, without subsuming them under the strictures of theoretical philosophy or of doctrine. The virtues hardly appear here, in what is one of the most beautiful records of the sheer delight taken by a grandfather in the babyish behavior of a grandchild.[1]

The child in question was male and still under four months old when this piece was composed (153, line 53). Apart from Styliane, who died before having any children, and an adopted daughter who was betrothed to Elpidios Kenchres, Psellos probably had no other children (see above, p. 13). We may therefore

---

1. For a brief literary appraisal, see Beck (1978) 115–116.

tentatively assume that his adopted daughter was the mother in this case. Perhaps there are hints of this in the text. In the first line Psellos addresses him as "the grandchild of my soul," which suggests that there was no biological relation. On 153, lines 49–51, he claims to be able to detect qualities in the child that his mother also had. But if the relation had been biological, he would have made comparisons to himself, his own mother, or others of his ancestors. In fact, he strictly avoids making comparisons between himself and the addressee, which grandfathers are generally highly prone to do. In *Letter S 72*, announcing the birth of this child to the Kaisar Ioannes Doukas, Psellos confesses that the midwives were only trying to please him by saying that the child was just like him in appearance, but he could see through this pleasing lie.

Ioannes Doukas was probably made kaisar shortly after the accession to the throne of his brother Konstantinos X in late 1059 and would have been referred to by that title by Psellos at any time thereafter, regardless of his political fortunes.[2] Which empress, then, sponsored the child's baptism? (154, line 90–91) The candidates are Eudokia Makrembolitissa, wife of Konstantinos X Doukas (1059–1067) as well as of his successor Romanos IV Diogenes (1067–1071), and Maria of "Alania" (actually of Georgia), the wife of Konstantinos X's son Michael VII Doukas (1071–1078) and then subsequently of Nikephoros III Botaneiates (1078–1081). The reign of Romanos should probably be excluded, for at the end of *Letter S 72* in which he announces the birth to Ioannes Doukas, Psellos adds that he has also sent word of the event to the emperor, which can only be one of the Doukas emperors, not the hostile Romanos, who had removed Ioannes from public life. In the 1060s Psellos was in his forties and, as far as we know, untroubled by illness and could probably expect and even hope to live until sixty at least (especially as he was a philosopher).[3] Therefore, at first sight a date in the mid-1070s, when he was in his mid-fifties, makes his pessimism about ever seeing his grandson reach adolescence more plausible (152, line 2).[4] But not all dates in the 1070s will do. It is likely that Psellos had either died or entirely lost favor at the court by 1076. We should not insist on this too much. Yet in *Letter S 157*, which he wrote to his friend, the *epi tôn kriseôn* Konstantinos (nephew of the former patriarch Keroularios), to congratulate him

---

2. See Polemis (1968) 35.
3. Talbot (1984) 267–270.
4. This date is preferred by Leroy-Molinghen (1969b) 292–295.

on the birth of a son, Psellos speaks in the past tense of the delight that he took in the children of the *vestarchês,* who is almost certainly his son-in-law (for a translation, see p. 174; for the latter's identity, see p. 15). Konstantinos attained the rank of *epi tôn kriseôn* after 1074 (see p. 14), and we must place the birth of the youngest of the *vestarchês'* children at least two years prior to Psellos' letter. Therefore, if the empress was Maria of Alania, Psellos' grandson must have been born between late 1071 (the elevation of Michael VII) and 1073 at the latest. Besides, for the winter of 1073–1074 Ioannes Doukas was out of favor and for most of 1074 he was away from the capital and in serious trouble, having been captured by the renegade mercenary Roussel de Bailleul in Asia Minor and forced by the latter to proclaim himself emperor against his own nephew Michael VII.[5]

On the other hand, in the early 1070s Psellos' adopted daughter would have been about thirty, a late age to be giving birth to grandchildren by Byzantine standards. A date in the 1060s seems more likely on these grounds, and perhaps we should not insist too much on Psellos' pessimism about seeing his grandson reach adolescence. After all, in the *hypomnêma* regarding the engagement of his daughter, an affair of the mid-1050s, Psellos likewise claims that he had betrothed her in fear that he would die before it could be done properly (145). Moreover, Eva de Vries-van der Velden has recently argued with some plausibility that Psellos' son-in-law was a certain Basileios Maleses, who was already married to Psellos' daughter by the early 1060s.[6] This identification makes a birthdate for his son unlikely for the years 1071–1073. As we know from the *History* of his friend Michael Attaleiates, Maleses was captured by the Seljuks along with the emperor Romanos IV after the battle of Mantzikert in 1071 (167) and held for at least two years (187). No sooner was he released than he was captured again in 1074 by Roussel (187–188) in the company of Ioannes Doukas, though Roussel honored him and treated him as a trusted advisor. Attaleiates claims that instead of pitying Maleses as a prisoner, Michael VII confiscated his property and stripped him of his children (188; it is unclear what this means exactly). But to which period of captivity does this refer? De Vries-van der Velden assumes that it was the first, by the Seljuks, but cannot explain

<hr>

5. Polemis (1968) 37–39.

6. De Vries-van der Velden (1996a). In my view, however (*pace* ibid. 118–119), the reference to Sabbaïtes does not by itself fix the date to the reign of Isaakios Komnenos (1057–1059).

the emperor's action.[7] Attaleiates' text is in fact ambiguous. It is more likely that Michael VII sought to punish Maleses for taking up with Roussel and for being close to the now disgraced Kaisar Ioannes. Maleses' standing in the rebel's camp would have been noted by the many embassies sent by the emperor at that time (187). This would have led to the punishment, which, in turn, would have embittered Maleses against the "tyranny of Michael," especially if, as his friend Attaleiates states, he was trying to advocate peace in the whole affair (188). When Roussel was finally defeated and captured, Michael exiled Maleses (who is not heard from again) and confirmed the confiscation of his property (192). It is, in addition, unlikely that a man whose property had been seized and children disgraced would have then been sent out on an expedition with Ioannes Doukas against a rebel in Asia Minor. So the disgrace occurred in 1074.

In fact, this explanation is required by the postulated identification of Maleses with the father of Psellos' grandson. In 1071, Psellos was very influential at the court and could have prevented, if not necessarily the humiliation of Maleses (perhaps the two did not get along), at least that of his beloved grandchildren. But by 1074 Psellos was losing ground, as was his and Maleses' friend and patron the Kaisar Ioannes. The attack on Maleses may then have been part of a broader attack against Psellos and the kaisar by the emperor Michael and his eunuch Nikephoros. It is in this context, then, that we should perhaps place Psellos' *Letter KD* 268, which expresses a great concern over the fate of the "children of the *vestarchês*." In his account of the events in question, Attaleiates consistently calls Maleses a *prôtovestês*.

To conclude, when was Psellos' grandson born? We are constrained here by the letter written on his behalf in 1093–1094 by Theophylaktos, the archbishop of Bulgaria and possibly a former student of Psellos himself (see above, p. 16, and below, p. 168). Theophylaktos calls him a young man (*neanias*), which means that, if a date in the early 1070s is precluded for the reasons discussed above, we should opt for a date late in the reign of Konstantinos X, perhaps 1066, making Psellos' grandson about twenty-six when he came to the archbishop's attention.

Editions and translations.   For a list of manuscripts and all studies referring to this text, see Moore (2005) 358. The text was first published by E. Kurtz and F. Drexl, *Michaelis Pselli scripta minora*, vol. 1: *Orationes et dissertationes* (Milan:

---

7. De Vries-van der Velden (1996a) 138.

Vita e pensiero, 1936) 77–81. It was reprinted with a French translation in Leroy-Molinghen (1969b) 306–315. A German translation appeared in Beck (1978) 321–323, which was in turn translated into Greek in Beck (1992) 435–437, though I have found both to be relatively unreliable and not entirely complete. The edition translated here is that of A. R. Littlewood, *Michaelis Pselli oratoria minora* (Leipzig: Teubner, 1985), with whose text I have taken issue only once (see n. 3). On p. xv, Littlewood lists the reviews of the original Kurtz and Drexl edition. The bold numbers in brackets correspond to the page numbers of the Littlewood edition.

To his grandson, who was still an infant

[**152**] Perhaps I will not live to see you, dearest newborn and offspring of my soul, when you reach adolescence, if God so wishes it, or when you mature; for the days of my life are failing and the time approaches when its thread will be cut short. I have therefore decided to address this speech to you in advance of that day and reciprocate your innate charm with the graces of speech. I should be ungrateful and entirely thoughtless if, at a time when your perceptions and thoughts are undeveloped (though as far as I alone am concerned you are perfect in these respects, insofar as you hear my voice and feel my affection, cling to my neck, slip into my embrace, and put up with my annoying kisses), I should be ungrateful, I say, if I myself failed to render to you a fitting return, given that I am wealthy in other respects but especially with regard to my fluency in speech.

Therefore, I offer this address to you as though it were an encomium, so that by reading my writing one day you may be able to know what skills your grandfather had in life and how proficient he was in the use of language. I shall praise you then, not by bringing in falsehoods from outside or inventing a good reputation for you, but merely by describing your disposition, which is such as I have never seen in another baby. Mind you, I am a terrific judge of character, if anyone is, and can see through the senses as though they were windows directly into the soul or, rather, to detect the qualities of your soul as they are settled on your brows and eyes.

Given that I have already mentioned these parts of your body, let me add that it could truly be seen right from the start that your eyes were kindly; not too rapid in motion nor slow and lethargic, which would have signified a dull disposition, but, rather, sometimes they were fixed as though lost in thought, at other times they moved [153] cheerfully, whenever a smile was about to come upon you. It sufficed for me to take note of this only once—I needed no Delphic tripod or bacchic ecstasy—to prophesy without hesitation from the kindly look in your eyes that you were about to laugh. And, true enough, you moved your lip slightly, blushed, and, behold! you laughed. Nor were your brows uninvolved in the meditation reflected in your eyes, but those too laid bare some aspect of your inner disposition by gently flexing and contributing their portion of prudence as well.

On the other hand, it was as though you were born not to cry: even when the sources of milk were blocked and the wet nurse deprived you of your customary drink, you did not break out in wailing nor thrash around convulsively; rather, it seemed as though you were contending with her and indicting her for injustice and hubris, especially whenever she looked at you with a stern face. In order to win over those watching you, the jurors as it were, you let a few tears roll down and by your utterances and looks caused the votes of the jury to incline in your direction. And as though you were then mollified, when the one who wronged you bared her breast again you swiftly changed back and regarded your tyrant more gently. With your lips then on the fountain, you drank, though not like one who guzzles greedily out of thirst, rather with moderation, and you immediately rewarded your nourisher with a friendly glance and a smile. And that which was contrary to your desire was for you a law chosen voluntarily; that which you had not thought out rationally had rational consequences. For most people the soul is born in a condition of irrationality, but for those in whom nature is settled by God in a more honorable way the spirit shines through this nature as through a lantern set upon a height, beaming its light far and wide. Something of this sort was foreseen by me, your grandfather, in your mother. It is nothing to marvel at if you have gleaned a portion of the nature of the one who bore you, like a stream issuing from the same source.

You see now why you were in other respects as well unlike most infants, but rather you were far more intelligent than others your age. Though you had not yet reached the fourth month of your life, the characters of those around you had already made a clear impression on your soul and you recognized each of us. It was as though you knew who paid you no attention and who cared deeply for you, and accordingly you responded with love or aversion. In my case alone did you make an exception to your rule[1] and regard me with affection

---

1. This phrase is possibly corrupt.

when I kissed you without restraint, crushed your lips with my rough touch, and embraced you too firmly; even when I rapped your right hand, you offered me your left, as though [154] you were obeying the Lord's commandment.[2] Perhaps you even knew that I struck you out of love, that I did not do so merely in order to do so, but in order to derive enjoyment from your natural grace in every way possible. And when I would see you becoming perplexed, I immediately snatched you away from your toys, took you up in my hands, and lifted you up in the air until you were full of joy.

And you detested, if any other baby ever did, being confined in swaddling clothes. When the wet nurse had expertly laved you in the basin and was about to bind you, straightening both of your arms along your sides and joining your feet together in a line, you immediately looked upset and cross. And then nothing else could give you joy, as though you were utterly unwilling to enjoy yourself in a prison. But as soon as your bonds were loosened and the swaddling bands removed, then you were up for anything! Your glance became more cheerful, your smile sweeter, and you moved your hands here and there, kicking your feet in every direction and, in your desire at least, took flight and soared through the air. You had quite a noble appreciation even of the pleasures of this world and, whenever your mother adorned your head or dressed you in a fancy outfit, you wriggled and turned in every direction, delighting in and preening yourself on account of your costume. The pleasures of the bath you did not accept as an infant would, but rather you loved them in a more rational way. I did not really want to bathe you myself, but in order that you, on the one hand, could delight in the bath while I, on the other, could delight in your grace and happiness, I often came to see you when you were bathed and became another baby with you as I leaned in close to your tub. You, in part because you were happy to see me, in part to get away from the water when it was a bit too hot, clutched at me in every way you could, wrapping yourself around me and clinging with all your might and, speaking in your baby talk, you said nothing that I could actually understand.

Moreover, your little body—may the evil eye never harm you!—was a thing so pleasant to hold in embrace and your limbs were so harmoniously arranged that you were truly a holy gift of nature. Your hair was curly and blond, your head had the perfect shape, you neck was nimble and free, and all the rest, lest I go on like this about every detail, was perfectly harmonized by nature.

2. Matthew 5:39.

May the rest of the days of your life be happy! But it is not in my power to make this certain. Yet the beginning, at any rate, was auspicious. The emperor and the empress quarreled over who would sponsor you, and the female sex won. And so you entered the palace and she hugged you adoringly; when she had finished, she took you up onto her neck and then, as though you were a load too heavy for her to bear, set you down upon the most soft and royal couch. Finally, she gave you back to your mother, giving as well the ornaments that she was wearing at that time.[3] In this way [155] was an imperial honor allotted to you, a lesser one than that deserved by your sex, but a greater one than by your age.

This, then, is the encomium that your grandfather wrote for you, incomplete to match your own incomplete state. But you, my living pearl, the ornament of my soul, when one day you will reach the age of reason and will realize what sort of man your grandfather was and what the first days of your life were like, take him as your model, steer your disposition toward moderation and honor your parents. Respect your teachers and professors and above all adorn your soul with reason and literary studies. After all, it was in this way that I too brought honor upon your mother and the family.[4] May you obtain all that you love, but especially education and good sense, which alone can elevate the soul to its proper beauty and which constitute understanding of the more profound things. I wrote all this for you while holding you in my arms and kissing you insatiably.

3. I prefer the ms. reading *kekosmêto* to G.C. Hansen's emendation *kekosmêso:* the ornaments that she, i.e., the empress, was wearing, not those that the baby was wearing, for why would the empress give them in that case?

4. Psellos may possibly be referring to his own mother here; the reference is ambiguous.

Letters regarding Psellos' family

Translated with introduction by Stratis Papaioannou

Introduction

The following six of Psellos' letters contain references to his immediate family. In *Letter S* 17, Psellos mentions in passing his affection and concern for his relatives, including some brothers not attested elsewhere. In *Letter S* 146, he informs the husband of his adopted daughter regarding her illness. *Letter KD* 233, a message of thanks for truffles received from a close friend includes a worried note about the same daughter's serious illness (or precarious condition in labor). In *Letter S* 72, Psellos announces with unabashed pride the birth of his grandson, while in *Letter S* 157 he describes in detail his passionate attachment to his grandchildren. Finally, in *Letter S* 177 Psellos expresses his distress about the illness of persons very close to him, probably his daughter Styliane.

The rhetoric of letter writing in Byzantium does not allow a clear portrait of Psellos' family members to emerge from these texts. Psellos focuses rather on himself, his passions and emotions (*pathê*), his nature (*physis*), and his character (*êthos*).[1] This rhetoric is moreover difficult to translate, as it is a mixture of obscurity, formality, and ambiguity. Obscurity was an accepted aspect of the genre: letters were expected to be allusive rather than informative of events,

---

1. For attempts at deciphering specific persons, details, and dates, see Ljubarskij (1978); Volk (1990); and de Vries-van der Velden (1996a) and (1996b). For an evaluation of Psellos' epistolographic *personae,* see Papaioannou (2000) and (2003). On the manuscript tradition of Psellos' letter collection, see idem (1998).

situations, and contexts. Formality was regulated by what Psellos calls the *charaktêr* or "expression"—the style and character—of friendship. Forms of address, demonstrations of loyalty and affection, praise, complaint, exaggeration, and playfulness shaped this formality. Lastly, ambiguity is a result of Psellos' usage of terms that have both rhetorical and philosophical meaning, terms that could describe both modes of being and modes of discourse. *Pathos*, for instance, means passion and passivity as well as emotion elicited by or present in discourse; *êthos* indicates moral comportment as well as a constructed image of self, while *charaktêr* denotes both personality and personal style. I have opted to translate these terms with a single word in English with the exception of *pathos*, which I have simply transliterated (or rendered as "affection"). I have also changed Psellos' frequent "we" to "I," as Psellos' formality accentuates rather than conceals the *I* that speaks.

Following Psellos' letters are two written by his student Theophylaktos, the archbishop of Ochrid (ca. 1050 to ca. 1108). These two letters, which pursue the same rhetorical strategies as those of Psellos, are translated here since they partly reveal the impact of Psellos' death on his family and friends as well as the fortunes of his surviving relatives.[2]

Editions and translations. Psellos' letters have so far been published in two large and many smaller (and scattered) collections. A new comprehensive edition is currently being prepared by E. Papaioannou: see idem (1998). The letters translated here are taken from the two major collections (by K. Sathas, and E. Kurtz and F. Drexl), and their publication details are given under *Letters S* and *Letters KD* in the bibliography. For a complete listing of the editions, translations, and discussions of Psellos' letters, see Moore (2005) 17–148.

---

2. On Theophylaktos' letters, see Mullett (1997) 48–49, 136, 143, 303, and 363.

Letters regarding Psellos' family

[256] For me, my eminent lord and brother,[1] philosophy is divided into two parts: the one, of which the mind alone receives images, appears to be dispassionate and implacable, while the other is compassionate to others and loving. Of these two parts, I praise the former yet I am not devoted to it; it is the latter which I admire less but which I pursue more. For this reason, I nursed parents in their old age, I was affectionate to brothers,[2] and I pay back what is appropriate to friends.

Thus since so-and-so is among those whom I cherish most, I consent often to his requests and I am carried about wherever he might wish to lead me. Although I could resist and fight back, I do the opposite because of my attachment to him. Thus, do not wonder that, although I am a friend, I often tire you with my requests about him. But know that philosophy does not disown even this portion. Now if you demand from me the highest, you will not obtain it, since [257] I have not even achieved the *detached* mode of life.[3] But if you are looking for the more sympathetic and, as it were, more benevolent portion, you will find it in abundance in me. I am moved by it and I also move my

1. Here "brother" is a term of friendship rather than kinship. On forms of address in Byzantium, see Grünbart (2000).
2. Here "brothers" might refer to biological brothers, close friends, or (most likely, in my opinion) relatives.
3. This word belongs to Psellos' Neoplatonic vocabulary; cf. Proklos, *Commentary on the* Kratylos 129 (Pasquali 77).

friends toward it. And who is such a friend to me as you are? What kind of man you are, I have often observed exactly for myself, to say it all in a word.

So this is the request and the matter that gave rise to it is the one for which the people from the first requester were sent to you. And I believe you will complete the requests of both as well as the mission in the most appropriate manner.

Letter S 146; date: unknown

[394] You wonder, my most honored brother,[4] why I honor you and retain the appropriate attitude toward you. How is this strange? If I retain unsullied the expression of friendship toward anyone I chance upon or people whom I met just once, how could I not preserve that form especially with you, whom I have placed as the first among the first of my friends, whom I then adopted into a spiritual relationship, upon whom I conferred the honor of becoming a member of my family, and (I should say) by whom I received honor in return? I am lying neither with respect to the promises to friends, nor about the familial, both bodily and spiritual, relationship. And if I had a power equivalent to my intentions I would show you what kind of a friend and relative I am. Circumstance, however, allows me neither to take pride in nor to carry out something worthy of praise and narration.

Thus with regard to what pertains to me, I have loved you in a pure way, I will love you even more sincerely, and I will care about you and about what is yours [395] by visiting or consoling and by neglecting nothing of what is beneficial. For, O most beautiful soul, the *magistrissa* is also worthy of being consoled and visited by me.[5] And she is a precise image of your noblest soul; for equally with you she honors and, so to speak, respects me.

Yet know also this. This admirable woman has received two blows. First, she fell terribly ill, with extreme pains in her side; then, she was wounded more terribly by the rumor that has been fabricated about you. If I was not there myself to console and counterfabricate, her soul would have fled to Hades. However, now she has recovered slightly.

---

4. Here the term is addressed to Psellos' son-in-law.

5. Psellos' son-in-law was a *magistros,* a high-ranking official (cf. *Letter KD* 70) and, as the end of the letter suggests, a judge.

As for your matters, I advise you as much: neither become more merciless in your verdicts, nor excuse entirely the accusers; for the former is irksome and the latter does not befit the rank of a judge. As for cases, choose to judge those that will be profitable to the locals.

I do not know exactly how you might accomplish things, but I fill the imperial ears with narratives about you such as the above. As for your succession, I honestly cannot give you any clear indications; for I see that the emperor is prepared for it in the same way for all the judges of the themes, yet he immediately holds back whenever someone, at the appropriate moment, keeps him back.

Letter KD 233; date: after 1059[6]
To the same (i.e., Ioannes Doukas[7])

[**281**] Do you not know, O Kaisar of transcending nature, that the truffle is an imperfect offspring of earth, a sort of aborted freak? For its mother does not give birth to it nor does she bring it to light in labor pains. It is rather those who are experts in the extraction of this marvelous offspring who, whenever they see earth's womb swollen, rend (if one must call it that) her inner parts in pieces and extract the truffle. Therefore, it is shapeless and lacks exterior beauty. Yet its mother, consoling its shapelessness, has placed in it an inexpressible pleasure, just as God implanted an orderly mind in the leader of the Athenians, Perikles, a man wise and of great nature, but born with an elongated head.[8] Aristotle too had a faltering tongue, Plato was round-shouldered, and Alexander, the famous Makedonian, had a crooked [**282**] neck.[9] For those who have a beautiful exterior are deficient on the inside, yet what those with a base covering conceal is marvelous. A thorn is set even before the rose and the cypress is fruitless. Such is the truffle as well; its appearance is shapeless, but what is hidden inside is nutritious.

---

6. Volk (1990) 24 and 328–333 relates this letter to the birth of Psellos' grandson, which he dates to 1072–1073; but see p. 159 above. Ioannes Doukas became kaisar after his brother Konstantinos became emperor in 1059.

7. On Ioannes Doukas, see D. Polemis (1968) 34–41; Ljubarskij (1973).

8. Cf. Plutarch, *Perikles* 3.3.

9. Cf. Plutarch, *How one can distinguish the flatterer from the friend* 9 (= *Moralia* 53c); see also *How the young should listen to poetry* 8 (= *Moralia* 26a–b) for Plato and Aristotle.

Still, your soul alone should be excepted from this argument or, rather, your mixture of body and soul; for the exterior of your body is truly marvelous and heroic, and the nature of your soul is full of intelligence and charm. Well, I have forgotten my misfortunes because of your good qualities; for my daughter is lying at her last gasp—or, rather now, after your gifts, she has been brought back to life. And while she is half-breathing, I am, O sacred one, breathless, re-covering and kept alive only by your nod and breath.[10]

Letter S 72; date: 1063–1065?[11]
To the same (i.e., Ioannes Doukas)

[307] Rejoice with me, greatest Kaisar. Rather, lead the joy, for another Psellos, rivaling me, his prototype, is born for you. For this is how those surrounding the mother persuade me to speak—perhaps lying yet speaking according to my desire. Indeed, did I even wait to see the newborn baby? No, O sacred one. I both embraced him and filled him with kisses and I almost stained my lips with blood, as if I had clasped a bravest warrior made red by blood returning from battle.[12]

As I profess philosophy, I should not be acquainted with precisely these things: what the womb is, what birth or a newborn child are. I should, rather, be attached only to the 'golden chain' of heaven.[13] But I do have, with regard to learning, perhaps a more masculine disposition, yet with regard to nature I am feminine. When my little daughter began to have her labor pains and someone surprised me by saying that [308] fierce pains were rendering the labor im-minent, I all but died on the spot. I was spinning and circling the bedchamber where she was in labor, and I was hanging upon her cries. But as soon as the infant emerged from the maternal womb, I forgot those pains. For I am not a Skythian in my soul, neither 'of oak nor of stone' was I born,[14] but I am a sprout of the delicate nature and I am softened by the natural affections.

---

10. According to the three mss. in which it survives, the letter ends here (Parisinus gr. 1182, f. 254v; Vaticanus gr. 483, ff. 60r–v, thirteenth-fourteenth centuries; and Laurentia-nus gr. 57–40, ff. 49r–v, fifteenth century). Kurtz and Drexl edit as part of *Letter* 233 (pp. 282.16–284.5) a text which is clearly a separate letter and survives only in the Paris ms.

11. So de Vries-van der Velden (1996a); Volk (1990) 328 ff. proposes 1072–1073.

12. Homer, *Iliad* 6.267–68 and 16.155 ff.

13. Homer, *Iliad* 8.19 ff.; cf. Psellos, *On the Golden Chain in Homer* (*Phil. Min. I* 46).

14. Homer, *Iliad* 22.126 as well as 16.34–35 and *Odyssey* 19.163.

And you, the great one, weighty in soul, stable in mind, when your bride was having a difficult labor (as I have heard from one of your people), even fell into laments. By contrast, I suffered deeply and passionately, yet I did not cry. Thus, I am at least more philosophical than you are so as to not shed a tear when my soul is in hardship.

But enough about these things. You should now think of how you might match two Pselloi. I have sent a letter about this to the emperor[15] as well. If it is superfluous, let it not be delivered; if not, let things be according to your ordinance.

Letter S 157; date: after 1063–1065?
To Konstantinos, nephew of the patriarch Michael Keroularios, when his son Romanos was born[16]

[**409**] The newborn baby is of the male gender; male, O earth and sun! Did you see him right away as he slid out, full of blood and tainted by gore as if coming from war and battle? Or did you wait so long that the midwife cut the navel-string, cleaned, and wrapped the baby in swaddling clothes? As I love both, O my friend, both the father and the mother, even if the child were female I would receive with pleasure the voice bringing the good news. What does it matter if the child is formed this way or that, more feminine or more masculine? In any event, he has been given his essence from both his parents. But that he is male moved me to greater pleasure. If he is also like his mother, especially in what regards his soul but also in his body to no less degree, then he will have perfection (unless his mother's form is resisting).

Well, I want to philosophize about everything, both words and things. Yet my character betrays me, as it is disposed in a nonphilosophical manner toward the natural affections (or perhaps this is philosophical too, for the other type of man is Skythian). Thus (how might one say it) I become excited about newborn babies, especially if they are dearest and of dearest parents, and when I am faced with their delights and charms.

15. If the letter dates to the 1060s, then this emperor is Konstantinos Doukas (1059–1067), Ioannes' brother; if it dates to the 1070s, then the emperor must be Michael Doukas (1071–1078), Ioannes' nephew. For the various possibilities, see p. 158 above.

16. The title is translated here following Vaticanus Barber. gr. 240, f. 163v (thirteenth century). On Konstantinos, see Ljubarskij (1974), (1978) 62–69; and Snipes (1981).

[410] In the distant past, the kings of Persia did not immediately place their newborn babies under their gaze, nor did they straightway embrace the progeny of their flesh, but they set a specific time when it was possible to see the offspring. Why did they do this? They were afraid that, with the strength of their hands, they might bring death to their infants, who were softer. Thus, they delayed seeing them, so that they might not become captivated through their eyes by the *pathos* of pleasure and then lament in full *pathos* the loss of their infants. Thus, without knowing it, they deprived themselves of the peak of charm.

As for myself, I could not stay away from the *vestarchês'* children, neither when they were being bathed nor when they were being swathed, but this was my most pleasing spectacle: the infant gently lying on the left arm of the wet nurse and held by the other arm, now with the face down, now supine. If the water happened to be too hot, my soul was suspended in extreme *pathos* and I would rail furiously at the bath nurse. The same was the case when the newborn would cry aloud in tears. And the songs of the wet nurse captured and enchanted me more than the Orphic songs or those of the Sirens. When she was about to swathe and wrap the baby, securing the hands while gently covering the head, holding and enveloping the entire body, I was shaken as if I were the one being wrapped, and I almost experienced the same as the baby.

Now whether this is a trait of a feminine soul, I do not really know; nevertheless, my character has thus been formed and my nature, like some kind of wax, soft and easily receiving an impression, both holds together the best of knowledge and receives the impression of the charms of what is dearest. I am not at all jealous of the so-called adamantines, whether they live on mountains or are suspended higher up. If they altered their nature toward what is more divine [411] through some higher conduct and became gods instead of men, this is the work of prayer, or something more than that. But if they are hardened in their character from their very first coming into being and if, since that beginning, their will and thought resists impression, then these neither pursue philosophy nor improvise it; indeed, they should not be called philosophers but 'stony and trodden' men.[17]

I would pray if necessary and ascend to God as much as divinity and time allowed. Still, I will also ponder philosophical pursuits together with others, I will converse with friends in gay spirit, and I will give my tongue free rein for

---

17. For the expression see Philon, *On Particular Laws* 2.169; *On the Contemplative Life* 62 (on soil); *On the Life of Moses* 2.202; and *On Prizes, Punishments, and Imprecations* 114–115 (on human souls).

jokes and witty charms. I will even deem the women's chambers worthy if I wish to please these as well. I will consider as my own those who are dearest to others, on account of the latter. I will converse with some from a superior, with others from an equal, and with still others from an inferior position. I will embrace my grandchildren with pleasure, I will kiss them full on the lips. I will say to the midwife that she should do this or that and how she should take care of the infants. On the other hand, I will explain to the wet nurse how the baby should drink the milk, eat these things and leave those. I will laugh and get upset, philosophize and lament, cry together with my dearest ones when they are crying, rejoice with them rejoicing. O my dearest *epi tôn kriseôn,* I will lift your child up in my arms many times; I will suspend him while holding him tightly; I will perform childish figures and funny faces. For my soul is fashioned toward every form of both the Muses and Graces. I am not like the strings that are either only high-pitched or only enharmonic, but my song is manifold, now sweet, flexible, and pleasing, now severe, noble, and virile.

I am thus. As for you, may you be strong first in your health, then, as you affectionately bounce and play with the newborn as [412] he now bounces, may you hold him securely, tightly in your hands whenever you lift him, because it worries me.

Letter S 177; date: 1069–1071?
To the prôtovestiarios[18]

[455] My Lord *prôtovestiarios,* I shared good Isaiah's pain when he was leaving Constantinople, for he was about to suffer much, but I also shared his pleasure

---

18. I have been unable to identify this *prôtovestiarios,* who, according to this letter, was participating in a military campaign. Is it Romanos Diogenes' second campaign in Asia Minor against the Seljuk Turks, which took place in April through December 1069? As has been argued, during that campaign Psellos wrote *Letter S 176* which precedes *Letter S 177* in their sole manuscript, Parisinus gr. 1182 (thirteenth century); cf. de Vries-van der Velden (1997) 287–291.

A *prôtovestiarios* was, according to Kazhdan (1991) 1749, a "post for a palace eunuch, second to that of *parakoimomenos* [see below] .... The role of the *prôtovestiarios* increased in the eleventh century." Psellos' close friend Konstantinos Leichoudes, who was to become patriarch under the emperor Isaakios Komnenos in 1059, was a *prôtovestiarios.* Leichoudes administered the government of the emperor Konstantinos Monomachos (1042–1055) at least until 1050 when he fell out of favor: see Weiss (1973) 79 ff. and Psellos, *Letter S 28.*

for he was coming to you who will shelter him.[19] He will be distressed, yet also receive consolation from you. And for me, who was hoping to do well here, first the separation from you is a great evil, and then other terrible things have happened: my dearest ones are ill—for the one I am entirely in despair, for the other I am close to it.[20] I may be called perhaps a wise man or a philosopher, but in unwanted misfortunes I can neither philosophize nor be magnanimous.

And to whom am I to express the sufferings of my soul after you are gone? [456] To whom am I to lament my calamities, unless you might wish to mention the *parakoimomenos*,[21] the imprint of your sacred soul, to whom indeed I go, in whom I find rest, and from whom I obtain countless consolations? Given your great reputation for virtue in your interactions with others, I think of both: how you might be eminent as well as prosperous, upon both your departure and your return.

We know nothing of what happens there, except for different rumors by different people. May you win better victories, and may we progress further than you into higher hopes, and may you remain healthy for me, the great asset of the Romans, my consolation, and breath, and life. Also, let all be greeted from me by you, especially those who care to be addressed by my eloquent tongue.

Theophylaktos of Ochrid, *Letter* 132; date: late 1070s? To Psellos' brother when Psellos died

That you are in pain and vexed, unable to bear the grief from the death of your brother, I know well. But I too am in pain, assailed by the spurs of friendship, upset doubly, when my friend is in sorrow and I am away, unable to be with him and offer consoling words. Therefore, even though I am absent, through

19. It is not possible to determine whether this Isaiah is identical to a certain *proximos* of the same name, to whom Psellos addressed a letter introducing one of his students: *Letter KD* 24.

20. It is uncertain who these "dearest ones" are. Volk (1990) 23, 317, 319 has suggested that it might have been Psellos' wife and daughter Styliane (or perhaps both of Psellos' daughters); if this is correct, the letter could date to the late summer of 1054. Psellos, however, may be also referring to his adopted daughter and her son, as he probably is with the same phrase in *Letter S* 186, dated most likely to 1071; cf. de Vries-van der Velden (1997) 305. *Letter S* 177 was then most likely written sometime in the years 1069 to 1071. See n. 18 above.

21. "The highest office conferred to eunuchs": Kazhdan (1991) 1585. This *parakoimomenos* is nowhere else mentioned by Psellos.

this very letter I speak to you as much as possible and urge your brother-loving as well as god-loving soul to receive great consolation by thinking, whenever his loss vexes your soul, that your brother has not died but has departed to God, freed from a painful life and illness; and if he, being human, acquired any stain during the course of that life, he was cleansed and thus came to the Lord, full of grace. Not only you, but all of us know what manner of man he was.

Theophylaktos of Ochrid, *Letter 27*; date: late 1070s?
To Kamateros

'Even if men forget their dead in Hades' chambers,'[22] I will return the favor owed to a friend now dead to those he has left behind. Well, to the thrice-blessed late Psellos, the *hypertimos,* the incomparably eloquent tongue, I owe, as is only fair, favors that are not easy to return; for I know that I benefited greatly from the Muse of that man. Now, as I am unable to be grateful to his entire self, I repay the favor to his offspring, as much as is possible, through your love for me. For the person handing your brilliancy this letter is Psellos' daughter's son, who, having experienced a bitter fate, is now in misfortune; you now ease his fate, that tyrant. If only you give your consenting nod, she will smile at him and embrace him, she might even lead his hand into her bosom and allow him to seize her goods. And do not think that I am writing this to you simply in order to ease my conscience. May I not benefit from my discourses or from my wish for salvation if I am not writing this to you from the depths of my heart. I feel for the young man, having seen him in happiness in the old days, and I also fear the soul of his grandfather, lest he might reproach my hardness and mercilessness; for I fear even to mention the One who, in the hour of judgment, reproaches the goats on his left for their inhumanity.[23] For if Psellos were to appear to me in a dream and loose his tongue 'from twelve springs,'[24] do you think that I will be able to bear the blame, the apparition, its horror and trembling? What if he introduces, next to others, God, and claims that He was

22. Homer, *Iliad* 22.389–390, where Achilles is speaking of his dead friend Patroklos. Synesios, bishop of Kyrene in the late fourth to early fifth centuries, begins two of his *Letters* (123 and 124) with the same Homeric phrase; Psellos too made use of it: *Letter S* 145 (Sathas 394, line 7) and *Letter KD* 134 (Kurtz and Drexl 156, line 25).
23. Cf. Matthew 25:31–46.
24. Cf. Philostratos, *Lives of the Sophists* 1.22.4.

protecting Jerusalem, a place otherwise unworthy and full of blood, through David, even when the latter was dead? What am I to say to this? O, I shall be persuaded by his charms, afflicted by justice, God, and Psellos' tongue.

Therefore, save me from these necessities by placing the one sent to you in some kind of a position; for, since many jobs are assigned to you, it is entirely easy for you to grant our request for the benefit of him who is recommended by such people—your means are by no means restricted. And may God keep you free from evil and harm.

On the festival of St Agathê

Introduction

This brief work by Psellos contains the only evidence that we possess regarding the Constantinopolitan women's festival of Agathê (Ἀγάθη). It was held annually on 12 May (529), forming a coda of sorts to the grand celebrations held in honor of the capital's foundation on the previous day,[1] though there does not appear to have been any organic connection between the two and certainly no imperial involvement in the festival of Agathê. It is difficult to reconstruct the phases and details of this festival from Psellos' allusive and explicitly philosophical account, which was, after all, addressed to an audience that already knew them. On the first page, we learn that images or paintings of some sort were put up on a wall (528). These were probably the same as those said later in the text to have been put up by priests in the vestibule or courtyard of a church whose gates they then opened to the crowd, which entered in an orderly fashion (530). These images depicted women working at the loom and being punished for making mistakes (530–531). The participants in the festival were themselves such weavers, who made votive offerings to the images and then sang and danced under the lead of the eldest and most accomplished among them. It is not clear when the procession and hymns mentioned by Psellos (530) took place, if not during the "orderly" entry of the crowd. Given that his description of weaving is confined to the *ekphrasis* of the images themselves, it does not

---

1. Dagron (1974) ch. 1.

appear that any such activity was actually a part of the festival itself. Laiou has proposed, more or less plausibly, that the women who were the chief participants either formed a professional guild of weavers or were part of such a guild.[2]

Why did Psellos write this curious little work? Laiou drew attention to the fact that in the manuscript it is included after a number of rhetorical exercises that praise various insects in order to demonstrate how the power of rhetoric can elevate what is normally considered low and unworthy. Certainly, a similar intention is announced at the beginning of our treatise, though the perspective here is philosophical rather than rhetorical, and there are other similarities which do indicate that Psellos is playfully and somewhat tongue in cheek making the most of his material, squeezing water from a rock, as he puts it, like Moses (527).[3] He even draws attention to the absurd and entertaining nature of the work (527–528), but the "foolery" in question is primarily his own philosophical interpretation of the festival, not the profession of the women who participate in it. Still, a serious purpose may be discerned behind this endeavor in some hints that Psellos drops. He likens himself to Moses, in that his philosophical interpretation will extract a lofty essence from an otherwise lowly subject matter, and at this point he calls Moses "the leader of the people" (*dêmagôgos*), which is an appropriate label given the context of the miracle of the water in the narrative of Exodus, but whose presence here seems unnecessary. On the next page, however, Psellos calls the founder of the festival of Agathê—a philosopher who implanted the lofty conception that he is now going to extract—a *katadêmagôgos* of the people. In short, those who imbue ordinary matters with deeper philosophical significance are in effect rulers, for they determine how people interpret their own lives, and may be likened to such prophets as Moses. We may, then, suspect that Psellos' own account of the origin of the festival is itself a philosophical "imposition" (528) that in reality serves his interests in ruling over his own people. The basic purpose of this treatise is then no different than that of all the treatises and lectures in which Psellos explains in Platonic terms the inner philosophical significance of various Christian practices and beliefs.

2. Laiou (1986) 116–122 and (2001) 262–263; for the guilds in the eleveth century, see Vryonis (1963). Subsequent or independent references have not added much to our understanding of the festival, e.g., Vergari (1987a) 406–408; Nardi (2002) 45; Connor (2004) 266. Angold (1995) 457–458 is unreliable in reporting the contents of Psellos' treatise and incorrect in interpreting his intention.

3. Laiou (1986) 111–114; for the manuscript, see Sathas (1876) oγ΄. The other works are now *Or. Min.* 27–29. For Psellos on the power of rhetoric, see Kaldellis (1999a) ch. 27.

The mention of *dêmagôgoi* and therefore the link to Moses may be important for another reason that has so far been overlooked. In a passage near the beginning of the work (528, lines 3–4), Psellos gives the impression that he is delivering it as an oration on the very day of the festival itself. The date is impossible to establish and the audience is not specified, though it is more likely to be his students than the court; it almost certainly was not the women who participated in the festival. At any rate, if he is addressing an audience, the references to *dêmagôgoi* acquire a more immediate relevance.

As was mentioned above, we know nothing regarding the festival of Agathê except what Psellos tells us in this treatise. What may its name have signified?[4] If it had once been celebrated in honor of a woman of that name, it is virtually certain that that was *not* how it was understood in Psellos' own time, for such an obvious explanation would have precluded his philosophical speculation and, at least, would have left some mark on his attempt to reinterpret its significance. Besides, no saint Agathê was honored on 12 May, though there were non-saintly women with that name in local Constantinopolitan history.[5] It seems that the origin of the name was a bit of a mystery in the eleventh century. Psellos' own explanation is not entirely impossible, though we do not have to go so far as to postulate a philosophical founder who had his eye on the ultimate Good. In other words, it is possible that the festival acquired its name from the generic "virtuous woman," the woman who is best at the work of the loom, and over time the accent did shift as Psellos suggests. More than this it is impossible to say at the moment.

Editions. For a list of manuscripts and two studies referring to this text, see Moore (2005) 397–398. The text has been published once, in Sathas (1876) 527–531, who gave it the title *On the women's festival in Constantinople called Agathê*. In the preparation of the following translation, the first in any modern language, a few corrections have been made to Sathas' text wherever necessary. The bold numbers in brackets correspond to the page numbers of this edition.

---

4. On this question, see Megas (1953) 104–108. Megas notes (106–107 n. 5) the coincidence that the Roman festival of the Bona Dea, who, according to Plutarch, was called Ἀγαθή, was celebrated exclusively by women, albeit in early December.

5. See the Agathê in pseudo-Kodinos, *Patria of Constantinople* 3.68 (Preger v. 2, 240), with Dagron (1984) 178–179.

On the festival of St Agathê

[527] It is not only with great matters that philosophy concerns itself but also with those things that seem childish to the many and not worth taking seriously. For it is not [only] every conception that it knows how to capture in a superior sense, but, if there should be some deed that is held in low regard, this too it elevates by reason to a higher level; so, it not only generates noble conceptions for the willing, but also transposes those things whose nature is not graceful to begin with, in accordance with the power and perfection of Moses, the leader of the people (*dêmagôgos*). For he too squeezed the clearest drinkable water out from the dry rock and transformed bitter waters into sweetness.[1]

As for women, then, and all those who hanker after the foolery of childish games, let the foolery of Agathê be played for them, whether one wishes to call it an afterthought or a reinterpretation or an entertainment that is both well suited [528] and unreasonable or, indeed, whatever a wit may say regarding our rendition; we, at any rate, will philosophize about the matter and, in accordance with reason and the appropriate level of elegance, will rise up to the occasion of this brilliant day, not by standing in a choir and singing various tunes nor by dancing or dancing ourselves away, but rather by philosophizing: What is the meaning of the festival? What does its name signify? What is the change of location?[2] How is it that the rite is given over to women? What is the

---

1. Water from the rock: Exodus 17:1–6; Numbers 20:1–11. Bitter water to sweet: 4 Kings 2:19–22 (?) (but this is Elisha).
2. It is unclear to what this question refers.

painting on the wall and what the various designs that they weave, showing that they have succeeded in some cases and failed in others.

For my part, at any rate, I am accustomed to impose more intellectual interpretations on things and have not understood Agathê's appellation in a crude way; rather, I believe that it was invented by a man who was philosophical in his soul and yet also wise in political matters, who was able to prevail over (*katadêmagôgôn*) and set to rights not only the men but likewise the women, especially in leading the souls of the more simpleminded up to superior conceptions through the clever use of appropriate proper names. For it was his intention to make clear to women in all possible ways the nature of the good and to reveal the most perfect end of every action. Yet because that class of people is not receptive to such discourses, the name was changed and made to conform to its gender. Given that the feminine adjective "good" does not have the same absolute sense as the neuter noun "the good," but requires a supplement, for instance to make a good nature, a good soul, and a good decision, for this reason he made the adjective into a noun by raising the accent,[3] in order to personify it and thereby move women upon a familiar feminine appellation. Indeed, how else might that gender have received the philosophy in that name, concerning which even the greatest philosophers have disagreed? But as for the ineffable good and what the end is of every action and motion, after which nothing has been found or remains left over, let these matters remain ineffable for now, reserved for when we philosophize in a loftier mode.

[**529**] Yet given that political activity, whether it already exists at the level of the good itself, or is perfected by the aid of discourse, or is a mixture of both, has the good as its end, let us not deprive of this name the women who work at the loom and weave and comb wool, but to these too, both to each individually in private and to all in common publicly, let us grant this symbolic Agathê, which is nothing other than the good suitable for each thing, that for which all other things are done and for the sake of which they endure misery and experience the bitterness of misfortune. Let us, then, dedicate to these women one specific day out of the entire year, on which we should experience and be instructed in the perfection of their art. And what day befits them more than the one that is now already established, namely the day after the festival in honor of the foundation of the city? If those things that are called goods in sequence after the first and most perfect good, I mean God, are indeed its images, then

---

3. Namely, from ἀγαθὴ to Ἀγάθη.

it is necessary for it, which is first by nature and truly the first cause, to exist in advance of them and only then for its reflection is to be present as well in this way.[4]

For a philosophical man, on the one hand, the good is neither circumscribed nor does it recur in cycles, for it is united with him and in no way whatever lost by him; but women, on the other hand, are content if its commemoration recurs even on an annual basis. Hence even our sacred festivals take place at set periods and in cycles of months: Christ is born on this day, he is then raised up on that one, and then does all the other things before being lifted up to the heavens. And these things he does not once, but many times on the same day for each celebration, every time that a year has passed.

The good, even as it proceeds from one [origin], is ranked as primary or secondary in accordance with the ordering of beings. On one level, it is of the mind; on another, of the soul, and the latter reveals itself in our bodies and professions. And the virtues are allocated on this basis and political activity is divided in itself. Legislative and judicial are separated by this, as are generalship and the art of making bridles, the arts of building and shipbuilding and, being prior to them, the art of architecture whose activity is directed toward it, and [530] in sum all things that do not act at random without a plan. That is why we subordinate handicrafts to it, for even the smith and the dyer practice their arts with a view to the good.

What then? Should we pay special honor to the masculine part of our species and deprive the feminine part of the end (*telos*)? To the contrary, to the contrary! For they do not whirl the spindle in vain nor turn the distaff nor harmonize their weaving with the shuttle, but they do so aiming at a goal and on account of that goal; and it is for the sake of the good, which they praise with hymns and honor with annual processions, that they fashion and paint, and all but worship with honors.

The priestly class are not themselves uninitiated in this matter, for which reason they do not turn these women out of the sacred places; rather, they set up the images as in a vestibule, open the gates to the rite, and the people come inside in an orderly file and attend to the designs, dedicating adornments upon the images and approaching the ineffable *telos* as though it were ensouled. They

---

4. In other words, the didactic significance of the festival is based on the premise that all subordinate goods, including the works of women, point to the first good: the presence of images and reflections testify to the existence of their prototype.

also burst into dance and sing songs, some composed in the distant past while others they improvise and sing on the spot.

Nor would one fault them on account of their age, for it is not only young girls who perform these God-revealing rites (*theophania*). This is to call them by a more fitting name, for the attainment of the good *is* a manifestation of God. But those also who are past their prime and superannuated and presbyters in a precise sense, those women who are regarded as the promoters (*promnēs-triai*) of the art, these, then, take the lead in the dance and initiate the song and reveal the most remarkable aspects of the rite. The others follow them, as in other respects, learning these things as well; they pay close attention to the images, hanging upon the designs, and examine the painting as though it were true to life. And the latter depicts various things. Here we see loom, thread, and woven garment, and there a smoothed-out linen cloth and the crafts-woman who accomplished it. And you might see her having failed at her task and simply frozen in her place, whether because she did not move the distaff in the prescribed way, or did not [531] bring the threads in alignment with the warp, having gathered twice as many of them with her fingers, or did not trans-fer that instrument skillfully to her thumb, or did not maintain a straight line in weaving the cloth. At that point, one will be shown hanging in suspense while another throws herself to the ground and comes close to crying aloud in an-guish. But the punisher looks at her in her face—a frightful look—and author-izes the women whip-bearers. The one being whipped wails loudly, painting a picture of the truth by the contortions of her body, and the women watching this wail along with her, recognizing this image of pain and fearing lest they suffer the same.

Yet the event quickly returns to gaiety and they join with each other by their hands and turn now this way, now the other, just like celestial bodies that both orbit and do not orbit, in the first case when they proceed toward the east, in the second toward the west. The rhythm is accompanied by music and the song is appropriate; the beat sets the time and the variations in the pattern typically adjust to the time.

We, however, should not concern ourselves with these things, with dances and patterns and such, but rather let us understand the nature of the true, on account of which they exist. If you wish, let a picture be painted for you too, but not of this kind, not in accordance with a more feminine pattern, and not somewhere outside of you; rather, let it exist immaterially in the mind, without being represented in a shape, just as the good itself exists, from which other things derive that appellation as well.[5] Whatever is formed in its likeness, this is exactly what philosophy wants and a proper education, for the most part, tends toward it. By formulating arguments, then, and exploring nature and practicing the sciences with precision, and by making use of the other steps in the argument that lead us up to the most elevated things, we will ascend and finally reach this *telos*.

5. Namely, of being good.

Bibliography

Editions of the works translated in this volume are listed and discussed at the end of the introduction to each chapter. The bibliography below lists (a) other works by Psellos cited in the introductions and notes; (b) other ancient and Byzantine sources (excluding the Church Fathers) cited in the notes; and (c) modern studies.

Other Works by Psellos

Chronographia. Edited by S. Impellizzeri, *Michele Psello: Imperatori di Bisanzio (Cronografia).* 2 vols. Introduction by D. Del Corno, notes by U. Criscuolo, translation by S. Ronchey. Milan: Fondazione Lorenzo Valla, A. Mondadori Editore, 1984.
   Edited and modern Greek translation by B. Karalis. 2 vols. Athens: Agrostis, 1992–1993.

De oper. daem. Edited by J. F. Boissonade, *Michael Psellus: De operatione daemonum.* Amsterdam: A. M. Hakkert, 1964. Reprint of Nuremberg, 1838.

Funeral Oration for Niketas. Edited and translated by A. M. Guglielmino, "Un maestro di grammatica a Bisanzio nell'XI secolo e l'epitafio per Niceta di Michele Psello." *Siculorum Gymnasium* 27 (1974): 421–462.

Funeral Oration for Nikolaos, Abbot of the Monastery of the Beautiful Source on Olympos. Edited in Gautier (1974) 33–69.

Hist. Byz. et alia = Sathas (1874).

Historia Syntomos. Edited and translated by W. J. Aerts. Berlin and New York: W. de Gruyter, 1990 (= *CFHB,* vol. 30).

Letters KD. Edited by E. Kurtz and F. Drexl, *Michaelis Pselli Scripta Minora,* vol. 2: *Epistulae.* Milan: Vita e Pensiero, 1941.

Letters S, in *Misc.,* pp. 219–523.

Letter to Keroularios. Edited and translated by U. Criscuolo, *Michele Psello: Epistola a Michele Cerulario.* Naples: Bibliopolis, 1990.

Letter to Xiphilinos. Edited and translated by U. Criscuolo, *Michele Psello: Epistola a Giovanni Xiphilino.* Naples: Bibliopolis, 1990.

Misc. ed. K. N. Sathas, *Μεσαιωνικὴ Βιβλιοθήκη (Bibliotheca graeca Medii Aevi),* vol. 5: *Pselli miscellanea.* Venice: Phoenix; Paris: Maisonneuve et Cie, 1876.

OFA. Edited by G. Dennis, *Michaelis Pselli Orationes, Forenses et Acta.* Stuttgart and Leipzig: Teubner, 1994.

Or. Min. Edited by A. Littlewood, *Michaelis Psellis Oratoria Minora.* Leipzig: Teubner, 1985.

Or. Pan. Edited by G. T. Dennis, *Michaelis Pselli Orationes Panegyricae.* Stuttgart and Leipzig: Teubner, 1994.

Phil. Min. I. Edited by J. M. Duffy, *Michaelis Pselli Philosophica Minora vol. I.* Leipzig and Stuttgart: Teubner, 1992.

Phil. Min. II. Edited by D. J. O'Meara, *Michaelis Pselli Philosophica Minora vol. II.* Leipzig: Teubner, 1989.

Poems. Edited by L. G. Westerink, *Michaelis Pselli Poemata.* Stuttgart and Leipzig: Teubner, 1992.

Theol. II. Edited by L. G. Westerink and J. M. Duffy, *Michael Psellus: Theologica II.* Munich and Leipzig: Teubner, 2002.

Other Ancient and Byzantine Sources (excluding Church Fathers)

Attaleiates, Michael. *Historia.* Edited and modern Greek translation by I. D. Polemis. Athens: Kanaki, 1997.

Blemmydes, Nikephoros. *A Partial Account.* Edited by J. A. Munitiz, *Nicephori Blemmydae autobiographia sive curriculum vitae.* Turnhout and Brepols: Leuven University Press, 1984.

Christophoros Mytilenaios. *Poems.* Edited by E. Kurtz, *Die Gedichte des Christophoros Mitylenaios.* Leipzig: August Neumanns Verlag, 1903.

Corpus paroemiographorum graecorum. Edited by E. L. a Leutsch and F. G. Schnei-dewin. 2 vols. Hildesheim: G. Olms, 1958. Reprint of Göttingen: Vanderhoeck and Ruprecht, 1839–1851.

Elpios (or Oulpios) the Roman. *Ecclesiastical Antiquities: On the Physical Appearance of the Saints.* Edited by M. Chatzidakis, "Ἐκ τῶν Ἐλπίου τοῦ Ῥωμαίου," Ἐπετηρὶς Ἑταιρείας Βυζαντινῶν Σπουδῶν 4 (1938): 393–414.
Edited by F. Winkelmann, "'Über die körperlichen Merkmale der gottbeseelten Väter': Zu einem Malerbuch aus der Zeit zwischen 836 und 913." In *Fest und All-tag in Byzanz,* edited by G. Prinzing and D. Simon. Munich: Verlag C. H. Beck, 1990. 107–127.

Eustathios Romaios. *Peira.* Edited by J. Zepos, *Jus Graecoromanum,* vol. 4. Athens: Phêxês, 1931.

Gregorios of Cyprus. *Concerning his own Life.* Edited by W. Lameere, *La tradition manuscrite de la correspondance de Grégoire de Chypre.* Bruxelles: Palais des Aca-démies; Rome: Institut historique belge, 1937. 176–191.

Hermogenes. *On the Method of Forcefulness* (*Peri methodou deinotêtos*). Edited by H. Rabe, *Hermogenis Opera.* Stuttgart: Teubner, 1969.

Ignatios the Deacon. *Life of Nikephoros I.* Translated by E. A. Fisher in *Byzantine Defenders of Images: Eight Saints' Lives in English Translation,* edited by A.-M. Talbot. Washington, D.C.: Dumbarton Oaks Research Library and Collection, 1998. 25–142.

Ioannes Geometres. *Lament on a judge as if spoken by his wife.* Edited by J. A. Cramer, *Anecdota graeca e codd. manuscriptis bibliothecae regiae Parisiensis.* Hildesheim: G. Olms, 1967. Originally Oxford, 1841. 320–321.

Kekaumenos, *Strategikon.* Text and modern Greek translation by D. Tsougkarakis. Athens: Agrostis, 1993.

pseudo-Kodinos. *Patria of Constantinople.* Edited by T. Preger, *Scriptores Origi-num Constantinopolitanarum.* 2 vols. Leipzig: Teubner, 1901–1907.

Komnene, Anna. *Alexiad.* Edited by D. R. Reinsch and A. Kambylis, *Annae Comne-nae Alexias.* Berlin and New York: W. de Gruyter, 2001 (= *CFHB,* vol. 40.1–2).

———. *Preface to the Diataxis.* Edited by E. Kurtz, "Unedierte Texte aus der Zeit des Kaisers Johannes Komnenos," *Byzantinische Zeitschrift* 16 (1916): 69–119, here 93–101.

Life of St Philaretos. Edited and translated by M.-H. Fourmy and M. Leroy, "La vie de S. Philarète," *Byzantion* 9 (1934): 85–170.
    The recent edition by L. Rydén, *The Life of St Philaretos the Merciful Written by his Grandson Niketas* (Uppsala: *Studia Byzantina Upsalensia* vol. 8, 2002) is not accessible in North America.

Manasses, Konstantinos. *Ekphrasis of the Earth in the Form of a Woman.* Edited by O. Lampsidis, "Der vollständige Text der ΕΚΦΡΑΣΙΣ ΓΗΣ des Konstantinos Manasses." *Jahrbuch der österreichischen Byzantinistik* 41 (1991): 189–205.

Mesarites, Nikolaos. *Funeral Oration for his Brother Ioannes.* Edited by A. Heisenberg, "Neue Quellen zur Geschichte des lateinischen Kaisertums und der Kirchenunion." *Sitzungsberichte der bayerischen Akademie der Wissenschaften: Philosophisch-philologische und historische Klasse* 5 (1922): 25–75.

Pardos, Gregorios. *[On Composition].* Edited in D. Donnet, *Le traité περὶ συντάξεως λόγου de Grégoire de Corinthe: étude de la tradition manuscrite, édition, traduction et commentaire.* Brussels and Rome: L'institut historique belge de Rome, 1967 (= *Études de philologie, d'archéologie et d'histoire anciennes,* vol. 10).

Photios. *Letter* 234. Edited by B. Laourdas and L. G. Westerink, *Photii Patriarchae Constantinopolitani Epistulae et Amphilochia,* vol. 2. Leipzig: Teubner, 1984. 150–158.
    Translated by D. S. White, *Patriarch Photios of Constantinople: His Life, Scholarly Contributions, and Correspondence together with a Translation of Fifty-Two of his Letters.* Brookline, Mass.: Holy Cross Orthodox Press, 1981. 115–124.

———. *Bibliotheke.* Edited and translated by R. Henry, *Photius: Bibliothèque,* vol. 2. Paris: Les Belles Lettres, 1960.

Proklos. *Commentary on the "Kratylos."* Edited by G. Pasquali, *Procli diadochi in Platonis Cratylum commentaria.* Leipzig: Teubner, 1908.

———. *On the Hieratic Art according to the Hellenes (De sacrificio et magia).* Edited and translated by J. Bidez, *Catalogue des manuscrits alchimiques grecs,* vol. 6: *Michel Psellus, Épître sur la Chrysopée. Opuscules et extraits sur l'alchimie, la météorologie et la démonologie.* Brussels: Lamertin, 1928. 139–151.

Skylitzes Continuatus. Edited by E. Th. Tsolakis, *Ἡ Συνέχεια τῆς Χρονογραφίας τοῦ Ἰωάννου Σκυλίτση (Ioannes Skylitzes Continuatus).* Thessalonike: Etaireia Makedonikon Spoudon, 1968.

Skylitzes, Ioannes. *Historical Synopsis.* Edited by J. Thurn, *Ioannis Scylitzae Synopsis Historiarum.* Berlin and New York: W. de Gruyter, 1973 (= *CFHB,* vol. 5).

Straboromanos, Manuel. *Poems and epigrams*. Edited by P. Gautier, "Le dossier d'un haut fonctionnaire d'Alexis Ier Comnène, Manuel Straboromanos." *Revue des études byzantines* 23 (1965): 168–204, here 201–204.

Theophylaktos Hephaistos. *Letters*. Edited and translated by P. Gautier, *Théophylacte d'Achrida: Lettres*. Thessalonike: Association de recherches byzantines, 1986 (= *CFHB*, vol. 16.2).

Timarion. Edited by R. Romano, *Timarione*. Napoli: Università di Napoli, 1974. Translated by B. Baldwin, *Timarion*. Detroit: Wayne State University Press, 1984.

Tornikés, Georges et Dèmètrios. *Lettres et Discours*. Edited by J. Darrouzès. Paris: Éditions du centre national de la recherche scientifique, 1970.

Modern Studies

Abrahamse, D. 1984. "Rituals of Death in the Middle Byzantine Period." *Greek Orthodox Theological Review* 29:125–134.

Agapitos, P. A. 1998. "Teachers, Pupils, and Imperial Power in Eleventh-Century Byzantium." In *Pedagogy and Power: Rhetorics of Classical Learning*, edited by Y. L. Too and N. Livingstone. Cambridge: Cambridge University Press. 170–191.

———. 2001. "Ὁ θάνατος στό Βυζάντιο: ἀποσπασματικές εἰκόνες ἑνὸς ἄγνωστου κόσμου." *Νέα Ἑστία* 1737 (September): 269–286.

———. 2003. "Ancient Models and Novel Mixtures: The Concept of Genre in Byzantine Funerary Literature from Photios to Eustathios of Thesssalonike." In *Modern Greek Literature: Critical Essays*, edited by G. Nagy and A. Stavrakopoulou. New York and London: Routledge. 5–23.

Agapitos, P. A., and I. D. Polemis. 2002. "Πρòς μια κριτική ἔκδοση των ἐπιταφίων λόγων του Μιχαήλ Ψελλοῦ: Η μονωδία Εἰς τόν ἀκτουαρίου Ἰωάννου ἀδελφόν (*OrFun*. 16)." In *Λόγια καὶ δημώδη γραμματεία του ἑλληνικού μεσαίωνα: Ἀφιέρωμα στον Εὔδοξο Τσολάκη*. Thessaloniki: Aristotelian University of Thessaloniki. 139–160.

Alexiou, M. 1974. *The Ritual Lament in Greek Tradition*. Cambridge: Cambridge University Press.

Angold, M. 1995. *Church and Society in Byzantium under the Comneni, 1081–1261*. Cambridge: Cambridge University Press.

———. 1998. "The Autobiographical Impulse in Byzantium." *Dumbarton Oaks Papers* 52:52–73.

Antoniadis-Bibicou, H. 1973. "Quelques notes sur l'enfant de la moyenne époque byzantine (du VIe au XIIe siècle)." *Annales de démographie historique.* 77–84.

Barbounis, M. G. 1994. Ὄψεις τῆς καθημερινῆς ζωῆς τῶν Βυζαντινῶν ἀπό ἀγιολογικά κείμενα. Athens: Herodotos.

Bassett, S. 2004. *The Urban Image of Late Antique Constantinople.* Cambridge: Cambridge University Press.

Beaucamp, J. 1982. "L'allaitement: mère ou nourrice?" *Jahrbuch der österreichischen Byzantinistik* 32.2:549–558.

Beck, H.-G. 1978. *Das byzantinische Jahrtausend.* Munich: C. H. Beck.

———. 1992. Ἡ βυζαντινα. Translated by D. Kourtovik. Athens: Educational Foundation of the National Bank of Greece.

Bidez, J. 1936. "Proclus περί τῆς ἱερατικῆς τέχνης." *Annuaire de l'institut de philologie et d'histoire orientales et slaves* 4 (*Mélanges Franz Cumont*): 85–100.

Browning, R. 1975. "Homer in Byzantium." *Viator* 6:16–33.

Buckler, G. 1929. *Anna Comnena: A Study.* London: Oxford University Press.

Cheynet, J.-C. 1999. "L'Asie Mineure d'après la correspondance de Psellos." *Byzantinische Forschungen* 25:233–241.

Clark, G. 1993. *Women in Late Antiquity: Pagan and Christian Lifestyles.* Oxford: Clarendon Press.

Connor, C. L. 2004. *Women of Byzantium.* New Haven and London: Yale University Press.

Criscuolo, U. 1981. "Tardoantico e umanesimo bizantino: Michele Psello," *Koinonia* 5:7–23.

———. 1982a. "πολιτικὸς ἀνήρ: Contributo al pensiero politica di Michele Psello." *Rendiconti dell'Accademia di Archeologia, Lettere e Belle Arti di Napoli* 57:129–163.

———. 1982b. "Pselliana." *Studi italiani di filologia classica* 4:194–215.

———. 1983. *Michele Psello: Orazione in Memoria di Costantino Lichudi.* Messina: Ed. Dott. Antonino Sfameni. 1983.

Dagron, G. 1974. *Naissance d'une capitale: Constantinople et ses institutions de 330 à 451*. Paris: Presses Universitaires de France.

———. 1984. *Constantinople imaginaire: études sur le recueil des "Patria."* Paris: Presses universitaires de France.

———. 2003. *Emperor and Priest: The Imperial Office in Byzantium*. Translated by J. Birrell. Cambridge: Cambridge University Press.

Dark, K. 2005. "Archaeology." In *Palgrave Advances in Byzantine History*, edited by J. Harris. Hampshire and New York: Palgrave Macmillan. 166–184.

Dennis, G. 1994. "A Rhetorician Practices Law: Michael Psellos." In *Law and Society in Byzantium: Ninth–Twelfth Centuries*, edited by A. E. Laiou and D. Simon. Washington D.C.: Dumbarton Oaks. 187–197.

Denniston, J. D. 1959. *The Greek Particles*. 2nd ed. Oxford: Clarendon Press.

Derderian, K. 2001. *Leaving Words to Remember: Greek Mourning and the Advent of Literacy*. Leiden and Boston: E. J. Brill.

Diehl, C. 1925. "Une famille de bourgeoise à Byzance au XIe siècle." In *Figures byzantines*, vol. 1, 291–316. Paris: A. Colin. Reprint Hildesheim: Georg Olms Verlagsbuchhandlung, 1965. Translated by H. Bell as *Byzantine Portraits*. New York: A. A. Knopf, 1927. 276–299.

Dölger, F. and J. Karayannopulos. 1968. *Byzantinische Urkundenlehre*, pt. 1: *Die Kaiserurkunden*. Munich: C. H. Beck.

Dyck, A. 1993. "*Psellus Tragicus*: Observations on *Chronographia* 5.26 ff." *Nineteenth Annual Byzantine Studies Conference: Abstracts of Papers*. Princeton: Byzantine Studies Conference. 71.

Emmanuel, M. 1995. "Some Notes on the External Appearance of Ordinary Women in Byzantium. Hairstyles, Headdresses: Texts and Iconography." *Byzantinoslavica* 56:769–778.

Fine, J. V. A., Jr. 1983. *The Early Medieval Balkans: A Critical Survey from the Sixth to the Late Twelfth Century*. Ann Arbor: University of Michigan Press.

Fortin, E. L. 1996. "Basil the Great and the Choice of Hercules: A Note on the Christianization of a Pagan Myth." In *Ernest L. Fortin: Collected Essays*, vol. 1: *The Birth of Philosophic Christianity: Studies in Early Christian and Medieval Thought*, edited by J. B. Benestad. Lanham, Md.: Rowman and Littlefield. 153–168.

French, V. 1987. "Midwives and Maternity Care in the Roman World." *Helios* 13:69–84.

Garland, L. 1988. "The Life and Ideology of Byzantine Women: A Further Note on Conventions of Behavior and Social Reality as Reflected in Eleventh and Twelfth Century Historical Sources." *Byzantion* 58:361–393.

Garzya, A. 1967. "On Michael Psellus' Admission of Faith." Έπετηρίς Έταιρείας Βυζαντινῶν Σπουδῶν 35:41–46.

Gautier, P. 1970. "La curieuse ascendance de Jean Tzetzès." *Revue des études byzantines* 28:207–220.

———. 1974. "Elogue funèbre de Nicolas de la Belle Source par Michel Psellos moine à l'Olympe." *Βυζαντινά* 6:9–69.

———. 1976. "Un chrysobulle de confirmation rédigé par Michel Psellos." *Revue des études byzantines* 34:79–99.

Graf, F. 2004. "The Bridge and the Ladder: Narrow Passages in Late Antique Visions." In *Heavenly Realms and Earthly Realities in Late Antique Religions,* edited by R. S. Boustan and A. Y. Reed. Cambridge: Cambridge University Press. 19–33.

Grünbart, M. 2000. *Die Anrede im byzantinischen Brief von Prokopios von Gaza bis Michael Choniates.* Ph.D. diss., University of Vienna.

Guilland, R. 1959. "Un compte-rendu de Proces par Psellos." *Byzantinoslavica* 20:205–230.

———. 1960. "A propos d'un texte de Michel Psellos." *Byzantinoslavica* 21:1–37.

———. 1967. *Recherches sur les institutions byzantines,* vol. 1. Berlin and Amsterdam: A. M. Hakkert.

Heinz, M. F. 2003. "Work: The Art and Craft of Earning a Living." In Kalavrezou (2003) 139–144.

Herrin, J. 1983. "In Search of Byzantine Women: Three Avenues of Approach." In *Images of Women in Antiquity,* edited by A. Cameron and A. Kuhrt. Detroit: Wayne State University Press. 167–189.

———. 1999. "L'enseignement maternel à Byzance." In *Femmes et pouvoirs des femmes à Byzance et en occident (VIe–XIe siècles),* edited by S. Lebecq et al. Villeneuve d'Ascq: Centre de recherche sur l'histoire de l'Europe du Nord-Ouest, Université Charles de Gaulle-Lille 3. 91–102.

Hill, B. 1996. "A Vindication of the Rights of Women to Power by Anna Komnene." *Byzantinische Forschungen* 23:45–54.

Hinterberger, M. 1999. *Autobiographische Traditionen in Byzanz*. Vienna: Verlag der österreichischen Akademie der Wissenschaften (= *Wiener byzantinische Studien*, vol. 22).

———. 2000. "Autobiography and Hagiography in Byzantium." *Symbolae Osloenses* 75:139–164.

Hondridou, S. D. 2002. *Ο Κωνσταντίνος Θ΄ Μονομάχος και η εποχή του (ενδέκατος αιώνας μ.Χ.)* Thessalonike: Herodotos.

Hunger, H. 1984. "Die Antithese: Zur Verbreitung einer Denkschablone in der byzantinischen Literatur." *Zbornik Radova Vizantološkog Instituta* 23:9–29.

Janin, R. 1969. *La géographie ecclésiastique de l'empire byzantin*, pt. 1: *Le siège de Constantinople et le patriarcat oecuménique*, vol. 3: *Les églises et les monastères*. 2nd ed. Paris: Institut français d'études byzantines.

Jeffreys, E. 1984. "Western Infiltration of the Byzantine Aristocracy: Some Suggestions." In *The Byzantine Aristocracy: IX to XIII Centuries*, edited by M. Angold. Oxford: British Archaeological Reports, International Series, vol. 221. 202–210.

Joannou, P. 1951. "Psellos et le monastère τά Ναρσοῦ." *Byzantinische Zeitschrift* 44:283–290.

Jouanno, C. 1994. "Michel Psellos: *Epitaphios logos à sa fille Styliané, morte avant l'heure du mariage*: Réflexions sur le cadavre défiguré et sur le rôle du corps dans le travail de deuil." *Kentron: Revue du monde antique et de psychologue historique* 10:95–107.

Kalavrezou, I., ed. 2003. *Byzantine Women and Their World*. Cambridge: Harvard University Art Museums; New Haven and London: Yale University Press.

Kaldellis, A. 1999a. *The Argument of Psellos' "Chronographia."* Leiden and Boston: E. J. Brill.

———. 1999b. "The Historical and Religious Views of Agathias: A Reinterpretation." *Byzantion* 69:206–252.

———. 2004. *Procopius of Caesarea: Tyranny, History, and Philosophy at the End of Antiquity*. Philadelphia: University of Pennsylvania Press.

———. 2005. "The Date of Psellos' Theological Lectures and Higher Religious Education in Constantinople." *Byzantinoslavica* 63: 143–151.

————. 2006. "Thoughts on the Future of Psellos-Studies, with Attention to his Mother's *Encomium.*" In *Reading Michael Psellos,* edited by C. Barber and D. Jenkins. Leiden: E. J. Brill. 229–245.

Kalogeras, N. 2000. *Byzantine Childhood Education and Its Social Role from the Sixth Century until the End of Iconoclasm.* Ph.D. diss., University of Chicago.

————. 2001. "What Do They Think about Children? Perceptions of Childhood in Early Byzantine Literature." *Byzantine and Modern Greek Studies* 25:2–19.

Karpozelos, A. 1982. *Συμβολή στή μελέτη τοῦ βίου καί τοῦ ἔργου τοῦ Ἰωάννη Μαυρόποδος.* Ioannina: University of Ioannina (= *Dodone* Suppl. vol. 18).

————. 2003. "When Did Michael Psellos Die? The Evidence of the Dioptra." *Byzantinische Zeitschrift* 96:671–677.

Kazhdan, A. 1983. "Hagiographical Notes. 3. An Attempt at Hagio-Autobiography: the Pseudo-Life of 'Saint' Psellus?" *Byzantion* 53:546–556.

————. 1998. "Women at Home." *Dumbarton Oaks Papers* 52:1–17.

————, ed. 1991. *The Oxford Dictionary of Byzantium.* 3 vols. Oxford and New York: Oxford University Press.

Kiousopoulou, A. 1990. *Ο θεσμός της οικογένειας στην Ήπειρο κατά τον 13ο αιώνα.* Athens: A. N. Sakkoulas (= *Forschungen zur byzantinischen Echtsgeschichte, Athener Reihe*).

Kolbaba, T. 2000. *The Byzantine Lists: Errors of the Latins.* Urbana and Chicago: University of Illinois Press.

Koukoules, Ph. 1948–1955. *Βυζαντινῶν βίος καί πολιτισμός.* 6 vols. Athens: Institut français d'Athènes.

Krallis, D. 2006. *Michael Attaleiates: History as Politics in Eleventh-Century Byzantium.* Ph.D. diss., University of Michigan.

Kyriakakis, J. 1974. "Byzantine Burial Customs: Care of the Deceased from Death to the Prothesis." *The Greek Orthodox Theological Review* 19:37–72.

Kyriakis, M. 1976–1977. "Medieval European Society as Seen in Two Eleventh-Century Texts of Michael Psellos." *Byzantine studies/Études byzantines* 3.2:77–99; 4.1:67–80; 4.2:157–187.

Laiou, A. E. 1981. "The Role of Women in Byzantine Society." *Jahrbuch der österreichischen Byzantinistik* 31.1:233–260.

———. 1985. "Observations on the Life and Ideology of Byzantine Women." *Byzantinische Forschungen* 9:59–102.

———. 1986. "The Festival of 'Agathe': Comments on the Life of Constantinopolitan Women." In *Byzantium: Tribute to Andreas N. Stratos*, vol. 1. Athens: Nia Stratos. 111–122.

———. 1992. *Mariage, amour et parenté à Byzance aux XIe–XIIIe siècles*. Paris: de Boccard (= *Travaux et Mémoires: Monographies*, vol. 7).

———. 2001. "Women in the Marketplace of Constantinople (10th–14th Centuries)." In *Byzantine Constantinople: Monuments, Topography, and Everyday Life*, edited by N. Necipoğlu. Leiden and Boston: E. J. Brill. 261–273.

Lambropoulos, K. 1988. *Ἰωάννης Ἀπόκαυκος: Συμβολή στην ἔρευνα του βίου και του συγγραφικού του ἔργου*. Athens: Basilopoulos.

Lampe, G. W. H. 1961. *A Patristic Greek Lexicon*. Oxford: Clarendon Press.

Lascaratos, J., and C. Tsiamis 2002. "Two Cases of Smallpox in Byzantium." *International Journal of Dermatology* 41:792–795.

Lemerle, P. 1967. "'Roga' et rente d'état aux Xe-XIe siècles." *Revue d'études byzantines* 25:77–100.

———. (1977). "'Le gouvernement des philosophes': L'enseignement, les écoles, la culture." In *Cinq études sur le XIe siècle byzantine*. Paris: Éditions du centre national de la recherche scientifique. 193–248.

Leroy-Molinghen, A. 1969a. "Styliané." *Byzantion* 39:155–163.

———. 1969b. "La descendance adoptive de Psellos." *Byzantion* 39:284–317.

———. 1971. "A propos d'un jugement rendu contre Psellos." *Byzantion* 40:238–239.

Leroy-Molinghen, A., and P. Karlin-Hayter. 1968. "A Basileopator's Descendant." *Byzantion* 38:280–281.

Littlewood, A. R. 1999. "The Byzantine Letter of Consolation in the Macedonian and Komnenian Periods." *Dumbarton Oaks Papers* 53:19–41.

————. 2006. "Imagery in the *Chronographia* of Michael Psellos." In *Reading Michael Psellos*, edited by C. Barber and D. Jenkins. Leiden: E. J. Brill. 13–56.

Ljubarskij, J. N. 1973. "Psell v otnoaenijach s sovremennikami 2. Psell i Duki." *Vizantiiskii Vremennik* 34:77–87.

————. 1974. "Psell v otnoaenijach s sovremennikami. Psell i semja Kerulariev." *Vizantiiskii Vremennik* 35:89–102.

————. 1978. *Michail Psell: Ličnost' i tvorčestvo. K istorii vizantijskogo predgumanisma.* Moscow: Nauka.

————. 2004. *Η προσωπικότητα και το έργο του Μιχαήλ Ψελλού: Συνεισφορά στην ιστορία του βυζαντινού πολιτισμού.* Translated by A. Tzelesi. Athens: Kanaki.

Ljubarskij, J. N., et al. 1998. "*Quellenforschung* and/or Literary Criticism: Narrative Structures in Byzantine Historical Writings." *Symbolae Osloenses* 73:5–73.

Macrides, R. 1990. "Kinship by Arrangement: The Case of Adoption." *Dumbarton Oaks Papers* 44:109–118.

————. 1996. "The Historian in the History." In *ΦΙΛΛΕΛΗΝ: Studies in Honour of Robert Browning,* edited by C. N. Constantinides et al. Venice: Istituto ellenico di studi bizantini e postbizantini di Venezia. 205–224.

Magdalino, P. 1984. "The Byzantine Aristocratic *oikos*." In *The Byzantine Aristrocracy, IX–XII Centuries,* edited by M. Angold. Oxford: British Archaeological Reports, International Series, vol. 221. 92–111.

————. 1994. "Justice and Finance in the Byzantine State, Ninth to Twelfth Centuries." In *Law and Society in Byzantium, Ninth-Twelfth Centuries,* edited by A. E. Laiou and D. Simon. Washington D.C.: Dumbarton Oaks Research Library and Collection. 93–115.

Maguire, H. 1981. *Art and Eloquence in Byzantium.* Princeton: Princeton University Press.

Majercik, R. 1989. *The Chaldean Oracles: Text, Translation, and Commentary.* Leiden: E. J. Brill.

Malamut, É. 1999. "Une femme politique d'exception à la fin du XIe siècle: Anne Dalassène." In *Femmes et pouvoirs des femmes à Byzance et en occident (VIe–XIe siècles),* edited by S. Lebecq et al. Villeneuve d'Ascq: Centre de recherche sur l'histoire de l'Europe du Nord-Ouest, Université Charles de Gaulle-Lille 3. 103–120.

Margarou, E. L. 2000. *Τίτλοι και επαγγελματικά ονόματα γυναικών στο Βυζάντιο: Συμβολή στη μελέτη για τη θέση της γυναίκας στη βυζαντινή κοινωνία.* Thessaloniki: Byzantine Research Center, Aristotle University of Thessaloniki.

McGuckin, J. A. 2001. *St. Gregory of Nazianzus: An Intellectual Biography.* Crestwood, NY: St. Vladimir's Seminary Press.

Megas, G. A. 1953. ''Ο Μιχαὴλ Ψελλὸς ὡς λαογράφος.' *Ἐπετηρὶς Ἑταιρείας Βυζαντινῶν Σπουδῶν* 23:99–109.

Misch, G. 1962. "Die Bruchstücke einer Autobiographie des byzantinischen Hofphilosophen Michael Psellos." In *Geschichte der Autobiographie,* vol. 3, pt. 2. Bern: A. Francke. 760–830.

Mitchell, J. F. 1968. "Consolatory Letters in Basil and Gregory Nazianzen." *Hermes* 96:299–318.

Moffatt, A. 1986. "The Byzantine Child." *Social Research* 53:705–723.

Moore, P. 2005. *Iter Psellianum.* Toronto: Pontifical Institute of Mediaeval Studies.

Mullett, M. 1997. *Theophylact of Ochrid: Reading the Letters of a Byzantine Archbishop.* Aldershot and Brookfield, VT: Variorum (= *Birmingham Byzantine and Ottoman Monographs,* vol. 2).

———. 2003. "Rhetoric, Theory and the Imperative of Performance: Byzantium and Now." In *Rhetoric in Byzantium,* edited by E. Jeffreys. Burlington, VT, and Aldershot: Ashgate. 151–170.

Munitiz, J. A. 1981. "Self-Canonization: The 'Partial Account' of Nikephoros Blemmydes." In *The Byzantine Saint,* edited by S. Hackel. London: Fellowship of St. Alban and St. Sergius. 164–168.

Nardi, E. 2002. *Né sole né lune: L'immagine femminile nella Bisanzio dei secoli XI e XII.* Leo S. Olschki: Fondazione Carlo Marchi (= *Quaderni,* vol. 16).

Nathan, G. S. 2000. *The Family in Late Antiquity: The Rise of Christianity and the Endurance of Tradition.* London and New York: Routledge.

Neville, L. 2004. *Authority in Byzantine Provincial Society, 950–1100.* Cambridge: Cambridge University Press.

Oikonomidès, N. 1963. "Le serment de l'impératrice Eudocie (1067)." *Revue des études byzantines* 21:101–128.

———. 1972. *Les Listes de préséance byzantines des IXe et Xe siècles.* Paris: Éditions du centre national de la recherche scientifique.

———. 1976. "L'évolution de l'organisation administrative de l'empire byzantin au XIe siècle (1025–1118)." *Travaux et mémoires* 6:125–152.

———. 1986. "The 'Peira' of Eustathios Rhomaios: An Abortive Attempt to Innovate in Byzantine Law." *Fontes Minores* 7:169–192.

———. 1990. "The Contents of the Byzantine House from the Eleventh to the Fifteenth Century." *Dumbarton Oaks Papers* 44:205–214.

Papadatos, S. I. 1984. *Περὶ τῆς μνηστείας εἰς τὸ βυζαντινὸν δίκαιον.* Athens: Academy of Athens.

Papaioannou, E. N. 1998. "Das Briefcorpus des Michael Psellos: Vorarbeiten zu einer kritischen Neuedition mit einem Anhang, Edition eines unbekannten Briefes." *Jahrbuch der österreichischen Byzantinistik* 48:67–117.

———. 2000. "Michael Psellos' Rhetorical Gender." *Byzantine and Modern Greek Studies* 24:133–146.

———. 2003. "Michael Psellos: Rhetoric and the Self in Byzantine Epistolography." In *L'épistolographie et la poésie épigrammatique: Projets actuels et questions de méthodologie,* edited by W. Hörandner and M. Grünbart. Paris: Centre d'études byzantines, néo-helléniques et sud-est européennes, École des Hautes Études en Sciences Sociales, 2003. 75–83.

Patlagean, E. 1973. "L'enfant et son avenir dans la famille byzantine (IVe–XIIe siècles)." *Annales de démographie historique.* 85–93.

———. 1976. "L'histoire de la femme déguisée en moine et l'évolution de la sainteté féminine à Byzance." *Studi Medievali* 3rd ser., 17:597–623.

———. 1987. "Byzantium in the Tenth and Eleventh Centuries." In *A History of Private Life,* vol. 1: *From Pagan Rome to Byzantium,* edited by P. Veyne. Translated by A. Goldhammer. Cambridge, MA, and London: Harvard University Press. 550–642.

Pizzolato, L. F. 1985. "La 'consolatio' cristiana per la morte nel sec. IV: Riflessioni metodologiche e tematiche." *Civiltà classica e cristiana* 6:442–474.

Polemis, D. I. 1968. *The Doukai: A Contribution to Byzantine Prosopography.* University of London: The Athlone Press.

Polemis, I. D. 1994. "Review of G. T. Dennis, ed., *Michaelis Pselli Orationes forenses et Acta.*" *Παρνασσός* 36:501–502.

Reinsch, D. R. 2000. "Women's Literature in Byzantium?—The Case of Anna Komnene. In *Anna Komnene and her Times,* edited by T. Gouma-Peterson. New York and London: Garland Publishing. 83–105.

Ringrose, K. M. 2003. *The Perfect Servant: Eunuchs and the Social Construction of Gender in Byzantium.* Chicago and London: University of Chicago Press.

Sathas, K. N. 1874. *Μεσαιωνικὴ βιβλιοθήκη (Bibliotheca graeca Medii Aevi),* vol. 4: *Pselli historia byzantina et alia opuscula.* Athens: A. Koromela Sons; Paris: Maisonneuve et Cie.

———. 1876. *Μεσαιωνικὴ βιβλιοθήκη (Bibliotheca graeca Medii Aevi),* vol. 5: *Pselli miscellanea.* Venice: Phoenix; Paris: Maisonneuve et Cie.

Scourfield, J. H. D. 1993. *Consoling Heliodorus: A Commentary on Jerome* Letter 60. Oxford: Clarendon Press.

Sideras, A. 1994. *Die byzantinischen Grabreden: Prosopographie, Datierung, Überlieferung 142 Epitaphien und Monodien aus dem byzantinischen Jahrtausend.* Vienna: Verlag der österreichischen Akademie der Wissenschaften (= *Wiener byzantinische Studien,* vol. 19).

Sigalos, L. 2004. "Middle and Late Byzantine Houses in Greece (Tenth to Fifteenth Centuries)." In *Secular Buildings and the Archaeology of Everyday Life in the Byzantine Empire,* edited by K. Dark. Oxford: Oxbow Books, 2004. 53–81.

Simon, D. 1973. *Rechtsfindung am byzantinischen Reichsgericht.* Frankfurt am Main: Klostermann.

Snipes, K. 1981. "A Letter of Michael Psellos to Constantine the Nephew of Michael Cerularios." *Greek, Roman, and Byzantine Studies* 22:89–107.

Spivey, N. 1996. *Understanding Greek Sculpture: Ancient Meanings, Modern Readings.* London: Thames and Hudson.

Spyridakis, G. K. 1950. "Τά κατά τήν τελευτήν ἔθιμα τῶν Βυζαντινῶν ἐκ τῶν ἁγιολογικῶν πηγῶν." *Ἐπετηρὶς Ἑταιρείας Βυζαντινῶν Σπουδῶν* 20:74–171.

Talbot, A.-M. 1984. "Old Age in Byzantium." *Byzantinische Zeitschrift* 77:267–278.

———. 1990. "The Byzantine Family and the Monastery." *Dumbarton Oaks Papers* 44:119–129.

————. 1997. "Women." In *The Byzantines,* edited by G. Calvallo. Translated by T. Dunlap et al. Chicago and London: University of Chicago Press. 117–143.

Tinnefeld, F. H. 1989. "Michael I. Kerullarios, Patriarch von Konstantinopel (1043–1058): Kritische Überlegungen zu einer Biographie." *Jahrbuch der österreichischen Byzantinistik* 39:95–127.

Van Dam, R. 2002. *Kingdom of Snow: Roman Rule and Greek Culture in Cappadocia.* Philadelphia: University of Pennsylvania Press.

————. 2003a. *Becoming Christian: The Conversion of Roman Cappadocia.* Philadelphia: University of Pennsylvania Press.

————. 2003b. *Families and Friends in Late Roman Cappadocia.* Philadelphia: University of Pennsylvania Press.

Vergari, G. 1985. "Sull' *epitafio* pselliano per la figlia Stiliana." *Studi di filologia bizantina* 3:69–76 (= *Quaderni del Siculorum Gymnasium,* vol. 15).

————. 1986. "Osservazioni sulla tradizione manoscritta dell'epitafio di Psello per la figlia Stiliana." *Orpheus* 7:345–355.

————. 1987a. "Per una riedizione dell' 'Epitafio per la madre' di Michele Psello." *Orpheus* 8:396–414.

————. 1987b. "Michele Psello e la tipologia femminile cristiana." *Siculorum Gymnasium* 40:217–225.

————. 1988. "Michele Psello: Per la figlia Stiliana." In *Cultura e politica nell'XI secolo a Bisanzio: Versioni di testi di Michele Psello e Giovanni di Euchaita,* edited by R. Anastasi. Catania: Università agli studi di Catania, Facoltà di lettere e filosofia. 153–184.

————. 1990. "Macro- e micro-ipotesti in un' orazione di Michele Psello." *Byzantinische Forschungen* 15:317–324.

Vogt, A. 1908. *Basile Ier empereur de Byzance (867–886) et la civilisation byzantine à la fin du IXe siècle.* Paris: Picard.

Volk, R. 1990. *Der medizinische Inhalt der Schriften des Michael Psellos.* Munich: Institut für Byzantinistik und neugriechische Philologie der Universität München (= *Miscellanea Byzantina Monacensia,* vol. 32).

de Vries-van der Velden, E. 1996a. "Psellos et son gendre." *Byzantinische Forschungen* 23:109–149.

———. 1996b "La lune de Psellos." *Byzantinoslavica* 57:239–256.

———. 1997. "Psellos, Romain IV Diogénès et Mantzikert." *Byzantinoslavica* 58:74–310.

Vryonis, S. 1963. "Byzantine Δημοκρατία and the Guilds in the Eleventh Century." *Dumbarton Oaks Papers* 17:287–314.

Walker, A. 2003. "Home: A Space 'Rich in Blessing.'" In Kalavrezou (2003) 161–166.

Walker, J. 2004. "These Things I Have Not Betrayed: Michael Psellos' Encomium of His Mother as a Defense of Rhetoric." *Rhetorica* 22:49–101.

———. 2005. "Michael Psellos: *The Encomium of His Mother.*" *Advances in the History of Rhetoric* 8:239–313.

Weiss, G. 1973. *Oströmische Beamte im Spiegel der Schriften des Michael Psellos.* Munich: Institut für Byzantinistik und neugriechische Philologie der Universität München (= Miscellanea Byzantina Monacensia, vol. 16).

———. 1977. "Die Leichenrede des Michael Psellos auf den Abt Nikolaos vom Kloster von der schönen Quelle." *Βυζαντινά* 9:219–322.

Wilson, N. G. 1983. *Scholars of Byzantium.* London: Duckworth.

Wolska-Conus, W. 1976. "Les écoles de Psellos et de Xiphilin sous Constantine IX Monomaque." *Travaux et Mémoires* 6:223–243.

Index

Emperors and empresses are listed under their first names, all others by their family or second names.

The subentries for Psellos and some of his relatives are listed in biographical rather than alphabetical order.

Psellos, Michael (*cont.*)
interest in physical beauty, 38–39,
43, 54, 55–56, 58, 113; motives for
writing *Encomium,* 31–36; motives
for writing *Funeral Oration,*
113–114; motives for writing *To his
grandson,* 157; his orations praised,
29; his philosophy different from
his mother's, 38, 87–88, 97, 99;
questions God's decision to take his
daughter, 114–116; in *Timarion,*
143–144; use of antithesis in
Encomium, 41–45; use of dreams
in *Encomium,* 46–47
—works: *Chronographia,* 8, 9, 29,
46, 47–48; *Life of St. Auxentios,*
33; *Theologica,* 47
See also Neoplatonism; Olympos,
Mt., in Bithynia
Psellos, Michael, twelfth-century
teacher, 16
Psellos' adopted daughter, 14–16; is
engaged and disengaged to Elpidios
Kenchres, 24, 139–156; gives birth,
18–19, 172; mother of Psellos'
grandson, 157–159, 164; married
to Basileios Maleses, 159; governs
Maleses' *oikos,* 23; is sick and visited
by Psellos, 170; is mentioned by
Theophylaktos, 177
Psellos' brother-in-law, 12, 72
Psellos' brothers, 12, 169, 176–177
Psellos' "children," 13
Psellos' daughter Styliane, 12–14,
15, 111–112; her ancestors, 119; as
an infant, 119–120; as a child,
120; education and upbringing,
20–22, 121–122; affection for
Psellos, 122, 129; piety, 122, 128;
physical appearance, 123–128;
virtues, 127–129; God decides she
must die, 130; her sickness, 130–132;
possible smallpox of, 111–112; death,
19, 27, 132; parents' lament, 132–134;

funeral, 134; Psellos wanted her to
marry, 23–24, 127–130
Psellos' father, 11–12, 26, 35, 46, 56–58;
mild character, 67–68; physical
appearance, 67; at daughter's death,
78–79; at her tomb, 78; enters a
monastery, 80; as a monk, 82–83;
confides doubts in Psellos, 83; dies,
84; appears to Psellos in dream,
86–87, 95
Psellos' "grandchildren," 15, 16, 174–175
Psellos' grandson, 15–16; birth, 18–19,
172; as infant, 157–165, 174–175; as
young man, 160; falls on hard
times, 177–178
Psellos' maternal grandparents, 10–11,
26, 35, 46, 53–55, 63, 66–67, 96
Psellos' maternal uncles, 11, 61
Psellos' mother (Theodote): birth,
11–12, 54; upbringing, 55; self-
educated, 21, 55; physical beauty,
43, 54, 55–56; public appearances,
25; marries, 23–24; submits to
husband, 26, 67, 68, 80; gives birth,
19, 58–59; affection for Psellos,
65–66; encourages Psellos' studies,
3, 20–21, 59–62, 68–69; virtue, 66;
piety, 64, 69; longing for asceticism,
70–71; association with monks
and nuns, 70–72; daughter dies,
78–79; decides to become a nun,
79–80; at daughter's tomb, 78;
enters convent, 18, 35, 46; extreme
asceticism, 44–45, 80–81, 88–90;
refuses to eat a fish, 89–90; her
theology of prayer, 81–82; at
husband's death, 84; consoles
Psellos, 85–86; becomes nun,
91–93; dies, 27, 34–35, 93; funeral,
46, 95–96; pronounced saint and
martyr, 96; Psellos' verdict on
her asceticism, 96–97; appears
to Psellos in a dream, 98–99;
canonized in *Encomium,* 33–34

Anthony Kaldellis

is professor of Classics at
The Ohio State University.
He is the author of many studies
of Byzantine intellectual and cultural
history, including *Hellenism in
Byzantium* and *The Christian Parthenon*.
He has also translated many Byzantine
historians into English.

Lightning Source UK Ltd.
Milton Keynes UK
UKHW011847100221
378571UK00001B/31